Modeling Citizenship

Modeling Citizenship

Jewish and Asian American Writing

CATHY J. SCHLUND-VIALS

Temple University Press
PHILADELPHIA

Temple University Press
Philadelphia, Pennsylvania 19122
www.temple.edu/tempress

Published 2011

LIBRARY OF CONGRESS CATALOGING-IN-PUBLICATION DATA

Schlund-Vials, Cathy J., 1974–
Modeling citizenship : Jewish and Asian American writing / Cathy J. Schlund-Vials.
p. cm.
Includes bibliographical references and index.
ISBN 978-1-4399-0317-9 (cloth : alk. paper)
ISBN 978-1-4399-0318-6 (pbk. : alk. paper)
ISBN 978-1-4399-0319-3 (e-Book)
1. American literature—Jewish authors—History and criticism. 2. American literature—Asian American authors—History and criticism. 3. Judaism and literature—United States. 4. Asian Americans—Intellectual life. 5. Judaism in literature. 6. Jews in literature. 7. Asian Americans in literature. I. Title.
PS153.J4S35 2011
810.9'8924—dc22

2010042417

051112P

THE AMERICAN LITERATURES INITIATIVE

A book in the American Literatures Initiative (ALI), a collaborative publishing project of NYU Press, Fordham University Press, Rutgers University Press, Temple University Press, and the University of Virginia Press. The Initiative is supported by The Andrew W. Mellon Foundation. For more information, please visit www.americanliteratures.org.

Contents

Acknowledgments vii

Preface: Modeling Citizenship and Modeled Selfhood xi

Introduction: Perpetual Foreigners and Model Minorities: Naturalizing Jewish and Asian Americans 1

1 "Who May Be Citizens of the United States": Citizenship Models in Edith Maude Eaton and Abraham Cahan 20

2 Interrupted Allegiances: Indivisibility and Transnational Pledges 52

3 Utopian and Dystopian Citizenships: Visions and Revisions of the "Promised Land" 86

4 Reading and Writing America: Bharati Mukherjee's *Jasmine* and Eva Hoffman's *Lost in Translation* 123

5 Demarcating the Nation: Naturalizing Cold War Legacies and War on Terror Policies 152

Epilogue: "A Sense of Loss and Anomie": Model Minorities and Twenty-First-Century Citizenship 177

Notes 185

Bibliography 207

Index 215

Acknowledgments

First and foremost, I owe an enormous debt of gratitude to Janet Francendese and the editorial staff at Temple University Press. Without Janet's willingness to see the early manuscript's potential and her guidance through multiple revisions, this book would have remained buried in a Microsoft Office folder labeled "future projects." Amanda Steele was especially helpful in the final preparations of the manuscript. The two anonymous readers gave insightful, instructive, and incisive comments that greatly improved and deepened the book's principal arguments. For the cover, Laura Kina generously gave permission to use her work, "Devon Avenue Sampler," which eloquently encapsulates the book's comparative and transnational frames.

Early on, at the University of Massachusetts, I was fortunate to take American studies classes with Sunaina Maira and Jules Chametzky. I am thankful that Nina Ha introduced me to Asian American studies and has always been a strong advocate. Joseph Skerrett, Margo Culley, and Maria Tymoczko bestowed an ideal mixture of support and critique. The Five Colleges ABD Fellowship program provided encouragement in the form of the Mendenhall Fellowship at Smith College. Others were responsible for productively pushing the project's scope: Randall Knoper, Suzanne Daley, Jenny Spencer, Mazen Naous, Donna LeCourt, Peggy Woods, Joe Donahue, Carol Bailey, Bridget Marshall, Laura Wright, Shannon Payne, Seongho Yoon, Roberta Uno, Yvonne Mendez, Priscilla Page, Marion Wright, Mary Muratore, Robert Reginio, Daniel Mahoney, Benjamin

Balthaser, Dawn Lundy Martin, Karen Cardozo, Lucy Burns, Stephanie Dunson, Amy Cheng, Albert Turner, Robert Hayashi, and Wendy Bergoffen. Tabitha Adams Morgan is a dear friend and confidante. Talvin Wilks pushed me to think critically about citizenship, as did Alice Tuan and Sunder Ganglani.

Modeling Citizenship reflects the conversations, exchanges, and discussions I have had with colleagues and graduate students at the Pennsylvania State University (Erie) and the University of Connecticut: Greg Morris, John Champagne, Tom Noyes, George Looney, Teri Caruso, Brenda Murphy, Robin Worley, Doreen Bell, Eleni Coundouriotis, Wayne Franklin, Tom Recchio, Shawn Salvant, Elizabeth Hart, Anna Mae Duane, Tom Deans, Amanda Bailey, Theodore Van Alst, Albert Fairbanks, Lisa Sanchez, Ross Lewin, Veronica Makowsky, Michael Meyer, Robert Tilton, Donna Hollenberg, Jean Marsden, David Benson, Claire Reynolds, Clare Eby, Lynn Bloom, Penelope Pelizzon, Ellen Litman, Manisha Desai, Diana Rios, Jorge Santos, Rebecca Nisitech, Mandy Suhr-Sytsma, Laura Bocon, Toni Fellela, Sarah McIntyre, Zara Rix, Patrick Lawrence, Michelle Yee, Margo Machida, Bandana Purkayastha, Roger Buckley, Maxine Smestad-Haines, Fe Delos-Santos, Sheila Kucko, and Angela Rola. Holly Welker made me see the value of the project in its early stages. Regina Barecca provided mentorship at a particularly difficult moment.

I benefited greatly from the UConn Foundations in Humanitarianism working group, and am indebted to Kerry Bystrom, Sarah Winter, Margaret Higonnet, and Kathy Libal. Christina Henderson, Gordon Fraser, Michelle Maloney-Mangold, and Christiana Salah were instrumental in the manuscript's completion. Martha Cutter is a model Americanist, as are Kate Capshaw Smith and Sharon Harris. Robert Hasenfratz consistently raised my spirits and kept me on track. Gregory Semenza and Charles Mahoney provided much-needed interruption in the form of good-humored support. Kathy Knapp gave excellent feedback on the preface and fourth chapter, and Karen Renner's comments on the introduction were incredibly instructive. Samantha Buzzelli meticulously reread portions of the final manuscript. A keen critic, Heather Turcotte was ever encouraging, and her questions always relevant. Jerry Phillips and Mary Gallucci read through multiple drafts, and their insights—along with their generous friendship—are invaluable.

Conferences hosted by the Association for Asian American Studies and the American Studies Association are ideal spaces to test ideas, and my colleagues in the field have provided support from near and afar: Viet

Nguyen, Fiona Ngo, Mariam Lam, Mimi Nguyen, Martin Manalansan, Scott Wong, Floyd Cheung, Jennifer Ho, Jonathan Lee, Kornel Chang, Mary Danico, Anna Gonazales, Rick Bonus, Pia Sengsavanh, Genevieve Clutario, Ligaya Domingo, Caroline Valverde, James Lee, Wei Ming Dariotis, Rudy Guevarra, Jason Chang, Kent Ono, Tina Chen, James Kim, Cindy Wu, Yoonmee Chang, Allan Isaac, Daniel Kim, Lan Dong, Robert Ku, Iyko Day, Anne-Marie Loy, Kathy Nadau, Nerissa Balce, Leakhena Nou, Joe Ponce, Madeline Hsu, Stephen Hohn Song, Paul Lai, Besty Huang, Victor Roman Mendoza, and Victor Jew. Further, as the East of California caucus reminds, the field is dynamic and geographically unbounded, and I want to thank Gary Okihiro and Jennifer Ho for their collaboration and guidance. Min Hyoung Song gave an excellent suggestion for the introduction and has proven a key mentor, as has Nitasha Sharma. Asha Nadkarni's sophisticated considerations of citizenship were essential in making this book a reality, as was her generosity of spirit. I want to also thank Anita Mannur for being a constant advocate for me and this project. She gently prodded me to think beyond particular frames and she did so with humor, good will, and undeniable style.

Though projects are often discussed by way of academic frames, I am equally thankful to friends outside the university: Tembi Bergin-Batten, Amanda Robinson, Gabe Kaparis, Judy Dillon, Leah Davis, Jeff Cook, Jared Quinn, Shelby Smith, Sean McWilliams, Peter Mitchell, and Dana Ong. Jason Townsend remains a tireless supporter who made me rethink certain arguments. Kevin O'Rourke provided a significant early reading of the project. Correspondingly, Michael Needham, who gave useful editorial suggestions, deserves great commendation as well. Finally, this project emerges from a personal experience with migration and naturalization. My parents—Charles Schlund and Ginko Schlund—deserve acknowledgement that I fear does not translate well. My brother, Charles, is also an integral part of this story. Judy Fennel Vials and Peter Vials provided welcome breaks over holidays. Last, but certainly not least, this book is dedicated to my husband, Christopher Reichert Vials, whose scholarship and activism are a source of extraordinary motivation. My best friend and best editor, he expertly read countless drafts with no complaint, was willing to push me to write at moments of incredible fatigue, and is a partner in every sense of the word.

Preface: Modeling Citizenship and Modeled Selfhood

> *Neil Diamond's remake of the 1927 Jolson vehicle isn't very good, but neither is it the vacuous, sentimental ego trip it's been painted as. The Jolson version was centered on the myth of the melting pot—the hero escaped his ethnicity and became something new, an "American." Here, the theme is more personal and psychological: Diamond must find a way to escape his father without renouncing his Jewishness. Nothing is followed through with much rigor, and the resolution is artificial, but the film at least has its teeth into something real.*
>
> —DAVID KEHR

As 1980 came to a close, the third week of December witnessed the cinematic premier of Richard Fleischer's remake of *The Jazz Singer* at New York City's Ziegfeld Theater.[1] Carrying the provocative tagline "Sometimes you have to risk it all," the 1980 version marked Jewish American singer/songwriter Neil Diamond's film debut.[2] Like its 1927 Al Jolson predecessor, Diamond's *The Jazz Singer* tells the tale of a Jewish American son who refuses to follow his traditional father's path. Drawn not to a life in his father's synagogue but to a career on the popular American stage, the protagonist (Yussel Rabinovitch) navigates the contested waters of intergenerational disagreements and familial conflicts, fulfilling in the process an overwhelming desire for fame and fortune. Addressing the assimilative cost of success alongside the benefits of cultural Americanization, by the century's end *The Jazz Singer* had emerged as a bona fide American immigrant fable, a legible corollary to official characterizations of the United States as "a nation of immigrants."[3]

Irrespective of the film's immigrant-focused frames and accessible narrative, Neil Diamond's entry into U.S. filmdom was largely unsuccessful. In fact, the film's byline about "risk" reads negatively given *The Jazz Singer*'s critical and commercial reception. Described by reviewers as "empty-headed," "ill-begotten," "unbelievable," and "forgettable," Diamond's *The Jazz Singer* failed to capture the public imagination like its predecessor of the same name.[4] Instead, the film was a box office bomb and a critical disappointment, though the film's soundtrack would reach multiplatinum heights. The combination of poor acting, trite screenwriting, and wooden direction reinforced criticisms that *The Jazz Singer* story had become all too familiar, foregrounding film commentator Paul Brenner's contention that this third version had become a "moth-eaten" narrative.[5]

Certainly, changes in the times undergirded such critiques. Nearly fifty years, a civil rights movement, cold war foreign policies, and sweeping immigration policy changes separated the acclaimed original from its panned successor. What is more, Diamond's *The Jazz Singer* revision suffered from its strict adoption of the original plot. Released two years after the airing of *Holocaust*, a popular four-part Emmy Award–winning NBC television miniseries, *The Jazz Singer*'s preoccupation with Jewish American identity, a hallmark theme in the 1927 version, struck an anachronistic chord among audiences accustomed to an alternative, potent narrative of the Jewish global experience.[6] In the aftermath of identity politics and black power protests, the 1980 version inexplicably included a blackface performance, eliciting ire from critics and audiences alike. Equally significant in the film's lackluster reception was its questionable applicability to an approaching millennial moment.

On the whole, *New York Times* critic Janet Maslin's observation that Diamond's fictional biopic "rehash[es] . . . a plot that makes not one bit of sense any more" makes plain the film's less-than-enthusiastic reception. Simultaneously, Maslin's characterization paradoxically bespeaks the film's obsolescence and relevance to contemporaneous immigration law.[7] In light of recent open-door immigration policies, apparent in the successful passage and deployment of the 1965 Hart-Cellar Act, the film's focus on a Jewish immigrant was presumably out of sync with a contemporary "America" changed by the mass mid-century arrival of Asian and Latin American immigrants. The film's primary narrative, centered on Jewish/Jewish American experiences, seemed more related to turn-of-the-twentieth-century waves of southern and eastern European immigrants than to post-1965 migrations from China, Korea, India, the Caribbean, and Mexico. Set within a cultural locale in which Jewish Americans occupied multigenerational positions as probationary white subjects, Diamond's Americanization arguments with his orthodox father and underdeveloped contemplations of hyphenated immigrant identity were incongruous when situated against a mainstream reading of Jews as "model minorities" and "amalgamated Americans."

Still, in the face of critical claims that the film's plot elements "made no sense" and appraisals that Diamond's *The Jazz Singer* was culturally irrelevant, a close analysis of the film's opening and closing scenes makes visible an oppositional reading. Without a doubt, *The Jazz Singer*'s perceived irrelevance is its specific historical relevance. The film's recuperations of one hundred years of U.S. immigration policy and experiences—which led reviewers to dismiss its central story as "old" and to overlook the "new" faces of immigration evident in the opening scene—foregrounds one of the central themes in *Modeling Citizenship: Jewish and Asian American Writing*, which explores "an American century" of immigration through cultural production.[8] Diamond's *The Jazz Singer*, despite its critical failings, clearly renders U.S. citizenship through immigrant acts and performance, discernible in emotional appeals to the nation and influenced by politicized understandings of belonging.

In turn, the politically affective citizenship performances that mark *The Jazz Singer*'s plot and characterization intersect with capitalistic and idealized notions of American selfhood. As cultural theorist Lauren Berlant maintains,

> In the United States, [citizenship] has often involved the orchestration of fantasies about the promise of the state and the nation to cultivate and protect a consensually recognized ideal of the "good life"; in return for cultural, legal, and military security, people are asked to love their country, and to recognize certain stories, events, experiences, practices, and ways of life as related to the core of who they are, their public status, and their resemblance to other people. This training in politicized intimacy has also served as a way of turning political boundaries into visceral, emotional, and seemingly hardwired responses of "insiders" and "outsiders."[9]

Guided by "politicized intimacy," *The Jazz Singer*'s use of sentimentality delineates political boundaries between insiders and outsiders through citizenship. Moreover, its overall intelligibility as an immigrant narrative within the larger U.S. body politic anticipates the critical sites at play in the present book. As the title suggests, *Modeling Citizenship* concentrates its critical attention on the multifold ways in which U.S. selfhood is performed, enacted, idealized, and challenged in Jewish American and Asian American cultural production.

Correspondingly, *Modeling Citizenship* examines the analogous yet divergent experiences of two "model minority" groups, Asian Americans and Jewish Americans. Scrutinizing articulations of sentimental citizenship alongside romanticized ethnoracial logics, *Modeling Citizenship* deconstructs citizenship formation through immigration policy and naturalization law. In this vein, *The Jazz Singer*'s focus on allegiances (ethnic and national), its brief but significant juxtaposition of Asian/Asian Americans and Jewish/Jewish Americans, and the film's negotiation of transnational citizenships at the outset concretize the theoretical foundations for *Modeling Citizenship*. Following suit, the book investigates convergent immigration histories, affective oaths to the nation, and "American" selfhood performances.

The film's inaugural visual montage, which utilizes "America" as the background song, is populated by multiple Asian/Asian American bodies. Latino/a, Latin American, European, white ethnic, African/African American, and Caribbean bodies also circulate in this multiethnic imaginary, yet Asian/American women, men, and children occupy a majority position. The en masse inclusion of these bodies gestures toward the previously referenced Hart-Cellar Act. The depiction of Asian/American subjects, moreover, attests to the impact of the abovementioned Refugee Act, which greatly increased Southeast Asian access to the United States and offered the "first permanent and systematic procedure for the admission and effective resettlement of refugees of special humanitarian concern to the United States."[10] Strategically, the use of "everywhere" and the collective deployment of "they" in the opening track brings to mind an all-encompassing sense of "America" as a global destination site for anyone—native born, asylum seeker, or immigrant—searching for "freedom" and "hope."

Accordingly, *The Jazz Singer* corresponds to Berlant's citizenship-circumscribed notion of "the good life." Set within the fantastical space of mass culture, Diamond not only performs as "the jazz singer," the renamed, revised, and Americanized Jess Robin; he also assumes the complementary "insider" role of a prototypical U.S. subject, willing to "risk it all" in the service of socioeconomic exceptionalism. Gambling familial affiliations and eschewing traditional ethnic identities, Jess Robin—in effect a cultural venture capitalist—pursues an "American dream," a recognizable national story forged in the crucible of U.S. commercial success.[11] True to American hero form, Diamond's protagonist is committed to "risking it all" in the face of minor personal and professional setbacks (a failed first marriage, a paternal disavowal, and doubts about his singer/songwriter abilities). Notwithstanding Jess Robin's perseverance, the secret to his success is not familial love but patriotic devotion, which eventually paves the way to—and cements a triumphal arrival on—the popular music stage.

In the film's melodramatic final scene, marked by a "make-or-break" performance, Diamond as Jess Robin sings "America," a patriotic composition filled with clichéd optimistic U.S. tropes. Onstage, bathed in red light, dressed in black pants, a sequined blue shirt, and a glittering white scarf, Diamond's Jess Robin is visually integrated into an American flag set.[12] Such nationalistic scenery is aurally reinforced by the singer's performance of a pro-American anthem; it is also visually underscored by what Michael Rogin notes is Diamond's closing iconic pose. The film's last shot features a deferential Diamond in front of a standing ovation and amid enthusiastic applause, head bowed, holding a microphone, with one arm raised à la Statue of Liberty.[13] Consistent with the patriotic "U.S.A." motif, Diamond's show-stopping performance bears more than passing resemblance to a pledge of allegiance. Indeed, as a de facto anthem of immigration and unabashed Americanism, codified via uncritical allusions to the nation as a welcoming site of rebirth and renewal, Diamond's "America" emphasizes democratic promise, sentimentally calling attention to Jess Robin's individual desire for (and achievement of) "the American dream." In so doing, the song affectively renders the immigrant experience for audience member *and* viewer, an interpretation made clear in romanticized lyrics about aspirations, homes, liberty, and fate.

Emotionally driven, the song "America" is a schmaltzy ballad about U.S. exceptionalism, where even the foreign-born can be witness and participant to maudlin forms of nation-building.[14] This nationalistic reading of "America" is substantiated by the song's concluding stanza, which lyrically alludes to Samuel Francis Smith's 1831 "My Country, 'tis of Thee" (alternatively and incidentally titled "America"). Diamond's choral incorporation of "My Country, 'tis of Thee" is fixed to "America's" overall premise, accordingly revised to accommodate a1980s immigrant present.[15] If the original "My Country, 'tis of Thee" favors a declaration of allegiance by the native-born, made plain in the lyric "my native land, thee," then Diamond's "America" verbalizes a comparable foreign-born assurance through lyrics about providential one-way journeys to the United States. Such allusions access the recent memory of Vietnamese boat people and Cuban raft refugees: contemporaneous seekers of "freedom" who occupy an expansive U.S. immigrant landscape. Stressing the ubiquity of newly arrived foreign bodies, Diamond typifies a contemporary immigration wave unimpeded by restrictionist policies, such as nation-state quotas and racially specific agendas, which characterized U.S. immigration law from the 1920s to the 1960s.

In this production, Asian/Asian American subjects are situated adjacent to Jewish/Jewish Americans, the other group most frequently quoted in the opening montage. Complementing stereotypical perceptions of "foreignness" associated with Asians and Asian Americans, Hasidic Jews appear in full traditional dress, intimating an analogous "alien" reading of Jewish/American selfhood.[16] The juxtaposition of Asian and Jewish engenders an ethnic comparison, fortified by images of "ethnic commerce" that accompany representations of immigrant bodies. The movement of these bodies toward "manifest destiny" Americanization is matched by the capitalist flow of "foreign" commodities. These commodities and foreign bodies are in turn, exchanged in a U.S. marketplace and citizenship economy. Collapsing the space between immigrant bodies and immigrant-run businesses, *The Jazz Singer*'s opening montage establishes New York City as a port of entry for immigrants and a viable channel for globalized economic practices. The mobility of such bodies—represented by countless numbers of men and women who crowd New York City streets and squares—is nevertheless contained within the confines of the capitalist metropolis. This "ethnic commerce" is evident in the quick back-and-forth movement of the camera, which pauses to highlight a business name (e.g., Helman's, a Jewish clothing store; O'Brien's Café; Zapatos Shoes; a Ukrainian Jewish bookstore; Shamoly Indian Seafood Restaurant; Hiro Japanese Restaurant, and Nishan Indian-Bengali Restaurant).

The dominance of Asian/Asian American businesses in such historically Jewish American spaces as Times Square, the Lower East Side, and Straus Square strengthens the film's negotiation of the historical and socioeconomic coherences between Asian and Jewish immigrants.[17] For instance, Times Square, "the Crossroads of the World," now filled with Asian-owned restaurants and shops (among other ethnic-run businesses), draws attention to the increased global current of people, capital, and culture within the United States. Situated at a crossroad where Asian and Jewish literally and historically converge, Times Square is delimited by a nation-state border, emblematized by a row of U.S. flags that confirm the film's setting in New York and the United States. Hence, the film's opening configures a transnational location, with porous borders that enable the rise of ethnic commerce and permit the migration of ethnic subjects.

The film's transnational accents, unmistakable in immigrant shops, bodies, and movement, are in time undermined by the presence of the American flags, indicating a cinematic return to the national. As Inderpal Grewal and Caren Kaplan argue, the term "transnational" carries the potential to "destabilize rather than maintain boundaries of nation, race, and gender." In this vein, *The Jazz Singer*'s acknowledgment of transnational subjectivities, or those who cross borders, temporarily makes less stable a reading of U.S. selfhood via singular ethnoracial categories. Equally compelling is Grewal and Kaplan's deployment of the transnational to "signal attention to uneven and dissimilar circuits of culture and capital" that highlight "links between patriarchies, colonialism, racisms, and other forms of domination."[18] The question then arises as to what groups in *The Jazz Singer* are cast as perpetually foreign "transnationals" and what groups are afforded the status of "transnational-nationals." This divergent reading of U.S. citizenship emerges out of late twentieth-century capitalist practices and cold war logics that enable the flow of individuals through fields of globalization.

Explicitly, such immigrants are border-crossing subjects *and* economic objects. The initial celebration of difference by way of ethnically marked spaces and faces starkly contrasts with their cinematic marginalization. Notwithstanding the film's multiculturalist leanings, the subsequent absence of these bodies obfuscates a celebratory reading of such subjects as American. In other words, introduced as transnationals yet undeveloped as Americans, these individuals remain unsettled. Such absences, which point to an unstable U.S. selfhood, lessen the role immigrants play in nation building. Alternatively, Diamond's American-born second-generation protagonist is allowed to marry his Jewish heritage and nationalistic aspirations. Afforded access to an accretive Jewish American identity, temporarily unsettled emotionally but established politically, Jess Robin makes firm his claim to state-authorized selfhood. A "transnational-national," Jess Robin's unfettered embodiment of "old" and "new" world values attests to the asymmetrical relationship between citizenship and race, native-born and foreign-born, pre-1965 American and post-1965 immigrant.

This "transnational-national" subjecthood is most evident in *The Jazz Singer*'s penultimate scene. When his father, Cantor Rabinovitch, is too ill to perform, the dutiful Jess Robin, clothed in traditional cantor robes, takes his place in the synagogue and sings "Kol Nidre," a traditional composition performed on the first night of Yom Kippur, or Day of Atonement.[19] Substantiating his Jewish roots through a performance of "atonement," Jess Robin reconciles with his estranged father. His confirmation of tradition through costume and concert—embodied by religious robes, Jewish prayer scarf, and "Kol Nidre"—foreshadows the singer's final act as not only an American but a Jewish American. The Jewish scarf is adapted to fit a patriotic set befitting Jess Robin, a "jazz singer" who sings nationalistic pop anthems. An actor and emcee, Jess

Robin's "America" performance signals his arrival as a viable citizen who successfully resolves his immigrant past with his U.S. present.

Along these lines, *The Jazz Singer* speaks to the turn-of-the-twentieth-century immigrant past and post-1965 immigrant present. At the same time, Diamond's confirmation of U.S. citizenship, evident in the final scene in which the protagonist declares his love of country in public, brings to the fore another site of inquiry in *Modeling Citizenship*: naturalization. An emblem of democratic virtue, Jess Robin's repudiation of the past in favor of the present reinforces his position as a natural immigrant subject who is, through performance, naturalized. Jess Robin's final act accentuates the cultural dimensions to a politicized process invested in public selfhood articulations. Likewise, for Jewish American and Asian American writers, naturalization and its tenets give rise to plots, characterizations, and conflicts that intimately relate immigrant experiences through dominant nationhood, state-authorized selfhood, and affective belonging. Suggestive at once of intrinsic understandings and seemingly contradictory alien subjectivities, to "naturalize" presupposes a process in which past difference gives way to modern sameness.

Within the United States, common parlance dictates an understanding of naturalization through multivalent citizenships. As defined by the current Immigration and Nationality Act, naturalization is a state-sanctioned system in which "U.S. citizenship is conferred upon a foreign citizen or national after he or she fulfills the requirements established by Congress."[20] Just as important in naturalization law are its demonstrative, less tangible stipulations. Relying on a convincing public performance, naturalization is equal part repudiation and declaration, affective and legislative, wherein the country of origin is dismissed in favor of the country of settlement. Therefore, naturalization as an identifiable practice produces a legally sanctioned, dismissively transnational "rebirth" via an emotional pledge of nation-state allegiance within a specific geographic location.

This alleged political virtue, manifest in characterizations of the United States as a democratic space of possibility, ostensibly offers immigrant subjects opportunities for metaphoric regenerations. Not surprisingly, immigrant subjectivity is often categorized generationally as well as ethnically. Focused on narratives of succession, the ethnic immigrant body is acculturated, manipulated, and assimilated into the greater U.S. body politic. Concerned with the "making of Americans" from "alien material," naturalization law is imbued with the task of domesticating the foreign. Further, it is fixed to the ever-growing project of *e pluribus unum* selfhood. Paradoxically, such legal citizenship frames unintentionally expose antithetical nation-building discourses through segregationist politics, xenophobic anxieties, and racialized forms of power. Naturalization pledges therefore intersect with particular understandings of immigrant bodies and citizenship at even the highest levels of U.S. state rule.

Modeling Citizenship: Jewish and Asian American Writing extends the exploration of naturalization law and immigration policy into the literary imaginary. Simultaneously, the book necessarily examines the impact of dominant ethnoracial logics and nationally approved narratives of American citizenship which, in form and content, exemplify the process of naturalization. This citizenship rubric brings to light the contradictory, discursive status of the United States as a place of unbounded possibility for recognized citizens. Concomitantly, naturalization underscores the nation as a potent site of limitation for denied aliens. *Modeling Citizenship* investigates naturalization tropes in immigrant literature, underscoring in the process questions of nation-state affiliation and senses of belonging. Conscious of literary performance and political play, *Modeling Citizenship* covers multiple titular meanings, highlighting "modeling" as performative act and "model" as ideal subject.

Introduction: Perpetual Foreigners and Model Minorities: Naturalizing Jewish and Asian Americans

At the front end of the American meritocratic machine, Asians are replacing Jews as the No. 1 group. They are winning the science prizes and scholarships. Jews, meanwhile, at our moment of maximum triumph at the back end of the meritocracy, the midlife, top-job end, are discovering sports and the virtues of being well-rounded. Which is cause and which is effect here is an open question. But as Asians become America's new Jews, Jews are becoming . . . Episcopalians.

—NICHOLAS LEHMANN

Over the last few years, Asian Americans have come to be known as the New Jews. The label is honorific. It is meant to accentuate the many parallels between these two groups of immigrants-made-good: Jews started out as outsiders; Asians did too. Jews dedicated themselves to schooling; Asians too. Jews climbed the barriers and crowded the Ivies; Asians too. Jews climbed faster than any other minority in their time; Asians too. Jews enjoy Chinese food; Asians—well, you get the picture. Somewhere in the half-lit region between stereotype and sociology, the notion has taken hold that Asian Americans are "'out-Jewing the Jews."

—ERIC LIU

Two years after the first Persian Gulf War, Robert Olen Butler's *A Good Scent from a Strange Mountain* was awarded the 1993 Pulitzer Prize in fiction.[1] Centered on Vietnamese refugees, Butler's debut collection of fifteen short stories was praised by critics for its revision of a then-established Vietnam War script. As *New York Times* reviewer George Packer averred, each first-person story "is told . . . from the viewpoint of a Vietnamese transplanted from the Mekong Delta to the Louisiana bayou. . . . The Americans have become foils; it's the Vietnamese who are now at the center, haunted by the past, ambivalent about their hosts, suffering sexual torments, [and] seeking a truce in their various wars."[2] If the Mekong Delta functions as the geographic epicenter not only for the American War in Vietnam but also for a 1960s Vietnamese civil war between north and south, then the Louisiana bayou is an analogously apt site, reminiscent of an 1860s North/South American Civil War.[3] And, if Americans were haunted by the unresolved Vietnam conflict, then the Vietnamese protagonists in *A Good Scent from a Strange Mountain* are similarly traumatized by war and relocation. By concentrating on the embodied remnants and affective reminders of war, Butler, a Vietnam War Army linguist-turned-author, joined the cultural ranks of other late-century Vietnam War–inspired productions like Michael Herr's *Dispatches* (1977), Oliver Stone's *Platoon* (1986), *Born on the Fourth of July* (1989), *Heaven and Earth* (1993), and Tim O'Brien's *The Things They Carried* (1993).

Even so, the *New York Times* review underscores a theme that is not war-specific in *A Good Scent from a Strange Mountain*. Specifically, at stake is a transplantation motif, epitomized by the collection's eleventh story, "Snow," which features a Vietnamese refugee and a relocated Jewish lawyer. Principally focused on two separate conversations that take place on Christmas Eve and New Year's Eve, respectively, "Snow" is nostalgic, bittersweet, and sentimental. In many ways an ideally coordinated pair, Giàu (the Vietnamese female protagonist) and Mr. Cohen (a Jewish émigré) share multiple coherences. They have both lost fathers in war; they are each without a partner; and, most significant, they are two U.S. "transplants." Combining interior monologues with back-and-forth dialogues about homelands, migration, and familial loss, "Snow" begins with a meeting of strangers and concludes with a possible love match. And, though the story takes place in the United States, the discussions between Giàu and Mr. Cohen are chiefly concerned with their respective countries of origin.

Hence, "Snow" is a conversational tale, and its plot is accordingly driven and characterized by "refugee talk." Through two geopolitical conflicts, the Vietnam War and the Second World War, Giàu and Mr. Cohen forge a connection by means of displacement and relocation. At the same time, the non-Asian American, non-Jewish American Butler accesses a legible, comparative ethnoracial frame of socioeconomic "kinship" that goes beyond the purview of foreign policy conflict or domestic negotiation. In so doing, Butler's "Snow" employs an oft-used ethnic comparison that marries "perpetual foreigners" and "model minorities."

"Free White Persons": Naturalized Subjects and Ineligible Aliens

Giàu and Mr. Cohen are "transplants" (or foreigners) who—with the exception of a brief interruption—remain uprooted and unrooted, despite distance, the passage of time, and their American relocation. This uprootedness is foreshadowed by Giàu's workplace, "The Plantation Hunan," which "does not look like a restaurant" and is "an old plantation house."[4] This built palimpsest—an emblem of the antebellum South—is the story's principal setting and functions as its primary transnational referent. For example, "Hunan" (Mandarin for "south of the lake") refers to a southeastern central province in the People's Republic of China. Thus, the Plantation Hunan carries a "southeasterly name" that geographically complements the narrative's Lake Charles, Louisiana location.

Such cartographic linkages correspond to the protagonist's own Vietnamese location and U.S. relocation. Indeed, if the Plantation Hunan hearkens back to the American Civil War, then Giàu's existence as a refugee underscores the dissolution of her former nation-state (South Vietnam/Republic of Vietnam) after the fall of Saigon on April 30, 1975. For World War II refugee Mr. Cohen, the 1939 Nazi invasion of Poland, which is alluded to in "Snow," renders impossible a consideration of his former home through non-Holocaust frames. Within this dislocated milieu of Louisiana, the Vietnamese protagonist fittingly opines, the Plantation Hunan "must feel like a refugee. It is full of foreign smells, ginger, and Chinese pepper and fried shells for wonton" (126).

Filled with foreign smells, the Plantation Hunan is witness to profound demographic shifts, and its transformation from an "American" to a "Chinese American" site brings to light late twentieth-century immigration and refugee flows composed of an increasing number of Asian bodies (à la Neil Diamond's *The Jazz Singer*). Like Giàu, the building is a doubly foreign (and alienated) subject. Following suit, though her employers are "very kind," they "know we are different from each other. They are Chinese and I am Vietnamese . . . but we are both here in Louisiana and they go somewhere with the other Chinese in town" (126). Accordingly, as a "stranger" among "foreigners," Giàu's alienated personhood (or alienhood) intersects with an unresolved selfhood vis-à-vis Vietnam and the United States.

Giàu's sense of nonbelonging foregrounds Mr. Cohen's seemingly "obvious" naturalized affiliation to the United States. In particular, Mr. Cohen's perceived Americanness is racially apparent early in the narrative. At the beginning of "Snow," Mr. Cohen places a take-out order at the Plantation Hunan, and this act sets the conversational stage for Vietnamese refugee and Jewish exile. Realizing that the order is delayed, Giàu apologizes, telling Mr. Cohen that he "should not have to wait for a long time on Christmas Eve" (129). Mr. Cohen responds, "It's okay . . . This is not my holiday." Giàu does not initially comprehend Mr. Cohen's ethnoreligious allusion, even though he clarifies, "I am Jewish. . . . A Jew doesn't celebrate Christmas." Giàu answers, "I thought all Americans celebrated Christmas," to which Mr. Cohen responds, "Not all. Not exactly." Giàu then asserts, "It felt a little strange to see this very American man who was not celebrating the holiday" (129). Collectively characterizing "all Americans" and insistent on Mr. Cohen's "very Americanness," Giàu unintentionally underscores a principal difference between the two refugees along past naturalization lines.

Expressly, Giàu's initial reading of Mr. Cohen's "very Americanness" attests to a proscribed physical "whiteness" (reminiscent of snow), which operates in contrast to Giàu's own racial identity. Indeed, "Snow" (like *A Good Scent from a Strange Mountain*) is by and large shaped by multiple allusions to Vietnamese culture, practices, and sites, which accordingly mark Giàu as "foreign protagonist." On another level, Giàu temporarily naturalizes Mr. Cohen, foregrounding a brief reconsideration of the original 1790 Naturalization Law. In particular, Giàu's naturalization of Mr. Cohen brings to bear the historic conditions that undergird how Americans are legislatively "made" from "foreign material." What is more, Mr. Cohen's reaction ("Not all. Not exactly") underscores asymmetrical (and probationary) relationships between ethnicity, race, and nation.

Such inequalities outline the ethnoracial politics at play in the 1790 Naturalization Act. Focused on converting "aliens" into "citizens," the first naturalization law stipulated that:

> any Alien being a free white person, who shall have resided within the limits and under the jurisdiction of the United States for the term of two years, may be admitted to become a citizen thereof on application to any common law Court of record in any one of the States wherein he shall have resided for the term of one year at least, and making proof to the satisfaction of such Court that he is a person of good character, and taking the oath or affirmation prescribed by law to support the Constitution of the United States, which Oath or Affirmation such Court shall administer, and the

> Clerk of such Court shall record such Application, and the proceedings thereon; and thereupon such person shall be considered as a Citizen of the United States.[5]

As is clear in the above passage, the 1790 Naturalization Act establishes residency requirements and legal processes, and necessitates an admittedly open-ended determination of "good character." In the face of explicit bureaucratic and legal frames, the original naturalization law appreciably commences with race: "free white personhood." If being "made American" is at once racially inflected, then Giàu's initial emphasis on Mr. Cohen's "Americanness" is forged through a de facto whiteness. Indeed, Giàu does not ascribe those same terms to her own personhood, which consequently places her outside a white imaginary. In the same way, Giàu indirectly models the exclusionary nature of American citizenship, which from the beginning was constructed via "free white persons" and concomitant whiteness.

Equally significant, though Giàu and Mr. Cohen are "kindred spirits," they are not so because of equivalent assimilation. Instead, the two are joined through parallel trajectories of alienation as well as divergent historic paths to U.S. naturalization. In this regard, "Snow" introduces the comparative frames at work in the present book, which examines the interplay between citizenship, performance, and immigration policy in the literatures of these two "kindred" groups. Robert Olen Butler's "outsider" position enables a dominant reading of Jewish and Asian Americans through connective histories of migration, relocation, and citizenship. In turn, affective performances in "Snow" foment an expansive exploration of how seemingly natural affinities between Jewish and Asian Americans are largely constructed (or modeled) through immigration law. In related fashion, Nicholas Lehmann's declaration that "Asians are replacing Jews" and Eric Liu's observation that "Asians are 'out-Jewing the Jews'" bring to light modes of social performance (or modeling). Taken together, Butler, Lehmann, and Liu make visible the ethnic and racial contours through which Americans and "model minorities" are both constructed and made.

To be sure, the 1790 Naturalization Act privileged the "free white person" over the indentured servant, the slave, and the Native American.[6] Whereas the Three-fifths Clause in the Constitution (along with the 1808 Importation Clause and the Fugitive Slave Clause) clearly delineated the role of slavery in the practice of antebellum enfranchisement, the original 1790 naturalization law depended on the category "free white person" as a prima facie requirement for citizenship. In so doing, the first naturalization law excluded particular groups through discourses of liberalism, rubrics of whiteness, and rhetorical omission. That is, the 1790 Naturalization Act relied on the narrative omission of other ethnoracial groups (such as Native Americans and Africans/African Americans). Within the legally fictive space of federal naturalization law, then, the requirement of "good character" masks a decidedly racist citizenship matrix, replete with innate moral values and assessments of racial inferiority. Indubitably, this racialized logic was used to deny Asian immigrant applicants until 1952, when the McCarran-Walter Act eliminated racial prerequisites from naturalization law. As Gary Okihiro argues, when "imposed upon [a racial binary]," Asian Americans "required a revision of categories from white and black to 'white' and 'nonwhite' that is equally arbitrary and hierarchical."[7]

Notwithstanding the overt exclusionary politics at work in the original 1790 Naturalization Act, the use of whiteness as a standard for U.S. selfhood benefited one ethnoracial group that had for centuries been denied naturalized citizenship in the former colonizer, Britain: Jewish immigrants. Expelled during the reign of King Edward I in 1290 and banned from settling in Britain and the territories until the latter part of the sixteenth century, British Jews, their descendents, and other Jewish subjects were largely rendered stateless.[8] This stateless condition changed during the pre-Revolutionary period, with improved British-Jewish relations. Such relational recuperation is apparent in the passage of the 1740 Parliamentary Act that allowed Jews naturalization access after seven years in a British territory or colony.[9] Nonetheless, absent from the colonial structure was a universal policy of naturalization.

Unquestionably, a potential impediment to Jewish naturalization in the territories could be found in colonial citizenship oaths, which frequently included the phrase "upon the true faith of a Christian."[10] For the Jewish would-be citizen in the years immediately following the Revolutionary War, to naturalize before the 1790 law was potentially tantamount to religious conversion. Further, in the pre–Revolutionary War period, this "citizenship matter" was mostly left to the discretion of independent colonial courts. The omission of a religious requirement in the 1790 law enabled Jewish access to U.S. naturalization as "free white persons," simultaneously signaling their legal selfhood status as "whites" within a nascent, foundational U.S. political imaginary.[11] If Jewish applicants for citizenship were—at the level of naturalization law—made "white," then their Asian counterparts in contrast were by and large rendered "not-white." Returning to "Snow," if Giàu's assumption of Mr. Cohen's "Americanness" hearkens back to the 1790 Naturalization Act, then her fundamental "foreignness" foregrounds a discussion of ineligibility via the citizenship franchise.

Emblematically, more then a century after the passage of the first naturalization law, Japanese applicant Takao Ozawa petitioned for American selfhood in the nation's highest court. Naturalization law had shifted slightly with an 1870 amendment that allowed both "free white persons" and "those of African descent" access to the citizenship process. Admittedly, Ozawa was not the first Asian applicant to petition for citizenship.[12] Nevertheless, Ozawa's case is noteworthy precisely because of the applicant's affective argument and naturalization rhetoric. For example, in his self-authored 1922 brief, Ozawa at length declared:

> In name, General Benedict Arnold was an American, but at heart he was a traitor. In name, I am not an American, but at heart I am a true American. I set forth the following facts that will sufficiently prove this. 1) I did not report my name, my marriage, or the names of my children to the Japanese Consulate in Honolulu; notwithstanding all Japanese subjects are requested to do so. These matters were reported to the American government. 2). I do not have any connection with any Japanese churches or schools, or any Japanese organizations elsewhere. 3) I am sending my children to an American church and American school in place of a Japanese one. 4) Most of the time I use the American (English) language at home, so that my children cannot speak the Japanese language. 5) I have lived continuously within the United States for over twenty-eight years. 6) I chose as my wife one educated in American schools . . . so it is my honest hope to do something good to the United States before I bid farewell to this world.[13]

Understandably, much of the scholarship about *Ozawa v. United States*, including Ian Haney Lopez's *White by Law* (1997) and *Whiteness of a Different Color* (1999) by Matthew Frye Jacobson, convincingly uses naturalization law to underscore the reification of whiteness as a shifting racial category.[14] Such a reading is undeniable given Ozawa's own appeal, which begins with his assertion that he was indeed a "free white person" and therefore a viable citizen subject.

Still, little scholarly attention is paid to the affective rhetoric Ozawa employs in his citizenship case. As I argue here, naturalization is in part a public, sentimental performance, requiring the "would-be American" to declare affiliation and loyalty. Without a doubt, such patriotic feelings are discernible in Ozawa's opening declaration of true Americanness. Ozawa's enthusiastic patriotism operates in stark (and deliberate) contrast to the situation of infamous turncoat Benedict Arnold, a stock villain of the Revolutionary War narrative. Regardless of Benedict Arnold's *jus solis* status (he was born in Norwich, Connecticut), Ozawa strategically emphasizes Arnold's heart-centered dislike of country to bolster a traitorous personhood. In juxtaposition, Ozawa argues that "at heart" he is a "true American," a point substantiated through a multivalent repudiation of his country of origin.

On another level, Ozawa's Benedict Arnold allusion fulfills one of the basic tenets of naturalization, which includes a demonstrable patriotism and knowledge of U.S. history. And in a more administrative vein, Ozawa recounts the bureaucratic and legal actions he has taken to demonstrate his loyalty to the nation. Imbued with tropes of "country love," and sentimental claims about "America," Ozawa is willing and able participant in a U.S.-specific bureaucracy of citizenship (full of American titles, marriage, and birth announcements). To be sure, the Supreme Court was convinced of Ozawa's affective "citizenship potential," evident in the juridical disclaimer that Ozawa "was well qualified by character and education for citizenship is conceded."[15] Even so, the Court ruled such patriotic attributes did not overturn the primacy of race in the making of Americans. In the end, though Ozawa was "well qualified," and despite Ozawa's assertions of Americanness, he was still Japanese and a member of the "Asiatic race." Neither a free white person nor someone of African descent, Ozawa was deemed an "alien ineligible for citizenship."

Earlier in the same year that Ozawa was denied naturalized citizenship on the grounds of racial ineligibility, the *New York Times* published a piece titled, "Americanizing Immigrant Jews." As suggested by the title, the January 15, 1922 article was primarily focused on the naturalization of Jews within the U.S. body politic. Drawing on sociologist Charles S. Bernheimer's essay in the contemporaneously released *Jewish Year Book*, "Americanizing Immigrant Jews" maintains that the "history, ethics, and ideals of the Jews have made them particularly impressionable to American ideals." Further, "Americanizing Immigrant Jews" details efforts by community organizers and educators to naturalize an estimated one million foreign-born individuals through rudimentary lessons in U.S. citizenship and English.[16] Though seemingly disconnected from the *Ozawa* case, the article's articulation of Americanization through the tenets of U.S. naturalization employs an analogous naturalized rhetoric.

To that end, Jewish immigrants are not only "impressionable"; they are deemed politically pliable because of innate "history, ethics, and ideals" that neatly correspond to dominant U.S. citizenship frames. Accordingly, the article casts immigrant Jews in the roles of romanticized, would-be American subjects. Indeed, such bodies become "model minority" holders of an "Americanization dream." Like their "good character" counterpart Ozawa, these agreeable, willing citizens fulfill the basic requirements of naturalization law. However, unlike Ozawa, such an Americanization dream is racially in reach for them.

Nevertheless, despite claims that Jewish immigrants were fit (and fitted) for naturalization, they still faced mounting nativism and persistent anti-Semitism. For example, a year before "Americanizing Immigrant Jews," Congress passed the alarmingly named Emergency Quota Act. Responding to rising native-born anxiety increasingly centered on the "perpetual foreignness" of immigrant bodies, U.S. senators and representatives reduced via legislative decree the number of eastern and southern European immigrants by 75 percent from previous years.[17] Given that eastern Europe was a point of origin for a majority of Jewish migrants, the Emergency Quota Act had dramatic effects on Jewish immigration. A precursor to the even more restrictive 1924 Johnson-Reed Act, the Emergency Quota Act signals a significant rupture in the idealized characterization of the United States as a heretofore open-door "nation of immigrants." Such restrictions would incontestably prohibit access to European Jews seeking asylum during World War II. In a similarly exclusionary vein, immigrants from the Asia-Pacific Triangle (including individuals from East Asia, Southeast Asian, and South Asia) were barred from entering the United States, reconfirming past anti-Asian immigration measures such as the 1875 Page Act, the 1882 Chinese Exclusion Act, and the 1917 Asiatic Barred Zone Act.

Taken together, despite nonparallel "racial access" to naturalization, both Jewish and Asian immigrants were expressly configured in and impacted by nativist law and policy. Situated within a reactionary anti-immigrant rubric, Jewish and Asian would-be Americans were therefore caught in what Gary Okihiro observes is fundamental to binaried citizenship characterizations. According to Okihiro, such nonwhite/white and native/foreign-born binaries in the United States "offer coherence, especially during times of social upheaval. They preserve rule amidst chaos, and stability amidst rapid change, such as during the late eighteenth, nineteenth, and twentieth centuries."[18] Focused on particularly frenzied periods in U.S. immigration policy, the texts examined in

Modeling Citizenship are organized alongside contemporaneous debates over immigrant bodies. Drawing on such "ends," *Modeling Citizenship* analyzes Jewish and Asian American writing produced during fin de siècle nativism, mid-century cold war model minoritization, and late twenty-first-century immigration amnesty and reform.

Within this late-century milieu, in the aftermath of war, amnesty, and reform, Robert Olen Butler's "Snow" is produced within the interstices of naturalization policy and immigration law. Further, a rereading of Mr. Cohen as both naturalized subject and concomitant "foreigner" reflects a concurrent and connective exclusionary history. All things considered, Mr. Cohen is a Polish Jew who has two other "homes": Poland and then England (132). After Mr. Cohen tells Giàu his migration story, the protagonist notes, "I was thinking how he was a foreigner, too. Not an American really" (133). Following suit, Giàu's revised declaration of foreignness and non-Americanness bespeaks the transnational conditions and affects that contextualize Mr. Cohen's migration from Europe to the United States. Simultaneously, Butler's strategic employment of foreign frames reinforces an outsider commonality between Vietnamese narrator and Jewish subject. As "perpetual foreigners," Giàu and Mr. Cohen are therefore socially and politically matched vis-à-vis expansive discursive and legal structures of U.S. immigration.

"Old" and "New" Model Minorities: Jewish Americans and Asian Americans

If Robert Olen Butler's "Snow" ends with two matched minorities, then Eric Liu's *The Accidental Asian* (1998) underscores like coherences between Jewish/Asian "foreigners" and Jewish American/Asian American "model minorities." From the outset, Liu's collection of essays autobiographically furthers Butler's cartographic narrative, for *The Accidental Asian* maps each group's migration from "outsiders" to presumably "insider" U.S. subjects. Indeed, prior to the "New Jews" chapter (from which the opening epigraph is taken), Liu recalls a past history of Asian exclusion from naturalization. Expressly, Liu evocatively asks, "What maketh a race?" He answers by briefly recounting a series of naturalization cases involving South Asian applicants. As Liu maintains: "To the judiciary system of the United States, Asian Indians were held to be: probably not white (1909), white (1910), white again (1913), not white (1917), white (1919 and 1920), not white (1923), still not white (1928), probably never again white (1939 and 1942)."[19] Undeniably circumscribed by whiteness, the abovementioned cases make visible the rise of nativism in the first half of the twentieth century. And though the judiciary system of the United States vacillated between "white" and "not white," Liu's list concludes with the decidedly pessimistic "probably never again white," signaling a concomitant perpetual foreignness.

Alternatively, within the racialized milieu of U.S. naturalization law, Liu's question of "what maketh a race" is indistinguishable from "what maketh a citizen." Alluding to *United States v. Thind* (the 1923 case), Liu emblematically underscores the primacy of race in the manufacturing of U.S. citizens. A Punjabi Sikh and World War I veteran, Thind claimed (vis-à-vis ethnology) that he was "Aryan" and therefore a member of the "Caucasian" (or white) race. Consequently, the Oregonian resident argued that he was an "alien eligible for citizenship." Revising the racialized logics of the *Ozawa* case, the Supreme Court nonetheless denied Thind's application. Notwithstanding Thind's "scientific whiteness," Associate Justice George Sutherland premised his rejection on "the [racial] understanding of the common man." Accordingly, the justice avowed that "It is a matter of familiar observation and knowledge that the physical group characteristics of the Hindus render them readily distinguishable from various groups of person in this country commonly recognized as white."[20] Focused on "common knowledge" and "familiar observation," the court summarily ruled that Thind's prima facie nonwhiteness was grounds for ineligibility.

In line with recent legislative action, the Supreme Court's verdict substantiated the constitutionality of the 1917 Asiatic Barred Zone Act, which banned immigration from East, South, and Southeast Asia. Simultaneously, as restricted foreign bodies, Asian Indians became nonnaturalizable domestic subjects.[21] Just as significant, Justice Sutherland's ruling included an intergenerational comparison between "the children of English, French, German, Italian, Scandinavian, and other European parentage" and those with "Hindu parents." Distinctively, the Supreme Court justice argued that the children of European parentage "quickly merge into the mass of our population and lose the distinctive hallmarks of their European origin." In contrast, Justice Sutherland observed, "it cannot be doubted that the children born in this country of Hindu parents would retain indefinitely the clear evidence of their ancestry."[22]

Legally, of course, both types of "children" enjoyed *jus solis* citizenship by sheer fact of birthplace.[23] Nevertheless, Justice Sutherland's homogeneity/heterogeneity binary foregrounds a specific child "problem" via dominant anxieties over nonwhite, second-generation U.S. subjects.[24] In particular, "Hindus" are not only "aliens ineligible for citizenship"; their American-born children were (according to early twentieth-century logics) racially non-naturalizable because they would "retain indefinitely" their ancestry. Hence, first-generation Asian bodies are cast as "perpetual foreigners," whereas second-generation Asian Americans are racially demonized minorities. In so ruling, Justice Sutherland articulates the uneasy, contradictory terms through which the mid-twentieth-century model minority myth is constructed.

If Asian ancestry proves to be a problem in the first half of the twentieth century, it is configured as a "solution" in the latter half.[25] As a second-generation Asian American, situated in the "in the half-lit region between stereotype and sociology," Eric Liu simultaneously embodies a problematic past and a solution-oriented present. Indeed, as Min Hyoung Song convincingly argues,

> in . . . *The Accidental Asian*, the former speech writer for the Clinton administration and graduate of Harvard Law . . . repeats what has already been said about the most visible of his generation: they are uniformly privileged and well-educated; little makes them different from their professional white peers; race is only a residual concern for them (not having felt the sharp pain of *de jure* discrimination nor in some cases *de facto* prejudice); being perceived as Americans is more important than whatever attenuated ties they might have to Asian countries from which their forebears may have departed, and their experiences are merely the most contemporary nay, albeit accelerated, iteration of the immigrant narratives as told by successive waves of ethnic Europeans.[26]

As Song maintains, Liu is in many ways an archetypal "child of 1965," the holder of a post-1965 Immigration Act "American dream" forged in civil rights–era reform. In dramatic fashion, this mid-century act eschewed nation-state quotas in favor of hemispheric designation. Such a shift marked the first time that en masse Asian migration to the United States was legally possible.

This "immigration possibility" in part foregrounds Song's argument about second-generation Asian Americans influenced less by resistance politics and shaped more by model minoritization schemas and professionalization frames. These concurrent "model" concerns prompt the "iteration of the immigrant narratives as told by successive waves of ethnic Europeans," foregrounding Liu's two-group juxtaposition. Correspondingly and indubitably, *The Accidental Asian* is predominantly focused on a mid-century, post-1965 Immigration Act imaginary despite brief mentions to early-to-mid-twentieth-century exclusion and naturalization. To be sure, this "after" space is typified by naturalized observations about U.S. selfhood. Particularly, such model minorities (including both Jewish and Asian Americans) are imagined through an amnesiac teleology of progress. Likewise, in tautological fashion, *The Accidental Asian* is invested in "honorific immigrants-made-good." Correspondingly, Liu's essay/memoir both gestures toward and emerges from the "model minority" stereotype.

Specifically, if Asian Americans are "out-Jewing" their principally eastern European predecessors, they are necessarily characterized (by means of the "model minority" label) as paragons of democratic and economic virtue. These "virtuous" frames are diametrically opposed to those of other groups of color, which remain undesirable. This divisive strategy is evident in an early articulation of the stereotype in a December 1966 article titled, "Success Story of One Model Minority Group in the U.S.," from the *U.S. News and World Report*:

> At a time when Americans are awash in worry over the plight of racial minorities—one such minority, the nation's 300,000 Chinese-Americans, is winning wealth and respect by dint of its own hard work. In any Chinatown from San Francisco to New York, you discover youngsters at grip with their studies. Crime and delinquency are found to be further minor in scope. Still being taught in Chinatown is the old idea that people should depend on their own efforts—not a welfare check—in order to reach America's "promised land."[27]

Conservatively couched and redolent of a late civil rights movement shift from integrationist to self-deterministic agendas, the *U.S. News and World Report* contrasts worrisome racial minorities with "winning" Chinese Americans. Explicitly, unlike those who allegedly depend on a welfare check, Chinese Americans rely on their own efforts, are by and large without vice, and are successful because of hard work. Drawing together a Protestant work ethic, self-reliance, and American exceptionalism, the *U.S. News and World Report* contends that Chinese Americans (and by extension, all Asian Americans) have the necessary "ingredients" to "reach America's 'promised land.'" Patient and persevering, Chinese Americans have overcome discrimination without protest and have achieved socioeconomic success (that is, the American dream).

Armed with Confucian determination, Chinese Americans have an extra edge in the "promised land." This cultural proclivity is akin to early twentieth-century claims of "impressionable" Jewish immigrants, who are willing and able Americanization subjects. If this comparative model minoritization is suggested in the *U.S. News and World Report* article, an earlier Asian American "success story" is more overtly comparative. In a *New York Times Magazine* piece from January 1966 titled, "Success Story, Japanese-American Style," sociologist William Petersen unequivocally states,

> Asked which of the country's ethnic minorities has been subjected to the most discrimination and the worst injustices, very few persons would even think of answering: "The Japanese Americans." Yet if the question refers to persons alive today, that may well be the correct reply. Like the Negroes, the Japanese have been the object of color prejudice. Like the Jews, they have been feared and hated as hyperefficient competitors.[28]

Arguing that Japanese Americans faced "the most discrimination and the worst injustices," Petersen (like the *U.S. News and World Report* article) at once relegates antiblack discrimination to the realm of nonexceptional "color prejudice." Cohering with the politics of "Success Story of One Minority Group in the United States," Petersen's discrimination declaration tactically locates Japanese Americans alongside other minorities, specifically Jews and African Americans.

At the same time, Petersen makes the larger claim that Japanese Americans were subjected to the most discrimination and the worst injustices, codifying a particularly troubling hierarchy of oppression. Though Japanese Americans are like African Americans and Jewish Americans, they nevertheless superlatively operate as the "most discriminated," making their success story all the more exceptional. In the process, the Berkeley sociologist mobilizes a now familiar divisive construction wherein Asian Americans have—despite a very real racist past—transcended de facto discrimination without making substantive demands for systemic change.[29]

Though brief, Petersen's allusion to anti-Semitism and Jewish personhood accesses the histories of two groups who referentially function within "model minority" frames. And, like Associate Justice George Sutherland, Petersen employs the figure of the naturalized European immigrant to illustrate a flattened ethnic futurity. Even so, Petersen revises this characterization to fit the perimeters of Asian American model minoritization. Indeed, Petersen maintains,

> Each new nationality from Europe was typically met with such hostility as, for example, the anti-German riots in the Middle West a century ago, the American Protective Association to fight the Irish, the national quota laws to keep out Italians, Poles, and Jews. Yet, in one generation or two, each white minority took advantage of the public schools, the free labor market and America's political democracy; it climbed out of the slums, took on better paying occupations and acquired social respect and dignity.[30]

The bulk of Petersen's argument in "Success Story, Japanese-American Style" relies on an opportune comparison among white ethnic groups (Italians, Poles, and Jews) that fails to individualize asymmetrical histories of whiteness and political struggle. Moreover, Petersen's successional narrative is premised on a typically American understanding of discrimination. In other words, Petersen argues that such systemic modes of oppression can be conquered by means of group agency, faith in capitalism, and patriotic allegiance.

On another level, such model minority characterizations render hyper-visible Jewish and Asian Americans within the dominant U.S. body politic. Nicholas Lehmann's turn-of-the-twenty-first-century pronouncement that Asians are at "the front end of the American meritocratic machine . . . replacing Jews" reminds us that ethnoracial frames of romantic selfhood and U.S. exceptionalism are alive and well. Indeed, if Liu's Asian Americans are the "New Jews," then Lehmann's Jewish Americans are undeniably even more naturalized, having become "non-Jews" or "Episcopalians." In so doing, Liu and Lehamman's collective characterization of Asian Americans as "New Jews" expressly confirms the "model minority" stereotype. In the face of such exceptionalist allegations, the model minoritization of Jews and Asians unavoidably intersects with a bifurcated U.S. racial logic that involves both "good" and "bad" subjects. Though the mention of "model minorities" makes seemingly stereotypical sense in the twenty-first century, it nonetheless elides an expansive history of anti-Semitism, nativism, and ethnoreligious/ethnoracial violence. To reiterate, as Liu notes, Jews and Asians "started out as outsiders," a point legislatively made clear in turn-of-the-twentieth-century calls to "shut the door" by means of exclusionary immigration policy. Jewish Americans and Asian Americans thus occupy a paradoxical selfhood position. Within the popular and political U.S. imaginary, they are both idealized citizens and marginalized minorities.

Reminiscent of Robert Olen Butler's "Snow," Liu's concluding articulation of identity—grounded in that "half-lit region between stereotype and sociology"—indubitably harnesses a long-standing comparison between Jewish Americans and Asian Americans. Such comparisons make visible connected ethnoracial logics and connective demographic correspondences. And, as evidenced by the comparative currency this frame holds, this tale of two model minorities continues into the twenty-first century. Indeed, almost ten years after the publication of *The Accidental Asian*, this relationship is apparent in a *New York Times* commentary from 2007 titled, "In Jews, Indian-Americans See Role Models in Activism."[31] In a more popular vein, these ethnoracial intersections are perceptible in the popular films *Harold and Kumar Go to White Castle* (2004) and *Harold and Kumar Escape from Guantanamo Bay* (2008), authored by two Jewish American screenwriters, Jon Hurwitz and Hayden Schlossberg, and featuring two Asian American male leads, Kal Penn and John Cho.

Notwithstanding such comparative currency, relatively little scholarship has taken up the comparative task of examining the connected literary productions of these two groups. Returning to Liu's *The Accidental Asian*, Jonathan Freedman rightfully reminds us that the "discursive criss-crossings evident in Liu's . . . reflections are just one of the many repeated moments of intersection between the experiences, real and imagined, of Jewish- and Asian-Americans for the last century. These crossings are both remarkably extensive and surprisingly under-studied."[32] Such "crossings" are undeniably present in past U.S. immigration policy and contemporary model minority characterizations. As important, these "crossings" occur at the legislative point at which immigrants are made into U.S. citizens via naturalization law and process. Taken together, the history of immigration and model minoritization underscore the racialization and deracination of Jewish and Asian Americans.

Writing Naturalization: Jewish and Asian American Literature

In drawing to a close, it is precisely the role of immigration and naturalization in U.S. nation building that structures *Modeling Citizenship*'s interdisciplinary analysis of Jewish and Asian American literature. In this analysis, *Modeling Citizenship* makes visible the contested terrain of citizenship, nationhood, and belonging. Concomitantly, the focus on immigration practice, policy, and discourse through legislation and representation coheres with Yen Le Espiritu's recent work on Filipino America, wherein she notes,

> The production of discourses of immigration, both popular and intellectual, is important because modes of representation are themselves forms of power rather than mere reflections of power. Immigration has become a key symbol in American culture, a central powerful concept imbued with a multiplicity of myths and meanings, capable of rousing highly charged emotions that culminate in violently unfair practices.[33]

Arguing that popular and intellectual representations "are themselves forms of power," Espiritu makes possible a reading of immigration as both a "key symbol in American culture" and an affective touchstone.

Turning to affective frames, immigration rouses highly charged emotions because it carries mythic meaning and prompts strong political reaction. From turn-of-the-twentieth-century nativist claims of Anglo-Saxon nationhood to turn-of-the-twentieth-century multiculturalist allegations of a U.S. nation of immigrants, the foreigner as would-be American undeniably marries past, present, and future notions of ethnicity, race, gender, and nation. Indeed, as is evident in immigration debate and policy, the question of how to make Americans out of foreign material necessarily brings to the fore a discussion about what culturally, socially, and politically constitutes the "right material." This evaluative rubric encompasses the naturalization processes through which non-native-born Americans are legally and bureaucratically "made." Often employed as a synonym for "assimilation," "naturalization" operates in divergently politicized fashion, connecting immigrant to both country of origin and settlement nation.

Both transnational and national, "naturalization" becomes a multi-sited means through which to configure different types of citizenship. To be sure, as Priscilla Wald argues, naturalization has "evolved as a keyword along with the modern conceptions of political belonging that we have come to associate with the nation."[34] Corresponding to "modes of political belonging," naturalization is defined through frames of personhood and selfhood that require a repudiation of past country affiliation and a declaration of commitment to present-nation civic practices.

What is more, as an "American keyword" (like Raymond Williams's notion of a viable and critical sociocultural vocabulary), Wald's "Naturalization" entry in Bruce Burgett and Glenn Hendler's edited *Keywords for American Cultural Studies* (2007) makes even more visible the multivalent function of the term within an ever-shifting U.S. cultural, political, and social imaginary. As Wald maintains:

> In this modern concept of the nation, political affiliation (citizenship) and common descent (kinship) are interfused rather than sedimentary modes of belonging. Kinship, no less than citizenship, is a taxonomic construction that registers, even as it masks, social and political hierarchies. The interweaving of the two is evident in early-twentieth-century debates over topics ranging from eugenics to migration policy. . . . Naturalization laws and policies register change not only in the legal contours of political belonging, but also in the terms by which that belonging is articulated.[35]

If naturalization—including "political affiliation and common descent"—is indeed taxonomic, then it functions as a focal point for examining the ways in which citizens are identified, read, and performed. Characterized by a particular grammar and patriotic rhetoric, naturalization becomes a heretofore underexamined literary trope. When considered in relation to two "model minority" groups, naturalization's affective and performative dimensions become potent poles upon which to evaluate idealized selfhood and exceptionalist nationhood. In other words, analyzing the specter, practice, and role of naturalization in Jewish and Asian American literary production makes such work taxonomic and indexical in scope.

Hence, *Modeling Citizenship* investigates a particular U.S. idiom of citizenship, inclusive of ethnic, racial, and national metaphors, which are then rearticulated and revised through the public act of writing. Accordingly, naturalization emerges as a useful signpost to measure the extent to which immigrant writers—particularly Jewish American and Asian American writers—negotiate shifting characterizations of monolithic U.S. selfhood through previously held affiliations. From Edith Maude Eaton's (Sui Sin Far's) short stories about Chinese immigrants to Abraham Cahan's novella, *Yekl*; from Israel Zangwill's *The Melting-Pot* to C.Y. Lee's *The Flower Drum Song*; from Mary Antin's *The Promised Land* to Gish Jen's response, *Mona in the Promised Land*; and from Bharati Mukherjee's *Jasmine* to Eva Hoffman's *Lost in Translation*, Jewish American and Asian American writing has been compellingly read through discourses of assimilation that evaluate the immigrant and refugee body through majority paradigms of U.S. selfhood. Focused on the literary negotiation of American selfhood via immigrant subjectivities, the inclusion of Zangwill despite his British citizenship highlights his work's resonance in contemporary immigration discourse, emblematized by his most famous dramatic (and U.S.-focused) production, *The Melting-Pot.*

Historically organized, the texts included in *Modeling Citizenship* speak to the multivalent and polyvocal role of cultural production in making visible the contested nature of citizenship at distinct moments in U.S. immigration policy and law. The final body chapter—which focuses analytical attention on two neoconservative model minorities—gestures toward a twenty-first-century reading of both groups vis-à-vis "War on Terror" logics, progressive resistance, and the ongoing immigration debate. This return to the political imaginary corresponds to the back-and-forth nature of U.S. immigration policy and ethnoracial formation, wherein immigrant and refugee subjects are considered either ideal American subjects or aliens ineligible for citizenship. Therefore, critical to *Modeling Citizenship* is the relocation of such Jewish and Asian American cultural productions from the margins of exclusively assimilative analyses to naturalized readings that necessarily take into account demographic upheaval and shift.

1 / "Who May Be Citizens of the United States": Citizenship Models in Edith Maude Eaton and Abraham Cahan

The anomalous spectacle of a distinct people, living in our community, recognizing no laws of this State except through necessity, bringing with them their prejudices and national feuds, in which they indulge in open violation of the law. . . . [The Chinese are] a race of people whom nature has marked as inferior . . . between whom and ourselves nature has placed an impassable difference.

—CHIEF JUSTICE HUGH MURRAY, 1854

There never has been any question heretofore of the right of a Chinaman to be naturalized in the same way as an Irishman or a German. Several native Chinese are at the present time citizens of the United States; it is fair to presume that they vote, and it is undeniable that they are useful members of the community in which they reside. In one point of view they remind one of the Jews of the Middle Ages—industrious, orderly, hard-working, money-getting—they are the natural traders of the Pacific shores. Yet it needs no great foresight to perceive that, at no distant day, they will be pariahs throughout our Pacific States.

—EDITORIAL, *HARPERS WEEKLY*, 1858

Four years after California was granted "free soil" statehood, a seemingly innocuous article appeared in the December 6, 1854, issue of the *German Reformed Messenger*, a weekly Chambersberg, Pennsylvania paper. Placed among alarmist reports of "An Immense Subterranean Lake in Michigan," touristic accounts of "Bird-Egging on the Pacific," and declarations that "Masons Must Not Fight," a headline unequivocally announced, "Chinese Not Competent to Give Testimony against Whites."[1] The *German Reformed Messenger* briefly focused its journalistic attention on a far-away California criminal case: *People v. George W. Hall* (1854). The appellant, a Nevada County resident, had recently been convicted for murdering Ling Sing, a Chinese miner. The prosecution's case principally rested on the testimony of three unnamed Chinese immigrants, the sole witnesses to the crime.

As suggested by the *German Reformed Messenger*'s byline, an integral part of *People v. Hall* was not so much a declaration of innocence as a proficiency petition. More important, the verdict reached by the California Supreme Court would have an impact that far surpassed its local purview. Initially concerned with Hall's appeal that Chinese were ineligible witnesses in a California court of law, the justification for acquittal makes visible a still-forming exclusionary matrix. The construction of such racialized logics in the mid-1850s directly corresponds to the concomitant emergence of Chinese immigrants on the U.S. socioeconomic landscape. Indeed, it is the mid-century Chinese immigration en masse to the United States that principally foregrounds the California Supreme Court's ruling.

Prompted by gold rushes, drawn to mining booms, and later recruited to labor on postbellum transcontinental railroads, Chinese immigrants embodied an emergent global Pacific imaginary that was replete with transnational flows of capital, labor, and commodities. In turn, rising numbers of Chinese bodies in California and the West Coast promulgated a nativist, racist redrawing of racial borders. As the *German Reformed Messenger* summarizes, "a white citizen of California was indicted for murder and convicted on the testimony of Chinese witnesses. He appealed on the ground that by the State law regulating criminal proceedings, 'no black or molatto [*sic*] person, or Indian, shall be allowed to give evidence in favor or against a white man.'" Central to the California court's decision was the issue of race, which to date had legally been categorized in a four-part manner ("white," "black," "molatto," and "Indian"). At stake in *People v. Hall* was the demarcation of racialized personhood within a shifting and increasingly more diverse immigrant/settler/native-born demographic. Additionally, the subsequent drawing of new racial borders anticipates late nineteenth-century naturalization rulings and immigration policies committed to excluding, prohibiting, and denying Chinese access to the U.S. nation.

In precedent-setting fashion, Chief Justice Hugh Murray turned to the 1790 Naturalization Act, which similarly commences with a delineation of citizenship by means of race. Correspondingly, the court ruminated on the constitutionality of Chinese selfhood, which encompassed (among other privileges) due process rights. For example, the Chief Justice opined:

> The Act of Congress in defining what description of aliens may become naturalized citizens, provides [for] every "free white

> citizen." . . . If the term "White," as used in the Constitution, was not understood in its generic sense as including the Caucasian race, and necessarily excluding all others, where was the necessity of providing for the admission of Indians to the privilege of voting, by special session? We are of the opinion that the words "White," "Negro," Mulatto," Indian," and "Black person," wherever they occur in our Constitution and laws, must be taken in their generic sense, and that even admitting the Indian of this Continent is not the Mongolian type, that the words, "Black person" . . . must be taken as contradistinguished from White, and necessarily excludes all other races other than Caucasian.[2]

In the spirit of "contradistinguishing" nonwhite from Caucasian, the court ruled (according to the *German Reformed Messenger* article) "that Chinese are not competent to give testimony against whites, in the courts of California, and accordingly the verdict in the case was set aside." As is apparent in the opening epigraph, Chief Justice Murray's ruling of incompetence was built on alleged illegality, transnational "prejudices," and innate "inferiority." Hence, *People v. Hall* undercuts the hopeful (albeit racist) *Harper's Weekly* assertion that "There never has been any question heretofore of the right of a Chinaman to be naturalized in the same way as an Irishman or a German."

At the same time, the "impassable difference" emblematized by the Chinese produces an analogous reading (as in the *Harper's Weekly* excerpt) between mid-century "Chinamen" and "Jews of the Middle Ages." Regardless of "industrious, orderly, hard-working, money-getting" talents, both Chinaman and Jew become inevitable pariahs. If *People v. Hall* confirmed this status for Chinese immigrants, Jewish Americans would face a related (but by no means identical) citizenship challenge eight years later. On December 17, 1862, while the nation was engaged in civil war, General Ulysses S. Grant issued a decidedly anti-Semitic decree. Known as "General Order Number 11," the military act pronounced the following: "the Jews, as a class violating every regulation of trade established by the Treasure Department . . . are hereby expelled from the department [in Kentucky, Tennessee, and Mississippi] within twenty-four hours from receipt of this order."[3] Although instantly protested and quickly overturned in January 1863, the act nonetheless attests to a probationary whiteness connected to citizenship. Tellingly, the absence of Jewish exclusion (analogous, for example, to Chinese exclusion) reconfirms the ostensible "whiteness" afforded both Jewish Americans and Jewish immigrants in the 1790 naturalization law.

Though predating them by almost half a century, such citizenship parameters and proposed expulsions unavoidably influence the works of Chinese Canadian American writer Edith Maude Eaton (Sui Sin Far) and Jewish American author Abraham Cahan. Dialogically situated, Edith Maude Eaton and Abraham Cahan necessarily write within the shifting fin-de-siècle contours of race, ethnicity, and nation. Correspondingly, both authors make visible the contested dimensions of U.S. selfhood vis-à-vis immigration. As the nation moved from antebellum selfhood to turn-of-the-twentieth-century personhood, the primacy of race in the "making of Americans" incontrovertibly persisted in five distinct (and connected) citizenship/immigration events: the above-mentioned *People v. Hall*, the amended 1870 Naturalization Act, the Page Act (1875), *In re Ah Yup* (1878), and the 1882 Chinese Exclusion Act. Unsurprisingly, the "raced" dimensions of naturalization and citizenship haunt the plots, characterizations, and themes in two Eaton short stories: "In the Land of the Free" (1909) and "The Story of One White Woman Who Married a Chinese" (1910). Specifically, Eaton strategically employs a more open characterization of Chinese immigrants as culturally and politically viable would-be citizens to engender an antiracist, anti-exclusion reading of such bodies.

Alternatively, despite access to naturalization as a viable citizenship subject, by means of extant law and policy, Abraham Cahan's Jewish protagonist in *Yekl: A Tale of the New York Ghetto* (1896) is faced with an equally uncertain selfhood future. In particular, Cahan's novella calls attention to the provisional dimensions of U.S. citizenship for Jewish immigrants (and, by extension, Jewish Americans). In the process, Cahan unintentionally reclaims a conditional immigrant past discernible in episodes like the December 1862 proposed expulsion and more contemporaneous calls to "shut the door" on eastern European immigrants. Suggestive of temporariness and surveillance (like a citizen "on probation"), probationary white selfhood circumscribes Cahan's novella about Jewish immigrant bodies in cultural transition.[4] Such histories and uncertainties destabilize readings of wholesale Jewish inclusion within a larger U.S. body politic.

"No Discrimination on Account of Color": The Making of Post-Bellum Citizenship

The antebellum question of "free white personhood," a pivotal inquiry in *People v. Hall*, would reemerge in amended fashion during the post-Civil War decade. Likewise, the issue of Chinese immigration would once again prove central in discussions over citizenship access and process. Indeed, on July 2, 1870, the United States Senate debated the fate of future Americans via a proposed amendment to naturalization law. The chief sponsor of the bill was Massachusetts abolitionist-turned-Reconstruction Republican Charles Sumner.[5] On the Congressional docket was the following amendment: "all Acts of Congress relating to naturalization [will] be, and the same are hereby, amended by striking out the word 'white' wherever it occurs, so that in naturalization there will be no distinction of race or color."[6] Proposed in the aftermath of war and in the midst of Reconstruction, the "raceless" naturalization law potentially afforded unimpeded citizenship access regardless of race and nation.

This was not the first time the Bay State senator had introduced such a bill. Sumner had tried to do so in 1867 and 1869, only to see his amendment languish in the Judiciary Committee. At first, the Massachusetts senator justified the bill by way of an expected black/white racial paradigm. Accordingly, Sumner averred, "Here . . . Africans in our country are shut out from rights which justly belong to them, simply because Congress continues the word 'white' in the Naturalization Laws."[7] Interestingly, Sumner's argument about "Africans" was principally directed not at immigrants but at native-born Americans (African Americans), who had ostensible *jus solis* citizenship in the post-bellum period. Nevertheless, Sumner's appeal tactically collapses the space between native- and foreign-born, making visible the full extent of African American disenfranchisement.[8] Mindful of a post-abolition, reactive and reactionary milieu, Sumner's declaration of unjustifiable exclusion coincided with a greater Reconstructionist agenda intent on righting—through multivalent selfhood—the constitutional wrongs of slavery by means of past deracination and present discrimination. Corresponding to political intentions at work in the Thirteenth, Fourteenth, and Fifteenth amendments, Sumner's proposed naturalization law eschewed race in the practice and process of citizenship.[9]

From the outset, Sumner appealed to the Declaration of Independence. Clearly a document of the "Founding Fathers," the Declaration operates—at the level of national discourse—in symbolic tandem with the Constitution. Despite their foundational coherences, critical to Sumner's petition was an issue of reconciliation between the two documents. Specifically, the Massachusetts senator publicly noted the disjuncture between a colorblind Declaration and a racialized Constitution. Unintentionally, Sumner returned to the original Declaration of Independence, which carried the abolitionist complaint that the King had "waged cruel War against human Nature itself, violating its most Sacred Right of Life and Liberty in the Persons of a distant People who never offended him, captivating and carrying them into Slavery in another Hemisphere, or to incure miserable Death, in their Transportation thither. This piratical Warfare, the opprobrium of infidel Powers, is the Warfare of the Christian King of Great Britain."[10] As the perpetuation of slavery in the United States attests, the "colorblindness" of the Declaration was principally achieved through omission. In spite of the revised Declaration's less-than-progressive slave politics, Sumner proclaimed the need to "bring our system into harmony with the Declaration of Independence and the Constitution of the United States."[11]

More important in relation to Sumner's amendment, the Constitution contemporaneously defined citizenship through "free white persons." A civil rights interventionist, Sumner reminded his fellow senators that in the Declaration of Independence, "all men. . . . not a race or color . . . are placed under the protection of the Declaration."[12] Admittedly, Sumner's plea for tolerance was not entirely inclusive with regard to gender. The Constitutional omission of women from the project of nation building (via the explicit privileging of male bodies and the absence of any mention of women) attests to an ongoing masculinist understanding of citizenship.[13]

In the face of a dominant black/white reading of the U.S. racial landscape, Sumner was more expansive in his call to remove from naturalization law "distinction[s] of race or color." Without a doubt, Sumner's petition addressed what was increasingly termed "the Chinese question" within the U.S. political and cultural imaginary. The question (or more accurately, the problem) was predicated on the increased presence of Chinese immigrants in the United States. Such "inassimilable" bodies focused policy anxieties over race, assimilability, and nation. Proposed a year after the completion of the transcontinental railroad, Sumner's amendment seemingly offered a "selfhood solution" to the "Chinese problem" via open-access naturalization. Furthermore, the direct mention of the Chinese in Sumner's appeal formed a more progressive response to racist denaturalization in *People v. Hall.*

To that end, Sumner professed, "We are told that they [the Chinese] are Imperialists; but before they can be citizens they must renounce Imperialism. We are told they are foreigners in heart; but before they can take part with us they must renounce their foreign character."[14] Apropos a naturalization agenda, Sumner's rhetoric draws attention to the two-sided nature of the "making of Americans" from "foreign material." Expressly, though the Chinese immigrant may be an "Imperialist," the would-be Chinese American must—according to naturalization law and oath—repudiate this past national affiliation. Similarly, though the Chinese immigrant is a de facto foreigner, the potential Chinese American is required to prove Americanization by means of language (English) and culture (a working knowledge of U.S. history). Sumner emphasized democratic intentionality vis-à-vis legislated naturalization: "If the Chinese come here, they will come for citizenship or merely for labor. If they come for citizenship, then in this desire do they give a pledge of loyalty to our institutions; and where is the peril in such vows? They are peaceful and industrious; how can their citizenship be the occasion of solicitude?"[15] Reminiscent of characterizations of "industriousness" in the *Harper's Weekly* passage, Sumner casts Chinese immigrants as voluntary subjects (either as prospective citizens or as "mere" laborers) who are simultaneously potential paragons of citizenship (as peaceful and loyal subjects).

Notwithstanding the senator's earnest support of Chinese immigration and naturalization, Sumner's appeal for "no discrimination on the account of color" failed. As Congress moved to revise the 1790 Naturalization Act, the "free white persons" clause remained, though the act carried an explicit provision for "those of African descent." Correspondingly, U.S. personhood—and specifically naturalized citizenship—was for the most part delineated along a polarized black/white axis. Consequently, the legibility of Chinese (and other Asian) immigrants through naturalization law continued to be ambiguous at best. The modified personhood stipulation paradoxically (and purposefully) "opened the door" for African immigrants seeking naturalized citizenship.[16] On the other hand, the 1870 Naturalization Act—principally by omission—"closed the door" for groups previously deemed "ineligible" or "incompetent" citizens.

The application of "closed door" personhood was apparent eight years later, when Ah Yup ("a native of China and the Mongolian race,") petitioned for U.S. citizenship in a District of California circuit court.[17] The 1878 case, *In re Ah Yup*, posed the first major suit vis-à-vis the recently amended law. Admitting that present-day naturalization provisions "exclude[d] all but white persons and persons of African nativity or African descent," the court all the same reasoned:

> Although the term "white persons" constitutes a whole variety of persons, none of which may be said to be literally white, the term has acquired a well-settled meaning within the common speech and literature of the country. Webster's dictionary describes 5 races, Caucasian (white) from Europe and western Asia; Mongolian (yellow) from China, Japan, and their region; Negro (black) from Africa; American (red) consisting of the natives of North and South America; and Malay (brown) occupying the islands of the Indian Archipelago region. Neither in popular language, literature, nor science do we find the words "white person" to be so comprehensive as to include those of the Mongolian race. When citizenship was extended to those of African decent, the term "white" was not deleted. This was done so as to exclude those of the Mongolian race.[18]

The court's reliance on Webster's dictionary, a recognizable reference standard, pitted the eligible citizen against the ineligible alien, as in *People v. Hall*. Further, the use of "popular language, literature, [and] science" to justify an exclusionary selfhood underscores a fixed whiteness (and concomitant blackness) within a late-nineteenth-century racial taxonomy. Indeed, this particular taxonomy would be deployed repeatedly in subsequent naturalization cases such as *Ozawa v. United States* (1922) and *United States v. Thind* (1923).

Still, the court's initial concession (that "free white persons" "constitute[d] a whole variety of persons, none of which may be said to be literally white") signals a less restrained conception of whiteness. Even so, this whiteness was necessarily "contradistinguished" from monolithic Asianness (specifically, Mongolianness). The court's pronouncement that "white person" was not "so comprehensive [a term] as to include those of the Mongolian race" reinforces the predominance of race in the formation of naturalized (and natural) Americans. Amid this racial backdrop, the court's substitution of "literal whiteness" in favor of "interpreted whiteness" produces a conditional personhood. In turn, such probationary selfhood makes visible dominant definitions of race and nation. Accordingly, it is within this interpretative space that Jewish immigrants continued to be "white" and hence "naturalizable."

If the 1870 Naturalization Act and *In re Ah Yup* cemented a domestic racial matrix for citizenship that privileged "white" over "Asiatic," then the 1875 Page Act and 1882 Chinese Exclusion Act achieved analogous effect at the level of immigration-oriented foreign policy. Focused on regulating foreign bodies, the 1875 Page Act prohibited the "importation" of Asian women for purposes of prostitution.[19] Though the directive specified a criminal act (prostitution), its widespread application effectively limited Asian women from entering the United States en masse until the 1945 War Brides Act.[20] As Susan Koshy maintains, the "representation of Asian women's sexuality as different from white women's sexuality not only corroborated the thesis of Oriental degeneracy; it justified the segregation of Asians and whites" (11). Further, Koshy significantly reminds us that, with the exception of Japanese immigrants, who by special provision were able to bring their families to Hawaii and the West Coast, Asian groups were prohibited from doing so.[21] By the same token, such ethnoracial regulation anticipates similar objectifying logics at work in the Chinese Exclusion Act, passed May 6, 1882.

Concerned with the increased "importation" of Chinese laborers, the Exclusion Act suspended the legal entry of Chinese laborers into the United States for a period of ten years. The policing purview of the Chinese Exclusion Act originally included both skilled and unskilled laborers. The law's initial provisions, expanded and renewed in the early twentieth century, largely succeeded in containing, policing, and stemming the flow of large numbers of Chinese immigrants into the United States until its 1943 repeal by Congress.[22] Indisputably and considerably, *In re Ah Yup*, the Page Act, and the Chinese Exclusion Act accentuate the value of race, ethnicity, and gender in politicized border control efforts. Without a doubt, such initiatives were aimed at solving the "Chinese question" through selfhood denial, regulation, and prohibition. Likewise, *Ah Yup*'s verdict of "ineligibility," the Page Act's assumption of immorality, and the Chinese Exclusion Act's characterization of illegality underscore the increasingly racialized dimensions of U.S. selfhood in the late nineteenth and early twentieth centuries. The racialized registers of U.S. selfhood foreground the political work in Edith Maude Eaton's short stories, which overtly assume the labor of rehabilitating Chinese immigrants (and by extension, Chinese Americans) via frames of eligibility and "rightful" personhood.

Models of Citizenship, Victims of Prejudice: Edith Maude Eaton's "In the Land of the Free" and "The Story of One White Woman Who Married a Chinese"

Situated within a decidedly anti-Chinese milieu, North American Chinese writer Edith Maude Eaton's pro-Chinese narratives "contradistinguish" racial stereotype from actual personhood via sentimental plot and characterization. As an example, Eaton's fin-de-siècle "In the Land of the Free" (1909) is an affective immigrant story of bureaucratization, detention, and exclusion. The narrative was originally published in *The Independent*, a liberal weekly magazine known for its progressive articles and stories on such subjects as abolition and the education of women.[23] Also included in the 1912 collection *Mrs. Spring Fragrance* (Eaton's one published volume), "In the Land of the Free" is emotionally and thematically driven.[24] As Amy Ling notes, the narrative makes legible "racial insensitivity, the human costs of bureaucratic and discriminatory laws, [and] the humanity of the Chinese."[25] Divided into four parts, the story follows the trials and tribulations of a Chinese immigrant family as they attempt to reenter and—more significantly—reunite in the United States.

Purposefully sentimental, "In the Land of the Free" commences with an idealized characterization of the United States. As the nationalistic title suggests, the United States is configured through familiar "country love" tropes, redolent of democratic virtue and U.S. exceptionalism. Indeed, the title is taken from the most patriotic of songs, "The Star-Spangled Banner." Eaton again engages the national anthem in the story's opening paragraph, which introduces the reader to Lae Choo and her son, the tenderly named "Little One." Eying the U.S. coastline, Lae Choo tells her son, "See, Little One—the hills in the morning sun. There is thy home for years to come. It is very beautiful and thou wilt be very happy there." Reminiscent of the "dawn's early light" which begins "The Star-Spangled Banner," the "morning sun" underscores Lae Choo's potential loyalty to the U.S. nation and anticipates a possible naturalization. Further, the mention of "home" (in tandem with the story's title) evokes "the land of the free" and the "home of the brave."

The use of the high diction and the absence of regional dialect straightaway contradict orientalist claims of inherent "Asiatic alienhood." Sinophobia—and attendant exclusion—in the United States was partly premised on language. Such elevated language allows Eaton to collapse the perceived gulf between English and Chinese. In other words, the use of formal English is a tactical translation of Chinese that militates against popular assertions of cultural depravity. Alternatively, if the story at once engages the immigration process, then the formal language used by its Chinese protagonists is analogous to official legal language. Be that as it may, such stilted grammar nonetheless breaks down when Lae Choo is faced with an impersonal bureaucracy. For example, when the couple are told that their son must be confiscated, Lae Choo declares, "No, you not take him; he my son too" (94). Such a linguistic rupture brings to light a multivalent emotional investment (that is, maternal love and anger) and an antagonistic encounter with an indifferent administrative state.

Such naturalized wordplay takes an affective turn, evident in the unidentified narrator's account of the "Little One's" response. As the narrator describes, "Little One looked up into his mother's face in perfect faith. He was engaged in the pleasant occupation of sucking a sweetmeat; but that did not prevent him from gurgling responsively" (93). Further countering anti-Chinese stereotype, Eaton stresses that Lae Choo (and "Little One") are not "temporary sojourners" but willing and responsive settler/pioneers in search of a permanent U.S. home. What is more, Lae Choo and Little One come to the United States in "good faith," indicating a desire for U.S. citizenship. With mention of "home" and "happiness," Lae Choo articulates a hopeful, householding vision of the United States.[26] Correspondingly, this romantic pronouncement of "home" coheres with a more nationalistic reading of promise and opportunity.

Even so, this arrival is complicated by immigration processes that require exact documentation. Lae Choo has the necessary paperwork for herself but not her China-born son. An undocumented and therefore "un-entitled" alien, the son is seized by the authorities and detained in an orphanage. Consequently, the customs agent and U.S. immigration policy recast Little One as a disenfranchised "Chinaman." Lae Choo initially protests, stressing her maternal rights. However, in the face of immigration law, Lae Choo has little choice but to acquiesce, and she quickly resigns herself to the process.

Despite this initial resistance, the unidentified narrator strategically brings to light Lae Choo's a priori lawfulness. The narrator observes, "accustomed to obedience she yielded the boy to her husband, who in turn delivered him to the first officer. The Little One protested lustily against the transfer; but his mother covered her face with her sleeve and his father silently led her away. Thus was the law of the land complied with" (95). Lae Choo is "accustomed to obedience," which paves the way for an innate legal compliance. Such law-abiding proclivities combat dominant assertions of non-rehabilitative Chinese criminality. In addition, Lae Choo's acquiescence to the law—characteristic of a "model citizen"—is dramatically subsumed within the bureaucratic, impersonal practice of immigration policy.

As the customs agent asserts, "Seeing that the boy has no certificate entitling him admission to this country, you will have to leave him to us" (94). Cast as a seize-worthy commodity, the Little One is consequently "delivered" and "transferred" to the U.S. customs agent. This confiscation prefigures the primary conflict between law, process, and family in the narrative. Undeniably, "In the Land of the Free" centers on Lae Choo and Hom Hing's attempts to retrieve, through legal and bureaucratic means, and be reunited with their indefinitely detained son. At the same time, Eaton's story speaks to a tension between the preservation of the family unit and an indifferent immigration processes. In the process, "In the Land of the Free" produces a critique of the nation-state via American family values and alleged racial logics about white superiority.

This contentious interplay between family, indifference, and whiteness is made plain in an episode involving James Clancy, a lawyer who claims he can facilitate Little One's retrieval. Up to this point, Lae Choo and Hom Hing have spent months negotiating the Little One's release, a fact implied through brief allusions to seasonal change (such as "winter rains"). At first, Clancy is met with gratitude; Lae Choo asserts, "You are a hundred man good"(98). However, Clancy exacts immediate (and exorbitant) payment without guarantee of result. Discouraged, Lae Choo tells the lawyer, "You not one hundred man good; you just common white man"(99). Highlighting the lawyer's "commonness" vis-à-vis his whiteness, Lae Choo destabilizes dominant claims of U.S. exceptionalism. Indeed, if the lawyer—a principal bureaucratic actor—stands in for the U.S. nation, then his interest in profit undermines grandiose (and racial) claims of moral high-groundedness.

The accented nature of Lae Choo's accusation—audible in the absence of "correct" grammar—draws attention to the critique of white masculinity through nonexceptionalist "commonality." In other words, whiteness is connected to a matrix of moral turpitude, replete with capitalist, antisentimental investment. Simultaneously, Eaton's story militates against stereotypical constructions of Chinese immigrants as disinvested in family values (such as claims of lawlessness and amorality). Equally important, the protagonists of "In the Land of the Free" are undeniably circumscribed by legality and invested in reunification. Taken together, Lae Choo's allegation tenaciously revises a hierarchy built on whiteness, which is racially presumptive of moral and ethical superiority. Correspondingly, the declaration of incompetence vis-à-vis the Chinese citizenship question is tactically manipulated within the narrative. To be sure, Lae Choo and Hom Hing must contend with an incompetent bureaucracy filled with ineffective actors, which refuses to follow its own set of rules and regulations. Within this milieu, Eaton employs a sentimental domestic plot that is indubitably fissured by U.S. immigration policy.

Combating Page Act logics about innate Chinese prostitution and *People v. Hall* "competency" verdicts, Eaton's characterization of Lae Choo as concerned mother produces an empathetic reading of Chinese womanhood through domestic frames. In the same way, Lae Choo's desire for family reunification overtly coincides with intelligible American family values, which hinge on the ability to reproduce traditional middle-class virtue. Concurrently, the characterization of the maternal Lae Choo challenges "fallen woman" tropes of Chinese femininity. Just as "In the Land of the Free" confronts the 1875 Page Act, the story also amends *People v. Hall* declarations of "bad citizenship." To that end, Eaton's Chinese protagonists are "competent," law-abiding subjects willing and able to work within established U.S. immigration processes.

Mindful of *In re Ah Yup*'s ruling of alien ineligibility, Eaton's "In the Land of the Free" domesticates the Chinese subject, eschewing transnational affiliation to China in favor of U.S. selfhood. At the same time, such domestication—or naturalization—turns tragic at the story's conclusion. Having secured "the precious paper which gave Hom Hing and his wife the right to the possession of their own child," the couple ventures to the orphanage. According to the narrator,

> The room was filled with children—most of them wee tots, but none so wee as her own. The mission woman talked as she walked. She told Lae Choo that little Kim, as he had been named by the school, was the pet of the place. . . . He had been rather difficult to manage at first and had cried much for his mother; "but children so soon forget, and after a month he seemed quite at home and played around as bright and happy as a bird."(101)

The unidentified narrator's description hearkens back to the beginning of the story in its use of "wee" (an affectionate term reminiscent of "Little One") and mention of "home." At the same time, Little One's domestication (revealed in his function as "the pet of the place") takes on naturalized importance. Adopted in an "adopted country" and renamed Kim, the Little One has (albeit unwillingly and unwittingly) taken on a new American identity, repudiating in the process his country-of-origin name. The Little One's name—Kim—at once calls to mind Ridyard Kipling's eponymous novel about an Irish orphan in India. Unlike Kipling's Kim, Little One is not a true orphan, for his parents are alive and seek reunification.

Lae Choo, who "did not hear what was said to her" due to "anticipatory joy," fails to comprehend the mission woman's assertion of her child's amnesia. The extent of Little One's naturalization is fully revealed when the family is reunited. As the narrator observes, Little One, "dressed in blue cotton overalls and white-soled shoes . . . shrunk from [his mother] and tried to hide himself in the folds of the white woman's skirt. 'Go'way, go'way!' he bade his mother" (101). As the final moment in the story, Little One's denial shows the high cost of naturalization. Refusing his Chinese parentage and Chinese name, Little One naturalizes, repudiating his Chinese mother and declaring loyalty to his American guardian. Provocatively, this affective performance occurs in the face of contemporaneous naturalization law, which codifies (by way of *In re Ah Yup*) the "Asiatic" subject as an "alien ineligible for citizenship." Consequently, Little One is culturally naturalized yet remains a denaturalized (or refugee) subject under racist naturalization law. Taken together, Eaton ironically reconfigures the story's title. In the end, the United States is not so much the land of the free but rather a site of detention, imprisonment, and forced naturalization.

If "In the Land of the Free" underscores the contradictions of U.S. nationhood through the rehabilitation of Chinese (and potentially Chinese American) personhood, Eaton's "The Story of One White Woman Who Married a Chinese" assumes a similar trajectory. Despite coherences, the familial dynamics at work in "Land of the Free" are dramatically modified in the second story vis-à-vis an interracial relationship. Like the earlier narrative, "The Story of One White Woman Who Married a Chinese" was initially published in *The Independent*, though with the markedly more sensational title, "A White Woman Who Married a Chinaman."[27] Whereas Little One's Americanization attests to a forced naturalization, "The Story of One White Woman" engenders a voluntary naturalization through intimacy, recuperation, and Americanization.[28]

As the title makes clear, what follows is a narrative about "one white woman"—Minnie—and her marital negotiation with "a Chinese." The interracial stakes of the story are immediately established. As Minnie professes: "Why did I marry Liu Kanghi, a Chinese? Well, in the first place, because I loved him; in the second place, because I was weary of working, struggling, and fighting in the world; in the third place, because my child needed a home" (66–67). Minnie's tripartite answer to the "marriage question" anticipates what will follow—a sustained and expanded domestic justification of interracial love. Implicitly, Minnie's opening interrogation addresses two distinct turn-of-the-twentieth-century issues: the "women's question" and the "Chinese question." Correspondingly, these questions—which were at the time largely answered by omission and exclusion—necessarily bring together gender, race, and nation.

Equally significant, Minnie answers both questions via romantic and affective declaration. Stressing the primacy of love in her decision to marry (apparent in the pronouncement of "in the first place"), Minnie is at once a voluntary and willing partner to Liu Kanghi, a "Chinese." Published after the passage of the 1907 Expatriation Law (which carried the punishment of denaturalization for women who married non-U.S. citizens), "The Story of One White Woman" promulgates a feminist politics through anti-racist, pro-Chinese frames. In the process, Eaton as author and immigration activist produces a resistive narrative that overtly critiques the sexist, racist, and nativist logics of the Page Act, Chinese Exclusion Act, *In re Ah Yup*, and Expatriation Act.

Minnie time and again calls attention to the humanity of her Chinese husband through the antithetical cruelty of her first husband—the white American James. As in "In the Land of the Free," the Chinese characters in "The Story of One White Woman" are more "American" than their native-born counterparts precisely because they embody "true" values (that is, family and morality). Eaton therefore characterizes them as subjects eligible and deserving of U.S. citizenship. To that end, Minnie is first and foremost a "traditional woman," invested in householding, housekeeping, and the "cult of domesticity." She is therefore an emblem of domestic middle-class virtue, making her decision to marry "outside her race" all the more unexpected.

In contrast, James carries an alleged commitment to women's suffrage and First Wave Feminism. Illustratively, James repeatedly criticizes Minnie because she is not "built for anything but taking care of kids" (68). As Minnie relates, James disapproves of her choices, making her "feel it a disgrace to be a woman and a mother" (70). Distrustful of feminist politics, Minnie confesses, "Once I told him that I did not admire clever business women, as I had usually found them, and so had other girls of my acquaintance, not nearly so kind-hearted, generous, and helpful as the humble drudges of the world—the ordinary working women" (67).

Minnie's admission (coupled with affectively charged observations of kind-heartedness, generosity, and helpfulness) establishes her conventional, conservative sensibility. Though Minnie eventually seeks nondomestic employment outside the home, it is only after her first husband insists. Consequently, Minnie's employment occurs in large part out of a desire to fulfill her husband's wishes, which bring to light her devoted wifehood. Be that as it may, Minnie loses her place as a stenographer because "her heart yearned over [her] child" (70). In this regard, Minnie's maternal imperative overcomes her spousal obligation, reconfirming a conservative characterization.

Despite her stated commitment to the marriage, Minnie obtains a divorce upon discovery of her first husband's infidelity. With young son in tow, a distraught Minnie wanders into Chinatown. Agitated, she contemplates suicide. As Minnie remembers, "someone touched my arm and I heard" Liu Kanghi's voice. Despite Liu Kanghi's warning that she "will fall into the water," Minnie's "answer was a step forward." In response, "a strong hand was laid upon my arm and I was swung around against my will" (71). Saving the protagonist and her son, Liu Kanghi is from the outset heroically characterized. By rescuing Minnie and her baby, Liu Kanghi is—like fellow Chinese immigrants Lae Choo and Hom Hing—introduced through sentimental family frames.[29] On another level, the Liu Kanghi's "strong hand" functions as a metonym for a universal reading of masculinity, revising extant views that Chinese men were effeminate, undeserving alien subjects when compared to their white American counterparts.

Concomitantly, Eaton's account naturalizes Liu Kanghi, a repeated move in "The Story of One White Woman Who Married a Chinese." Indeed, Liu Kanghi is described as "wearing American clothes"; he "wore his hair cut, and, even to my American eyes, [he] appeared a good-looking young man" (72). Hence, Minnie naturalizes Liu Kanghi and other Chinese bodies through family frames and domestic spaces. As Minnie narrates,

> The Chinese family with which he [Liu Kanghi] placed me were kind, simple folk. The father had been living in America for more than twenty years. The family consisted of his wife, a grown daughter, and several small sons and daughters, all of whom had been born in America. Liu Jusong, the father, was a working jeweler; but, because of an accident by which he had lost the use of one hand, was partially incapacitated for work. Therefore, their family

> depended for maintenance chiefly upon their kinsman, Liu Kanghi, the Chinese who had brought me to them. (72)

"Kind" and "simple," the Chinese family represents a "complete" unit (with husband, wife, "grown daughter," and several children). The completeness of the Liu Jusong family operates in stark contrast to Minnie's current familial status (without a husband). Noting that the father had lived "in America for more than twenty years" and that all the children "had been born in America," Eaton presents the reader with a familiar (and sympathetic) portrait of Chinese and Chinese Americans. The first-generation Chinese father's job—as a jeweler—also produces a reading of Chinese subjects outside the dominant purview of "unskilled sojourners." And Minnie's emphasis on "native-born" children gestures to the 1898 *United States v. Wong Kim Ark* case, wherein a 6–2 Supreme Court decision upheld the *jus solis* U.S. citizenship of Asian Americans born in the United States.

Additionally, Minnie contrasts her first husband's directive toward nondomestic employment with her Chinese husband's acceptance of conventional domestic labor. For example, within "The Story of One White Woman Who Married a Chinese," Minnie seeks outside employment to repay the Liu Jusong family. In response, Liu Kanghi offers a "domestic solution," suggesting that she work as an at-home embroiderer. This resolution, which marries domestic frame to affective labor, makes socioeconomic sense for Minnie, who happily acquiesces. As Minnie relates,

> So gladly I gave up my quest for office work. I lived in the Liu Jusong house and worked for Liu Kanghi. The days, weeks, and months passed peacefully and happily. Artistic needlework had always been my favorite occupation, and when it became a source both of remuneration and pleasure, I began to feel that life was worth living after all. I watched with complacency my child grow amongst the Chinese children. My life's experience had taught me that virtues do not all belong to the whites. I was interested in all that concerned the Liu household, became acquainted with their friends, and lost altogether the prejudice against the foreigner in which I had been reared. (74)

Maintaining that "virtues do not all belong to the whites," Minnie directly challenges assertions of white superiority and allegations of Chinese depravity. Simultaneously, by enabling nonalienated labor, Liu

Kanghi contradicts a dominant "coolie" image. Minnie recuperates a Victorian notion of family life focused on children, home spaces, and domestic duties. Minnie becomes a "rehabilitated" subject able to engage in her favorite occupation, which in turn foregrounds a feeling "that life is worth living." In so doing, Minnie's account revises the Chinese home through legible American (or naturalized) frames.[29]

As the protagonist watches "with complacency" her child's growth in a Chinese household, Minnie loses "altogether the prejudice against the foreigner," highlighting the degree to which she has been naturalized (by progressive politics) into the Liu Jusong home. Armed with a transformed racial view, Minnie's new outlook is structured by means of familiarity, family, and affective moral virtue. Amid a more traditional backdrop of gender roles and practices, Eaton situates Liu Kanghi, the Chinese husband, within a middle-class imaginary composed of conservative family politics. In deliberate contrast, James—the would-be First Wave Feminist/first husband—operates outside a conventional political milieu. All the same, though James may seem "progressive" in relation to "the woman question," he is less so on the "Chinese question." Strikingly, when Minnie refuses to reconcile, James threatens legal action, telling his ex-wife that she "has sunk. . . . The oily little Chink has won you" (76).

If James is a conservative with regard to the "Chinese question," then Minnie is an outright progressive. As the protagonist retorts,

> Won me! . . . Yes, honorably and like a man. And what are you that dare sneer at one like him. For all your six feet of grossness, your small soul cannot measure up to his great one. You were unwilling to protect and care for the woman who was your wife or the little child you caused to come into this world; but he succored and saved the stranger woman, treated her as a woman, with reverence and respect; gave her child a home, and made them both independent, not only of others but of himself. Now hearing you insult him behind his back, I know, what I did not know before—that I love him, and all I have to say to you is, Go! (76–77)

Affectively couched, Minnie's reply returns to the question of "why" with regard to her marriage to Liu Kanghi. But the order of this latter justification is reversed—instead of beginning with a declaration of love, Minnie concludes with it. In naturalizing fashion, Minnie's declaration of love enables a repudiation of her past "American husband" in favor of her "Chinese husband." Tellingly, the protagonist's response to her "American husband" generates a reading of the "Chinese husband" through masculinist virtue. Accordingly, Liu Kanghi emerges as an American gender traditionalist despite his initial foreignness. Unlike James, Liu Kanghi is willing and able to "protect and care" for Minnie and her child. Further, he is able to provide permanent domestic refuge (or "home"). Liu Kanghi is also responsible for the protagonist's "independence," which attests to a liberation forged not through James's suffragist agenda but via the "cult of domesticity." Last but certainly not least, Minnie's marriage to Liu Kanghi in the concluding portion of "The Story of One White Woman Who Married a Chinese" undeniably underscores the connection between family, nation, and naturalization.

Paradoxically, this marriage leaves open the question of Liu Kanghi's full naturalization. As Minnie admits,

> I accept the lot of the American wife of a humble Chinaman in America. The happiness of the man who loves me is more than the approval or disapproval of those who in my dark days left me to die like a dog. My Chinese husband has his faults. He is hot-tempered and, at times, arbitrary; but he is always a man, and has never sought to take away from me the privilege of being but a woman. I can lean upon and trust in him. I feel him behind me, protecting and caring for me, and that, to an ordinary woman like myself, means more than anything else. (77)

As the "American wife of a humble Chinaman in America," Minnie problematically characterizes (via racist label) her own spousal location. The reinscription of citizenship (American versus Chinese) simultaneously highlights the understanding of nation in the wake of exclusion, citizenship ineligibility, and the Expatriation Act. Minnie repeatedly refers to her second husband as a "Chinese husband," which confirms her husband's foreignness. Consequently, it is unclear by the narrative's conclusion whether or not Minnie considers Liu Kanghi a fully naturalized "American husband." This marital ambiguity suggests an intimate probationary personhood; such marital citizenships would be accessed more directly (and with a different racial register) in Abraham Cahan's *Yekl: A Tale of a New York Ghetto* (1896).

The "Quintessentials of Good Citizenship": Performing Citizenship in Cahan's *Yekl*

> *They are a harmless race when white men either let them alone or treat them no worse than dogs; in fact they are almost entirely harmless anyhow, for they seldom think of resenting the vilest insults or the cruelest injuries. They are quiet, peaceable, tractable, free from drunkenness, and they are as industrious as the day is long. A disorderly Chinaman is rare, and a lazy one does not exist. So long as a Chinaman has strength to use his hands he needs no support from anybody; white men often complain of want of work, but a Chinaman offers no such complaint; he always manages to find something to do.*
>
> —MARK TWAIN, *ROUGHING IT*, 1871

Evocative of Charles Sumner's appeal for Chinese inclusion on grounds of industriousness and moral rightness, the "Chinaman" of Mark Twain's *Roughing It* is "quiet, peaceable, tractable . . . and . . . industrious as the day is long."[30] Twain produces (racial slur aside) a rehabilitative reading comparable to Edith Maude Eaton's pro-Chinese narratives. Similarly, he eschews claims of inherent vice, privileging instead an idealized reading of redeemed Chinese personhood. Twain's characterization brings to light a particular connection between Chinese immigration, discriminatory whiteness, and labor competition. After all, Twain's Chinese are "a harmless race" especially when contradistinguished from "white men" who refuse to let them alone and complain of want of work.

Less generously, Twain's Chinese are sentimentalized "coolies" who subsist on work and manage to "always . . . find something to do." Importantly, the Chinese are not only juxtaposed against other working-class subjects; in the end, Twain claims that they ethically and morally fare better than their white counterparts. Consequently, the American author counters emergent "yellow peril" anxiety (rooted in economic and cultural competition) and dominant claims of alienated Asiatic criminality with a romantic characterization. Twain's nonthreatening Chinese are both gentle and inoffensive, making possible a strategic casting of Chinese immigrants as de facto nineteenth-century model minorities. Even with the best recuperative intent, Twain's characterization is largely illegible within the dominant political imaginary of the time, a reading substantiated by soon-to-be-passed legislative acts of anti-Chinese exclusion, prohibition, and regulation.

In the face of such illegibility, Twain would nevertheless return to these "model minority" frames twenty-six years later, though for a decidedly different agenda. Specifically, the renowned writer would focus his attention not on the "Chinaman" but rather the "Jew." In a September 1899 *Harper's Magazine* article titled "*Concerning the Jews*," Twain maintained, "the Jew is a good and orderly citizen. Summed up, they certify that he is quiet, peaceable, industrious, unaddicted to high crimes and brutal dispositions; that his family life is commendable; that he is not a burden upon public charities; that he is not a beggar; that in benevolence he is above the reach of competition. These are the very quintessentials of good citizenship." [31] Responding to politics abroad (in France, Austria, and Germany), "Concerning the Jews" criticizes intensifying European anti-Semitism central to foreign threats of expulsion and disenfranchisement. Accused of inciting political unrest, Jewish subjects abroad faced immanent forced relocation, and Twain's opinion piece confronts this potential deracination by deconstructing "bad citizenship" frames. As an ethnoreligious starting point, Twain examines the "word Jew as if it stood for both religion and race." Continuing, he addresses and engenders multivalent readings of Jewish personhood. Twain significantly revises his past "model minority" characterization as he moves from redeeming the "Chinaman" to rehabilitating the "Jew."

Expressly, the author omits any mention to "whiteness," which underscores the nonreligious dimensions of a 1790/1870 naturalization law that privileged race in the making of new Americans. In particular, Twain notes that "in the United States [the Jew] was *created free* in the beginning" (emphasis added). Arguing that "the Jew is not a disturber of the peace of any country," Twain reassembles the tenets of "good citizenship," as in his 1872 discussion about the Chinese as paragons of U.S. virtue. Committed to family, "unaddicted" to crime, "industrious," and "peaceable," Twain's Jews embody ideal selfhood. Indubitably, Twain's depiction of "good Jewish citizenship" relies on a parallel racial construction of lawfulness, strong work ethic, and economic acumen.

Divergently, Twain's emphasis on the Jew as isolated subject—apparent in the article's title (and its subsequent acknowledgement of exclusionary practices abroad)—brings to the fore Jewish global marginalization vis-à-vis an "otherwise" politics. Though "Concerning the Jews" is directed at foreign frames, the article unavoidably addresses a domestic immigration configured through globalization. Acknowledging anti-Semitism in the United States (predicated largely–the author surmises—on economic competition during the Reconstruction era), Twain, in spite of everything, locates the problem (or "Jewish concern") elsewhere. In transnational fashion, Twain remarks, "the Jew is being legislated out of Russia. . . . The Jews are harried and obstructed in Austria and Germany, and lately in France; but England and America give them open field and yet survive."

Maintaining that England and America offer an "open field" and still thrive as nations, Twain explicitly attempts to assuage anxieties about the viability of a Jewish citizenry abroad. Alternatively, the American author implicitly underscores a domestically relevant cause-and-effect relationship: that anti-Semitism abroad is responsible for the present-day en masse relocation of Jewish émigrés to Boston, Philadelphia, and New York City. In mapping the connection between foreign politics and domestic policies, Twain concomitantly challenges characterizations of a "Jewish immigration problem" in the United States, which engaged exclusionary logics manifest in claims of "bad subjectivity" and inassimilability.

Purposely and temporally situated amid such U.S. fears of alien inassimilability and bad citizenship, Twain's declaration of ideal selfhood challenges existing U.S. legislative "solutions," which attempted to contain undesirable personhood (such as that of Chinese immigrants and other newly arrived bodies) via prohibition, taxation, and categorization. For instance, three months after the restrictive Chinese Exclusion Act, Congress passed immigration legislation that levied a fifty cent tax on all "aliens" entering the United States. Armed with a classification agenda, the August 3, 1882, act carried an added regulatory provision: entry denials for "convicts (except those convicted of political offenses), lunatics, idiots, and persons likely to become public charges."[32] Within this multisided context, Twain's emphasis on the "quintessentials of good citizenship" therefore references regulatory impulses in immigration policy and tactically elevates Jewish personhood precisely through model minoritization.

In highlighting Old World problems and romantic personhood, Twain simultaneously undercuts New World polemics such as the "immigration question," which undoubtedly concerned Jewish (inclusive of eastern and southern European) migration. After all, the "immigration question" (unlike the analogous "Chinese question") was not limited to one specific group. Even so, it did encompass the majority—if not all—of Jewish immigrants from eastern Europe and Russia. Moreover, though Jewish subjects were granted access to naturalization, the issue of assimilation and worthy selfhood continued to "haunt" (drawing briefly from Donald Weber's work) immigrants in the New World.[33] Such immigration debates and naturalization frames are certainly at play in Abraham

Cahan's *Yekl: A Tale of the New York Ghetto* (1896), which is both a "tale" of New York and (to a lesser extent) a tense, nostalgic story about Russia.

Unlike Twain's universal characterization, Cahan's novella individualizes—through its titular protagonist—the flow of immigrant bodies from Europe. As Robert M. Dowling argues, *Yekl* was significant in part because it was the first account written "by a Lower East Side insider and set in that district with fellow insiders as protagonists. In it, Cahan dissects the motives and tendencies of two immigrant Jews in New York whose stories were paradigmatic of the eastern European immigration experience."[34] Further, if Edith Maude Eaton directly answered the "Chinese question" and the "women's question" in clearly delineated stories about Chinese immigrants, then Abraham Cahan's *Yekl: A Tale of the New York Ghetto* critically engages the "immigration question" and the "great ethnic question" via ambiguity and open-endedness.[35]

Invested in the "quintessentials of good U.S. citizenship," Cahan's eponymous protagonist negotiates the contested terrain of culture and nation. However, in order to invest, Yekl must simultaneously disinvest in the country of origin. Such back-and-forth movements between investment and disinvestment produce an immigrant identity crisis forged in (and ultimately meditated through) the crucible of naturalized citizenship. Despite Yekl's declarations of U.S. superiority, he remains involuntarily and perpetually tied (via culture and family) to the country of origin. As Yekl moves away from "old country" family and practice, his partially naturalized self continues to exist at the margins. In the end, Yekl's selfhood is simultaneously conditional and probationary, an unfinished and haphazard assemblage of "quintessentials."

The protagonist's bifurcation—between immigrant and would-be American—is at once established by means of names and through a transnational cartography. The first chapter, titled, "Jake and Yekl," initially suggests two primary characters.[36] This expectation is soon subverted when the reader is introduced to Jake. As the unidentified, omniscient narrator later relates, "It was some three years before the opening of this story that Jake had last beheld that very image [of his wife and child] in the flesh. But then at that period of his life he had not even suspected the existence of a name like Jake, being known to himself and to all Povodye—a town in northwestern Russia—as Yekl or Yekele."[37] Yekl/Yekele is thus an a priori figure (from "some three years before"). Comparing "a name like Jake" to Yekl or Yekele, the narrator underscores the protagonist's titular naturalization. This nominal past/present binary is directionally matched—Yekl/Yekele is "northwestern" whereas Jake is "southeastern" (the Lower East Side).

If "old country" Yekl does not suspect the existence of a name like Jake, then "new country" Jake is likewise uncomfortable with his past self. According to the narrator, "Three years had intervened since he had first set foot on American soil, and the thought of ever having been a Yekl would bring to Jake's lips a smile of patronizing commiseration for his former self. As to his Russian family name, which was Podkovnik, Jake's friends had such rare use for it that by mere negligence it had been left intact" (12). Indicative of naturalized self-loathing, Jake has developed a "patronizing" relationship to his "former self," marked by condescension and dismissal. Unsettled by the "thought of ever having been a Yekl," the narrator typifies a successional immigrant narrative, inclusive of allusions to U.S. rebirth and revision. Though the protagonist retains his Russian surname (Podkovnik), Jake and his friends have such rare use for it that it has been neglected and ignored. Like his wife and child (who also carry his surname), Jake's last name is an "absent presence," a transnational reminder of former selves and affiliations nevertheless left intact.

Despite connotations of wholeness (or intactness), Jake is principally a composite figure. Composed of a "little sweltering assemblage," the garment factory workplace resonates with Jake's selfhood, which is similarly assembled in piecemeal fashion (1). According to the unidentified omniscient narrator, "He [Jake] had been speaking for some time. He stood in the middle of the overcrowded stuffy room with his long but well-shaped legs wide apart, his bulky head aslant, and his bared mighty arms akimbo. He spoke in Boston Yiddish, that is to say, in Yiddish more copiously spiced with mutilated English than is the language of the metropolitan Ghetto in which our story lies" (2). Jake's "Boston Yiddish" speech, "copiously spiced with mutilated English," represents a transnational amalgamation. Nevertheless, this linguistic mixture is far from complete or indistinguishable. Instead, suggestive of an additive, the spiced affect of Yekl/Jake's language, distinctively "Boston Yiddish," is incongruous within the metropolitan Ghetto (the Lower East Side). Still, it is the Yiddish—*not* the English—that is copiously spiced, bringing to light the invasive quality of the latter. Cahan reverses an assimilative U.S. trajectory wherein the foreign is subsumed by the domestic. In this case, Yiddish is the principal ingredient in the transnational recipe of Boston Yiddish, and English is both mutilated and ancillary.

The resilience of Yiddish disrupts the cohesion of Jake's American performance, betraying a priori cultural ties. Such a rupture is dramatically revealed in an earlier exchange between Jake and his audience of co-worker/compatriot workers. Jake declares, "Once I live in America . . . I want to know that I live in America. *Dot'sh a kin' a man I am*! One must not be a *greenhorn*. Here a Jew is as good as a Gentile. How, then, would you have it? The way it is in Russia, where a Jew is afraid to stand within four ells of a Christian?" (5). From the outset, Jake conflates geography, culture, and politics in his monologue, and brings to light his desire to not only reside in the United States but also to comprehend through experience what it means to be American.

The juxtaposition of correct grammar and accented, italicized English (*Dot'sh a kin' a man I am!*) produces a bilingual Yiddish and English speech act (evocative of Eaton's "In the Land of the Free" translation). This reading is explicitly confirmed within the text, which carries the following footnote: "English words incorporated in the Yiddish of the characters of this narrative are given in italics" (2). Accordingly, Cahan's *Yekl: A Tale of the New York Ghetto* is a *translated* text that engages transnational linguistic, cultural, and political frames. All the same, such transnational frames are undermined by a protagonist principally invested in U.S. citizenship and vociferously disinvested in Russian selfhood. Indeed, Jake imperatively points out that one "must not be a greenhorn," dismissing outright the inexperienced newcomer unfamiliar with U.S. customs and practices.

Moving from culture to politics, Jake privileges a religion-blind tolerance, apparent in the proclamation that "Here a Jew is as good as a Gentile." In line with Mark Twain's "Concerning the Jews" (published a mere two years after *Yekl*), Jake's declaration of U.S. equality calls attention to a very real anti-Semitism in Russia. However, when examined vis-à-vis "separate but equal" logics in *Plessy v. Ferguson* (1896), Jake's assertion of alleged universal equality falls short. Concurrently, Jake's assertion of ethnoreligious parity reinforces an implicit (albeit probationary) whiteness. Imbued with U.S. exceptionalism, the protagonist indirectly delineates Yekl the immigrant from Jake the settler. Whereas the former must contend with Old World anti-Semitism, the latter is afforded equal standing with his gentile counterpart.

In line with such declarations to idealized U.S. nationhood, and despite the persistence of transnational accents, Jake repeatedly engages naturalization performances. As is apparent in the previous discussion, the novella's performative dimensions are supported by the narrator's attention to Jake's stance, location, and arm movement ("He stood in the middle of the overcrowded stuffy room with his long but well-shaped legs wide apart, his bulky head aslant, and his bared mighty arms akimbo"). Such specificity calls to mind stage directions; this dramatic reading is corroborated following a dispute Jake has with co-worker, Meester Bernstein over the merits of American prize fighting. As the narrator relates, the two are interrupted by a female coworker (the "comely, milk-faced blond" Fanny), prompting "the theatrical pair [to break] off their boasting match to join" the ongoing debate about "the American cause" (4).

If Jake resembles a theatrical performer, he is also a seasoned naturalization actor who willingly defends his new home country via a patriotic "American cause," inclusive of a virtuous discussion of American authority in sport and politics. Still, Jake's citizenship performance is challenged by his audience, who undermine the protagonist's self-celebratory claims of U.S. exceptionalism and superiority. Responding to Jake's declaration of U.S. preeminence, the abovementioned Bernstein interjects, "America is an educated country, so they won't even break bones without grammar. They tear each other's sides according to 'right and left.' . . . I do think a burly Russian peasant would, without a bit of grammar, crunch the bones" (4). Noting that Americans "won't even break bones without grammar," Bernstein introduces a set of rules that in the end are meaningless in a boxing ring, wherein all that matters is the physicality of "a burly Russian peasant."

On another level, Bernstein's grammatical insinuation furthers a naturalized reading. The very notion of grammar carries with it a specific set of rules for speech and citizenship acts. Likewise, the Bernstein/Jake argument reflects the basic rhetorical structure for U.S. citizenship, which requires a repudiation (or battle) between two opposing sides. Such naturalized wordplay is accessed when Bernstein accuses Jake of being a false "Yankee." As Jake's early foil asserts, "He thinks that *shaving* one's mustache makes a Yankee!" (6). The term "Yankee," indicative of a native or resident of the United States, resembles Jake's "Boston Yiddish," which was born in New England and transplanted to the Lower East Side. The argument escalates between Bernstein and Jake, culminating in the former's accusation that the protagonist is uneducated. Angry and hurt, Jake "felt wretched. He uttered an English oath, which in his heart he directed against himself as much as against his sedate companion, and fell to frowning upon the leg of a machine" (7), The oath—reflexively conceived and directed "against himself as much as against his sedate companion"—foreshadows a profound identity crisis (or "wretchedness") within Jake/Yekl.

This personhood predicament (of being interstitially located between two worlds) is for the most part exposed vis-à-vis Jake/Yekl's familial obligations, which include a Russian wife (Gitl) and son (Yossele). Prior to the novella's opening, Jake has spent the previous three years performing the role of a bachelor. To that end, Jake has kept the "narrative fact" of his marriage a secret from co-workers and a potential love interest, fellow Jewish immigrant Mamie. It is only after news of his father's death—and his grieving mother's subsequent wish that Jake/Yekl be reunited with spouse and son—that the protagonist is forced to reconcile his bachelor present with his marital past. Correspondingly, the collision between "Old World" and "new country" shifts the story's focus. In particular, this family plot transforms Cahan's novella from prototypical immigrant narrative (culminating in successful amalgamation) into conflicted narrative of Americanization and concomitant naturalization.

In so doing, *Yekl* reengages a transnational focus by means of family frames. And, despite the passage of three years, Jake maintains a nostalgic familial connection. As the narrator observes, "if his attachment for the girls of his acquaintance collectively was not coupled with a quivering of his heart for any individual Mamie, or Fanny, or Sarah, it did not, on the other hand, preclude a certain lingering tenderness for his wife" (25). This "certain lingering tenderness" suggests a sentimentality that is idealized, abstracted, and ultimately nostalgic. Though Jake's "wife had long since ceased to be what she had been of yore," she nevertheless emerges "from a reality . . . [that had] gradually become transmuted into a fancy" (25). The wife's transmutation from reality to fancy evokes an alchemy rooted in distance and maintained through the passage of time. On another level, such transmutation partially mirrors Jake's own transformation from greenhorn to imagined "American."

Nevertheless, what begins as a fanciful remembrance quickly takes a decidedly unsentimental, realistic turn. Like Eaton, Cahan explicitly mentions the bureaucratic immigration process. To that end, the narrator relates, "A few weeks later, on a Saturday morning, Jake, with an unfolded telegram in his hand, stood in front of one of the desks at the Immigration Bureau of Ellis Island. . . . All the way to the island he had been a flurry of joyous anticipation. The prospect of meeting his dear wife and child, and, incidentally, of showing off his swell attire to her, had thrown him into a fever of impatience" (34). Tellingly, Jake's family reunification takes place on the Sabbath (Saturday) and at Ellis Island, which signals the protagonist's secularism and his family's immigrant status. Despite the potential for sentimentality (hearkening back to

Eaton's "In the Land of the Free"), the family reunion is largely anticlimactic. Jake is at first in a "flurry of joyous anticipation" because of the prospect of meeting his wife and child. However, romantic frames are undercut by Jake's impatient capitalist desire, emblematized by his enthusiasm to show off his swell attire. Hence, the very notion of "prospect" shifts from a benign reading of futurity to a more self-interested financial enterprise.

Jake's capitalist investment speaks to a "quintessential" U.S. citizenship, predicated on a belief in free market economies, consumption, and supposed American superiority. In contrast, Gitl is representative of a bucolic Russia that fits uneasily within New York urbanity and capitalist-driven modernity. According to the narrator, Jake

> caught a glimpse of Gitl and Yossele through the railing separating the detained immigrants from their visitors, and his heart sank at the sight of his wife's uncouth and un-American appearance. She was slovenly dressed in a brown jacket and skirt of grotesque cut, and her hair was concealed under a voluminous wig of a pitch-black hue. This she had put on just before leaving the steamer, both in honor of the Sabbath and by way of sprucing herself up for the great event. (34)

Uncouth, slovenly, and—most important—"un-American" in appearance, Gitl emblematizes Jake's previously spurned "greenhorn" characterization. Correspondingly, if Jake is the representative immigrant-turned-Yankee, then Gitl becomes his uncouth and un-American antithesis. Such an antithetical relationship is evident to an unnamed immigration official, who was so struck by "the contrast between Gitl and Jake . . . that [he] wanted to make sure—partly as a matter of official duty and partly for the fun of the thing—that the two were actually man and wife" (35).

As the couple leaves Ellis Island, Jake is profoundly disappointed and disparages both Gitl and his son, Yossele. The narrator relates, for example, that:

> presently . . . the illusion took wing and here he was, Jake the Yankee, with this bonnetless, wigged, dowdy-ish little greenhorn by his side! That she was his wife, nay, that he was a married man at all, seemed incredible to him. The sturdy, thriving urchin [Yossele] had at first inspired him with pride; but as he now cast another side glance at Gitl's wig he lost all interest in him, and began to regard

> him, together with his mother, as one great obstacle dropped from heaven, as it were, in his way. (36)

Incredulous and simultaneously disinterested, "Jake the Yankee" explicitly dissociates from "Yekl the Russian." On one level, the unidentified narrator telegraphs Jake's disbelief that a familial connection exists between "dowdy-ish greenhorn" Gitl and his "urchin" son. Such doubt is rooted in a transnational disavowal, wherein Yankee Jake renounces family—and, by extension, Russia—through disinvestment, or "no interest."

On another level, this renunciation acquires significance when placed adjacent to naturalized citizen and nation. Collectively characterized as a "great obstacle dropped from heaven," Gitl and Yossele embody not only the proverbial Old World but (more important) Jake's intimate connection to that imaginary. If, as Robert G. Lee maintains, the family stands in for the nation, then Gitl and Yossele (along with patriarch Jake) symbolize a transnational, albeit unstable, combination of U.S. and Russian nationhood.[38] Incompatible with U.S. naturalization law, such multivalent citizenship is illegible vis-à-vis requirements of absolute repudiation. Jake's privileging of Americanness—in contrast to his family's alienness—makes the latter a "great obstacle" for the former. To be sure, this mixed-nation combination proves predictably explosive and destructive, as Jake and Gitl's marriage dissolves along a naturalization axis.

Such dissolution takes the form of composite U.S. citizenship "quintessentials." Impelled and compelled to naturalize his family, Jake charges himself with the task of domestic Americanization. As a starting point, Jake at once orders his wife and child to speak English in the home and wear "American" clothes. Demanding his wife address him as "Jake," the protagonist nominally naturalizes his wife and son with the seemingly more "American" names Goitie and Joey. Tellingly, Gitl's new name—"a word phonetically akin to Yiddish for Gentile"—reinforces Jake's secularist, naturalization agenda (41). In the face of Jake's *e pluribus unum* mission, the unnamed narrator nevertheless reinscribes a Russian familial affiliation. Accordingly, Jake's wife is referenced as "Gitl" and not "Goitie." This narrative employment of Gitl's "old country" name contrasts with the protagonist, who is by and large referred to as "Jake."

Even with Jake's totalitarian attempts to naturalize Gitl, she fails to live up to her "Yankee" husband's expectations. As a result, Jake repeatedly repudiates his wife on the grounds that he is an "American feller" and that she is a lowly "greenhorn." Invested in all things American, Jake slowly but surely disinvests in Gitl and Yossele, who become unwanted foreign goods. In contrast, fellow Jewish immigrant Mamie (who, by the novella's conclusion, will become Jake's second wife) is very much "American made." Continuing in a materialistic vein, Jake idealizes Mamie because (according to the protagonist) she dresses and "speaks English like one American born" (52). Indeed, Mamie emerges as the focus of Jake's commodity fetish. In turn, this fetish is chiefly embedded in a desire (drawing from an earlier moment) to "know that he lives in America." As the novella time and again reveals, such "knowing" is based on legible American performances, including speech and custom.

Purportedly adept at using American idiomatic expressions, wearing contemporary American styles, and armed with fluency in English, Mamie is Jake's aspirational selfhood counterpart. All the same, the unnamed narrator intervenes and undermines Jake's reading of Mamie through "quintessentials" of naturalization. Indeed, when Mamie is introduced, she is "a girl with a superabundance of pitch-black side bangs," which ironically foreshadows Gitl's "greenhorn" wig. Although Jake professes that Mamie "speaks English like one American born," she is nonetheless marked by foreign accent and affect. Responding to Jake's invitation to dance, Mamie dismissively asserts, "Dot slob again? Joe must tink if you ask me I'll get scared, ain't it? Go and tell him he is too fresh." The narrator concedes that like "the majority of the girls in the academy, Mamie's English was a much nearer approach to a justification of its name than the gibberish spoken by men" (19). Though her English is "a much nearer approach," Mamie remains (like Yekl) an accented, composite subject.

If *Yekl: A Tale of the New York Ghetto* begins with a protagonist invested in the "quintessentials" of naturalized citizenship, it fittingly ends with the naturalization of its most "foreign" elements. To be sure, Jake's greenhorn ex-wife Gitl is transformed in spectacular American fashion. As the narrator describes, "her general Americanized makeup, and, above all, that broad brimmed, rather fussy, hat of hers nettled him [Jake]. It seemed to defy him, as if devised for that purpose" (84). Bothered by Gitl's appearance, Jake is confronted with the mundane dimensions of Americanization. No longer exceptionally "American," the protagonist is momentarily confronted by the possibility that *any* subject can gain access to U.S. selfhood, including the seemingly "un-naturalizable" Gitl.

What is more, if Jake is "nettled" by Gitl's Americanization, he is also—true to character—paradoxically drawn to it. In the novella's final moments, Jake and Mamie make their way to City Hall, where the two will presumably obtain a marriage certificate. As Jake reflects,

> What if he should now dash into Gitl's apartment and, declaring his authority as husband, father, and lord of the house, fiercely eject the strangers, take Yossele in his arms, and sternly command Gitl to mind her household duties. . . . But the distance between him and the mayor's office was dwindling fast. Each time the car came to a halt he wished the pause could be prolonged indefinitely; and, when it resumed its progress, the violent lurch it gave was accompanied by a corresponding sensation in his heart. (84)

Circumscribed by multiple types of "return," the above passage underscores Jake's transnational ambivalence. On one level, Jake expresses a temporal desire to return to the past. This wish to "go back" coincides with a domestic reimagining of familial relationships. To that end, Jake momentarily embraces traditional roles as "husband, father, and lord of the house." Reminiscent of *The Odyssey,* Jake assumes the role of Odysseus, who analogously "ejected strangers" upon returning from an epic journey. Needless to say, it is Jake's own desire to "know America" that has led him astray, and such a "what if" return is impossible.

Equally, Jake engages an a priori "Yekl" identity, for his nostalgic reenvisioning incorporates Russian—and not American—names (that is, Gitl and Yossele). The employment of former names counters the protagonist's previous (domestic) directive to speak English and use American names. Further, Jake's desire for return embodies a sentimentality, emblematized by a "sensation in his heart," that underscores the protagonist's reinvestment in Gitl. Nevertheless, in a story concerned with speculation and exchanges, Jake is ultimately caught within a bind wherein he is unable to return what he has purchased.[39] Desirous of all things American, the seemingly naturalized Jake has effectively traded his Russian past for a U.S. present.

Invested in appearances, or "quintessentials," Jake has bought—via his impending marriage to the more naturalized Mamie—an American household complete with an American wife. And, suggestive of a naturalization ceremony, Jake and Mamie's imminent (and public) nuptials require a repudiation of the past and vow to the present. All the same, as the open-ended conclusion affectively reveals, it remains unclear whether such investment will lead to anything more than further rupture, mixed feelings, and concomitant disinvestment. And Yekl remains a probationary subject, constructed according to conditions that are both within and outside his control.

Yekl's ending anticipates what Abraham Cahan would later characterize as "ill comport." Published almost a decade after *Yekl*, Cahan's *The Rise of David Levinsky* (1917) concludes with the eponymous protagonist's confession that "I can never forget the days of my misery. I cannot escape from my old self. My past and my present do not comport well. David, the poor lad swinging over a Talmud volume at the Preacher's Synagogue, seems to have more in common with my inner identity than David Levinsky, the well-known cloak-manufacturer."[40] Similarly focused on the Jewish immigrant experience, *The Rise of David Levinksy* is in large part an expanded version of *Yekl*. Like Jake, David Levinsky is invested in U.S. selfhood, and the novel explores this desire via cultural and economic exchanges. Though more economically successful than garment worker Jake, cloak-manufacturer David Levinksy nevertheless arrives (in more direct fashion) at the same conclusion. Stressing that his "past and [his] present do not comport well," David Levinksy underscores an internal tension between his immigrant and American selves. Like to his predecessor, David Levinksy cannot escape "his past self," despite previous claims to the contrary.

Affectively configured, Yekl and David Levinsky are not so much paragons of American selfhood. Instead, Cahan's protagonists model the naturalized costs of U.S. citizenship. Further, each titular character makes visible the transnational frames that necessarily undergird the immigrant experience. As the principal source of strife and conflict, such transnational identities militate against the logics of naturalization, which presuppose the ability to shed past selves and privilege a monolithic personhood. Taken together, Cahan's composite characters are faced with "ill comport" for they are unable to fit neatly within established (and at times conditional) citizenship frames. Though granted access to the U.S. political franchise via naturalization law, Jewish immigrants nonetheless had to negotiate Old World sensibilities (including religion and custom) within a dominant New World schema. In contrast, Edith Maude Eaton's pro-Chinese narratives (which attest to policies of exclusion, acts of prohibition, and claims of ineligible alienhood) deliberately produce model minority subjects willing—though politically unable—to be made into Americans. As the course of U.S. empire continued into the twentieth century, such transnational allegiances and citizenships would tactically employ model minority frames in the service of foreign policy. Concomitantly, the characterization of undesirable alienhood would become even more pronounced in an increasingly more nativist domestic imaginary.

2 / Interrupted Allegiances: Indivisibility and Transnational Pledges

From time to time there has been born [sic] in upon this community the intimation that in "The Melting Pot" Mr. Israel Zangwill had written [sic] a most important play. The bill-boards have carried the indorsements [sic] of men of prominence in civic and National affairs, and even Col. Roosevelt, while still President, was quoted as among its most enthusiastic admirers. This merely goes to prove that even a President may be mistaken.

— *NEW YORK TIMES*, SEPTEMBER 7, 1909

San Francisco's Chinatown nowadays is no milieu for the novelist who is an outsider. With the slave girls vanished, also the racketeering tongs, the social life of the quarter is other than what it was, or had seemed to be. And you get a notion of this in The Flower Drum Song. *Mr. Chin Y. Lee has an objective eye on the scene.*

—IDWAL JONES, *NEW YORK TIMES*, MAY 19, 1957

On December 21, 1898, following the fin-de-siècle U.S. victory in the Spanish-American War, President William McKinley addressed American citizens at home and newly annexed Filipino subjects abroad. The twenty-fifth commander-in-chief maintained that American forces came "not as invaders or conquerors, but as friends, to protect the natives in their homes, in their employment, and in their personal and religious rights." McKinley buttressed such "friendly" foreign policy claims with the assertion that "all persons who, either by active aid or by honest submission, cooperate with the Government of the United States to give effect to these beneficent purposes will receive the reward of its support and protection." The president solemnly concluded that:

> it should be the earnest and paramount aim of the military administration to win the confidence, respect, and affection of the inhabitants of the Philippines by assuring them in every possible way that full measure of individual rights and liberties which is the heritage of a free people, and by proving to them that the mission of

> the United States is one of the benevolent assimilation, substituting the mild sway of justice and right for arbitrary rule.[1]

Replete with allusions to democracy, householding, and asylum, McKinley euphemistically (albeit unintentionally) dictated the course of twentieth-century U.S. empire. More to the point, McKinley's address reads foreign bodies through voluntary affiliation and naturalization.

Specifically, the imperial project that began with the Spanish-American War, built on the assimilation of Filipino bodies into the larger body politic, proved an oft-deployed template for subsequent U.S. excursions abroad. Indeed, as Amy Kaplan, Allan Isaac, and Victor Bascara contend, the characterization of U.S. nationhood through sentimental democratic principles (reminiscent and reflective of past exceptionalist claims) was primarily exported through military power and cultural influence.[2] Correspondingly, McKinley's recipe for "benevolent assimilation" used naturalistic ingredients to U.S. imperialistic ends. Constitutive of natural law (that is, political universality) and naturalization (which, as Priscilla Wald argues, "evinces the alchemy of the state"), McKinley's address exalted democratic desire and reified sociopolitical sameness.[3] In so doing, the president accessed an alchemical process wherein foreignness naturalistically gives way to "benevolent" American selfhood. McKinley was certainly not alone in his manipulation of domestic frames to serve foreign policy agendas. From Theodore Roosevelt to President Harry S. Truman, from the Spanish-American War to the cold war, utopian articulations of unproblematic assimilation were positioned alongside the forceful spread of U.S. democracy. McKinley's declaration of "benevolent assimilation" and later cold war policies engendered a global (although asymmetrical) U.S. citizenship practice.

Even so, the very notion of "benevolent assimilation" was by no means limited to the political arena. Indeed, if Abraham Cahan and Edith Maude Eaton negotiated domestically driven "ethnic questions" at the turn of the twentieth century, then British Jewish playwright Israel Zangwill and first-generation Chinese American novelist Chin Y. Lee were analogously invested in foreign policy-determined "ethnic solutions." The most well-known (or infamous) of their literary productions—Zangwill's *The Melting-Pot* (1908) and Lee's *The Flower Drum Song* (1957)—concentrate on two immigrant groups who lack clear nation-state affiliation because of pogram (Russia) and communism (China). Likewise, *The Melting-Pot* and *The Flower Drum Song* test, to different ends, the viability of state-authorized belonging for de facto political refugees. Significantly, Zangwill's dramatic test and Lee's literary assessment of selfhood engaged contemporaneous arguments over the present and future of immigration policy. Most important, the emphasis on refugees—implicit in Zangwill's play and explicit in Lee's novel—brings to the fore extrastatal identities formed through involuntary frames, such as forced relocation. The "refugee" as legible figure is at once a U.S. asylum seeker and the victim of civil war or international conflict, judged according to naturalization (im)possibility. When juxtaposed, *The Melting-Pot* and *The Flower Drum Song* appreciably render visible a half century of U.S. foreign policy and immigration legislation.

What is more, *The Melting-Pot* and *The Flower Drum Song* bring attention to the interplay of foreign policy and domestic initiative. The promise of "benevolent assimilation" abroad undeniably impacted U.S. immigration practices at home. Such naturalized frames ostensibly militated against domestic claims that new tides of immigrants were unassimilable because of political, cultural, and social difference. Nevertheless, "benevolent" discourses characteristic of turn-of-the-century foreign policy were in direct conflict with domestic calls to "shut the door." The contradiction between the verbalization of ideal foreign subjects and the stigmatization of aliens at home was most manifest in early twentieth-century restrictive immigration policies. Within the political interstices of immigration debate and shifting immigration policy, Zangwill's *The Melting-Pot* in particular strikes a relevant chord, for it directly confronts xenophobic anxiety while supporting the virtues of open-door domestic strategies.

Despite *The Melting-Pot*'s pertinent (and at times prescient) message, until the present day the play has occupied a litigious position within ethnic American literary studies. Typified by Jules Chametzky as the "*locus classicus* of assimilationist narratives," scholarly considerations of Zangwill's most eminent dramatic work privilege the play's reception history and essentializing amalgamation theme.[4] On another level, the play's political significance is more visible through its correlation with McKinley's nascent imperialist foreign policy. Expressly, *The Melting-Pot* extends the benevolent assimilation project into the U.S. cultural imaginary through a series of "good faith" citizenship performances. Circumventing divisiveness and transnational affiliation in favor of indivisibility and U.S. allegiance, Zangwill's play casts the Jewish immigrant as a "model minority" in a "comedy of Americanization." This "comedy of Americanization" employs stock white ethnic characters and concludes with an at-the-time impossible love match between the Jewish protagonist David and his love interest, the Christian Vera. Further, the play's handling of nativist anxiety strategically depends on the rhetoric of naturalization as applied to the grammar of U.S. exceptionalism.

Equally, the grammar of U.S. exceptionalism, naturalization, and alienation is very much present in Chin Y. Lee's 1957 novel, *The Flower Drum Song*. Even with reviewer Idwal Jones's assertion that Lee offers an "objective eye" to view a Chinatown in the moment of transition, the work continues to dwell in the scholarly margins. Like *The Melting-Pot*, Lee's novel has been ignored within Asian American literary studies. For example, in *Asian American Literature* (1982), Elaine Kim observes, "*The Flower Drum Song* presents a highly euphemized portrait of Chinatown life," suggesting an emphasis on sentimental and assimilationist characterizations and plot.[5] Notwithstanding Kim's dismissive reading, I resituate and reevaluate *The Flower Drum Song* within and through the contested terrain of immigration policy.[6] To that end, I argue that *The Flower Drum Song* constructs a historically specific Chinatown imaginary bounded by mid-twentieth-century policies of containment.

Lee characterizes San Francisco's Chinatown as a transitional space that exists in the shadow of the first decade of the cold war. Set after the Chinese Communist Revolution in 1949 and focused on the lives of Chinese refugees in San Francisco's Chinatown, Lee's novel is among the first Asian American texts published after the passage of the 1948 Displaced Persons Act and the 1952 removal of racial requirements from naturalization law in the McCarran-Walter Act. Additionally, the linkage between refugee and naturalized subject is conveyed in the characterization of first-generation Chinese subjects. This political negotiation—which brings into focus policy and law—occurs through the rhetoric and processes of naturalization.

Such narrative "give and take" takes the form of repudiation of the country of origin combined with uncritical acceptance of the country of settlement. Yet neither *The Melting-Pot* nor *The Flower Drum Song* offers uncontested paths to U.S. citizenship. In fact, naturalized rejections and approvals are challenged by ancillary characters. These secondary characters temporarily undercut the validity of monolithic citizenship, productively interrogating claims of indivisibility through transnational schema. Therefore, within this milieu and embedded in *The Melting-Pot* and *The Flower Drum Song* are a series of polemics (between primary and ancillary characters) about the very nature of U.S. citizenship. Alternatively, Zangwill's Jewish protagonist—who counters dominant U.S. ethnoracial logics yet is complicit with imperialism—anticipates and resonates with subsequent cold war characterizations of the "model minority" Asian immigrant.

The Flower Drum Song likewise employs transnational frames, enacts citizenship performances, and illuminates the interplay of mixed feelings. However, Lee's novel about Chinese refugees and intergenerational conflicts in San Francisco's Chinatown implicitly reworks and revises Zangwill's "comedy of Americanization." Within *The Flower Drum Song*'s imaginary, multiple "dramas of alienation" converge on relocated and dislocated cold war subjects. In the midst of effected, affective, and disaffected citizenship pledges, *The Flower Drum Song*'s open-ended transnational resolution destabilizes Asian/American model minoritization as a naturalized category. As a close reading makes clear, the novel's ambiguous conclusion undercuts the stereotype's decidedly inflexible logics of assimilability. In the process, Lee facilitates a refugee-specific critique of U.S. cold war policy.

Roosevelt's "Corollary": Naturalizing Immigrant Amalgamation and *The Melting-Pot*

Notwithstanding the triumphalism of his 1898 address, McKinley would not live to witness the long-lasting impact of U.S. imperialist forays in the Philippines. Instead, the legacy of American manifest destiny in the Pacific would fall to the vice president, Spanish-American War hero Theodore Roosevelt. Appropriately, in light of the Spanish-American War, McKinley's death occurred within a backdrop of celebratory expansionism and alleged Western superiority. These emphases on U.S. imperial conquests domestically and abroad were spectacularly revealed in the 1901 Pan-American Exposition in Buffalo, New York, which included electricity exhibits, the debut of the x-ray, and an "Ethnology Building" containing a tableau of Western hemisphere "primitive peoples" and Native American village maps.[7] McKinley survived a week after Leon Frank Czolgosz fired his fateful shot on September 6, 1901, eventually succumbing to his injuries on September 13. Sworn into office on September 14, Roosevelt's first presidential proclamation predictably and sentimentally addressed his predecessor's passing. Roosevelt declared that "McKinley crowned a life of largest love for his fellow men, of earnest endeavor for their welfare, by a death of Christian fortitude; and both the way in which he lived his life and the way in which, in the supreme hour of trial, he met his death will remain forever a precious heritage of our people."[8]

Though seemingly incidental, the use of "heritage" and "our people" in Roosevelt's memorial proclamation foreshadows the Republican president's subsequent proclivity toward collective national characterizations. Such communal claims were time and again used by Roosevelt in the ongoing immigration debate. Cast in recent memory as a Progressive-era populist president and antitrust advocate, Roosevelt, both during and after his presidency, was very much invested in the ever-pressing "immigrant problem." To that end, the Rough Rider president publicly deployed an identifiable antagonistic rhetoric against unassimilated, marked, immigrant bodies. For instance, Roosevelt cautioned his 1919 contemporaries:

> In the first place, we should insist that the immigrant who comes here in good faith becomes an American and assimilates himself to us, he shall be treated on an exact equity with everyone else, for it is an outrage to discriminate against any such man because of creed, or birthplace or origin. But this is predicated upon the person's becoming an American and nothing but an American. . . . We have room for but one flag, the American flag. . . . We have room for but one language here, and that is the English language . . . and we have room for but one sole loyalty and that is a loyalty to the American people.[9]

Roosevelt's emphasis on indivisibility as foundational to U.S. selfhood effectively marries the imperial foundation of McKinley's policy in the Philippines to domestic anxieties about difference in the United States. To be sure, the notion of "good faith" and the stress on assimilation reinforced contempraneous understandings of "benevolence" as a contested but nonetheless intelligible characterization of U.S. exceptionalism abroad and at home.[10]

Central to Roosevelt's 1919 letter is its accent on naturalization. Roosevelt's initial antidiscrimination stance, "predicated upon the person's becoming an American and nothing but an American," accesses naturalization in its declaration of "one flag . . . one language . . . and . . . one sole loyalty." According to Roosevelt's *naturalized* ideal U.S. selfhood, immigrants acting in good faith would naturally become assimilated American subjects. Eschewing hyphenation in favor of amalgamation, Roosevelt's citizenship doctrine by and large utilizes affective modes of pledging, allegiance, and English. The illegibility of multiple affiliations in the "making of new Americans" is even plainer in an earlier October 12, 1915, speech. Before a gathering of the Knights of Columbus in New

York City, the president asserted: "There is no room in this country for hyphenated Americanism. . . . The one absolutely certain way of bringing this nation to ruin, of preventing all possibility of its continuing to be a nation at all, would be to permit it to become a tangle of squabbling nationalities."[11] The singularity of Roosevelt's immigrant-focused resolve simultaneously acknowledges and dismisses difference according to an alchemical spectrum of naturalization. In the face of such acculturated arguments, Roosevelt's interest in the power of affective selfhood performances was dramatically revealed in 1908, with the premiere of Israel Zangwill's play, *The Melting-Pot*.

In fact, Roosevelt was among the play's most animated supporters. Throughout the performance, the president reportedly declared that Zangwill's play was "all right!"[12] Roosevelt's enthusiasm continued into the second act, which bore witness to a standing ovation led by the president. No doubt attracted to the play's use of amalgamation as a solution to the "immigrant problem," Roosevelt's reaction confirms *The Melting-Pot*'s naturalized themes. Moreover, Roosevelt's presence would go beyond the play's premiere. Roosevelt's enthusiastic reaction in part foreshadows the dedication that appears in the published version of the play. Fittingly, Zangwill dedicated the play to the twenty-sixth president, "in respectful recognition of his strenuous struggle against the forces that threaten to shipwreck the Great Republic which carries mankind and its fortunes."[13] In so doing, the British Jewish playwright culturally cemented the politicized relationship between foreign and domestic, "benevolence" and amalgamation.

Regardless of avid presidential support, contemporaneous reviews of the play were less than stellar. In the 1909 review quoted above, the critic panned *The Melting-Pot*, averring that it was "sentimental trash masquerading as a human document," "a very bad play viewed from almost any point of view," and "awkward in structure, clumsy in workmanship, and deficient as literature." In addition, the reviewer took to task the play's narrative overreliance on long monologues, "sermons," and "long labored speeches," which resembled repeated pledges of allegiance to the United States by the immigrant protagonists.[14] Notwithstanding aesthetic critiques, *The Melting-Pot*'s "long labored speeches" necessarily link allegiance to naturalization and foreign policy. Besides, *The Melting-Pot* dramatically revived a century-old metaphor that intersected with the "birth" of the United States as a distinct immigrant nation.

In 1782, Congress adopted the national motto, *e pluribus unum* ("out of many, one"). That same year, French immigrant-turned-naturalized-American writer Hector St. John Crèvecoeur distinctively observed that the newly arrived immigrant "becomes an American by being received in the broad lap of our great *Alma Mater*. Here individuals of all nations are melted into a new race of men."[15] Reminiscent of John Winthrop's assertion of possible New World rebirth, Crèvecoeur (in *Letters from an American Farmer*) characterizes a form of U.S. selfhood premised on the ability of the immigrant body to transform or "melt" into an indistinguishable American. Crèvecoeur individualizes *e pluribus unum* processes with a focus on the singular immigrant subject, bonding the sole citizen to a larger "race of men." "The new race of men" engendered by Crèvecoeur's *Letters from an American Farmer* reproduces the end product of an alchemical equation and metaphorically mobilizes naturalization as a process with a clear beginning and end. After all, according to Crèvecoeur, seemingly disparate ingredients combine and turn out an identifiable form of sociocultural citizenship.

Irrespective of previous geographic location, Crèvecoeur's "Alma Mater" suggests indivisibility forged from the crucible of democratic possibility. Such indivisibility is part of a larger American project that ideally grows through immigration, which in turn enables the "making" of new citizens. Still, the 1790 codification of naturalization as a political and politicized means of transformation from immigrant to U.S. citizen counters Crèvecoeur's assimilationist and expansionist assertion. On the one hand, the 1790 naturalization law outlines an oppositional, exclusionary citizenship practice, marked by overt racial logics and implied class privilege. This "privileged" reading is apparent in the deliberate multisited divisiveness that elevates the "free white person" over the indentured servant, the African/African American slave, and the Native American.

On the other hand, the 1870 revision of naturalization law to superficially include black and white bodies in the process of "making Americans" seemingly concretizes Crèvecoeur's notion of a "new race of men." Nonetheless, this "new race" of American men circulated in a segregated political economy, apparent in emergent Jim Crow legislation and evidenced by increased U.S. immigration prohibitions such as the 1882 Chinese Exclusion Act and the 1924 Johnson-Reed Act. Hence, Crèvecoeur's assertion of natural amalgamation, formed within an assimilationist immigration flow, was largely undecipherable to nativist politicians and cultural producers. Such lawmakers reconfirmed the dominantly held a priori nature of U.S. citizenship through geography (location) and, to varying degrees, race (Anglo-Saxon whiteness).

The "crucible of democratic possibility" vital to Crèvecoeur's casting of nascent U.S. nationhood and McKinley's "benevolent" assimilationist U.S. foreign policy foreground Zangwill's "comedy of Americanization," *The Melting-Pot.* Originally calling it *The Crucible*, Zangwill admitted in a 1908 pre-premiere interview that he had spent three years writing a play that had no plot. Yet the play "without a plot" would enjoy, as mid-century literary critic Maurice Wholgerten observed, a "significance quite disproportionate to its literary importance," reviving enduring metaphor of immigration, amalgamation, and naturalization into the larger U.S. body politic.[16] *The Melting-Pot* effectively situated the United States within an essentializing discourse of reconciliation, wherein centuries-old ethnoreligious conflicts could be resolved. Likewise, the United States functions as an idealized location in which the stateless Jewish subject (or, for that matter, any immigrant) could be an American citizen.

In the process, Zangwill rearticulates the "melting-pot" metaphor so that it directly responds to the rise of nativism and increased immigrant-focused anxiety. Zangwill's "comedy of Americanization" translated well in light of a U.S. imperialism built on assimilative objectives. Fusing a Romeo and Juliet narrative of star-crossed lovers to an immigrant story dominated by patriotic desire, *The Melting-Pot* features two Russian protagonists—David Quixano, a Jewish male, and Vera Revendal, a Christian female—who, through the course of four acts, overcome not only a violent Russian history of pogroms but the outwardly insurmountable and multigenerational divide between Jew and gentile, foreigner and American.

Nevertheless, multiple stories threaten the intended love match between David and Vera. David's Uncle Mendel is anti-Christian and from the outset refuses to acknowledge the viability of his nephew's romantic relationship with a gentile. The American-born Quincy Davenport, the son of wealthy capitalists, is also interested in Vera, a relocated socialist alienated from her parents due to their tsarist views. This romantic investment, coupled with Davenport's position as a capitalist patron of the arts, figures keenly within the play's plot. An accomplished musician/composer, David initially relies on Davenport's orchestra for employment. Davenport's eventual (and opportunistic) refusal to hire David underscores a selfish (and capitalist) desire for Vera, who becomes a contested love commodity. Davenport attempts to solidify the dissolution of the David/Vera match by funding Vera's father and stepmother in their trip to the United States.

In financing Vera's parents, Davenport makes possible a nonimmigrant transit for foreign bodies that circulates in direct opposition to the play's dominant immigration imaginary. Both father and stepmother literally and historically represent Russia. Given their tourist purpose, neither expresses an interest in permanent relocation to the United States. As such, they remain nonimmigrant Russian nationals, committed to the country of origin in citizenship and allegiance. Further complicating matters in *The Melting-Pot*, Vera's Russian baron father oversaw the massacre of Jews in David's home village, including the protagonist's immediate family members. Following an argument with his daughter at the end of the third act, the baron asks David to avenge his familial loss and kill him accordingly. Against all affective odds, David refuses, dramatically forgiving (through lack of action) the Baron's crime against his family. David's willingness to forget past conflicts corresponds to the play's larger naturalized message, which hinges on the repudiation of Old World politics.

A secondary plot within the play involves David's symphony, which is composed during the real time of the play. This symphony is based on and reflective of David's early and repeated assertions that the United States is a "great Crucible" for foreign bodies. Therefore, David's symphony, aesthetically driven by immigration, emblematically engages the melting-pot metaphor. For the premiere, David insists that the symphony be performed before a *newly arrived* immigrant audience, reinforcing the composition's pro-immigrant stance. This symphonic "masterpiece," as labeled by David and the orchestra's conductor, Herr Pappelmeister, is scheduled in none-too-subtle fashion for the Fourth of July, which incidentally sets the temporal stage for the final act. The most patriotic of holidays, the Fourth of July setting is a significant, albeit predictable, site for a spectacular naturalization ceremony. What is more, the Independence Day premiere foreshadows a naturalized and naturalization ending. With regard to *The Melting-Pot*'s primary players, David and Vera dramatically express in the concluding scene their U.S. loyalties in imagined and real time. On stage, the protagonists pledge allegiance before their fellow immigrants; off-stage, this affective citizenship performance is witnessed (and verified) by American audience members, including the aforementioned President Roosevelt.

This date-oriented discussion between conductor and composer takes place in act 3. In this penultimate act, David and the conductor Herr Pappelmeister also confer on the appropriate venue for the protagonist's "masterpiece." The conductor originally proposes Carnegie Hall, which prompts David to ask, "But what certainty is there your Carnegie Hall audience would understand me? . . . It was always my dream to play it first to the new immigrants—those who have known the pain of the old world and the hope of the new." Herr Pappelmeister disagrees and argues that such an audience would not do as a result of inferior "breeding." The conductor tells David, "I fear neider dogs nor men are a musical breed." David responds, "The immigrants will not understand my music with their brains or their ears, but with their hearts and their souls," revising the "hearts and minds" discourse of McKinley's "benevolent assimilation" to accommodate an emotional, rather than intellectual, citizenship project (151). Herr Pappelmaster acquiesces, and this decision to play to "hearts and minds" cements *The Melting-Pot*'s multivalent message, which brings together sentimental readings of U.S. foreign policy and romantic characterizations of the United States as a "nation of immigrants."

Needless to say, immigrant bodies undeniably dominate the heterogeneous demographic imaginary of *The Melting-Pot*. The degree of each character's assimilation is indexed through accented speech and adherence to traditional custom. Protagonist David is a first-generation "unaccented" Russian Jewish immigrant composer who falls for the similarly "unaccented" first-generation Russian Christian Vera. Minor characters include David's grandmother (the non-English-speaking orthodox Frau Quixano) and David's abovementioned uncle (the less orthodox, first-generation Mendel). Frau Quixano and Mendel signal varying degrees of foreignness and Jewishness. Further, there is Herr Pappelmeister, a German immigrant conductor, and the previously discussed Quincy Davenport, the only native-born American. In addition, *The Melting-Pot* cast of characters employs the stereotypical white ethnic character Kathleen, a heavily accented maid.

In *The Melting-Pot*, Kathleen's role is configured primarily through cultural conversion. The Irish Kathleen initially dismisses Frau Quixano's orthodox beliefs, particularly the grandmother's kosher practice of separating the cookware in accordance to Jewish custom and biblical law. Indeed, Kathleen threatens to leave the Quixano home in protest. As the stage directions dictate, Kathleen (after hearing from David about Frau Quixano's experiences in Russia and the United States) "hysterically burs[t] into tears, dropping her parcel, and untying her bonnet strings." The Irish domestic declares, "Oh, Mr. David, I won't mix the crockery, I won't –," validating Frau Quixano through traditional food practices (151). At play are an identifiable politics of empathy that involve

Kathleen and Frau Quixano. Kathleen's empathetic reaction suggests to audience and fellow cast member alike that she too has suffered alienation as a consequence of her foreign location. Kathleen subsequently elects to remain in the Quixano employ, which corroborates her newly found understanding of faith and confirms her acceptance of Jewish difference. In a later scene, Kathleen enthusiastically celebrates Purim with Frau Quixano, a festival that celebrates the victory of Jews of Persia over Haman, who unsuccessfully plotted their extermination.

David's role in converting Kathleen from an antipathetic to empathetic position takes on the valences of naturalization, replete with loyalty pledges and declarations to the U.S. nation-state. Still, as the play progresses, the audience is introduced to both willing *and* unwilling converts to U.S. selfhood. Kathleen's empathetic shift operates in direct contrast to the actions of Mendel, who repeatedly destabilizes claims of U.S. exceptionalism through citizenship. These character dynamics are apparent early in the play. For example, in *The Melting-Pot*'s first act, David declares:

> Not understand that America is God's Crucible, the great Melting-Pot where all the races of Europe are melting and re-forming! Here you stand, good folk, think I, when I see them at Ellis Island, here you stand in your fifty groups, with your fifty languages and histories, and your fifty blood hatreds and rivalries. But you won't be long like that, brothers, for these are the fires of God you've come to. . . . A fig for your feuds and your vendettas! Germans and Frenchman, Irishmen and Englishmen, Jews and Russians—into the Crucible with you all! God is making the American. (37)

Reminiscent of Crevécoeur's articulation of "melted sameness," Zangwill's protagonist updates the 1782 amalgamation metaphor, signaling the emergence of Ellis Island as a viable entry point for immigrants and would-be Americans. Addressing Vera, Mendel, and the audience, David's emphasis on "languages, histories, blood hatreds, and rivalries" characterizes the potential diversity of immigrants through negative frames. Such frames are by no means permanent in the United States, nor are they secularly contained, a point made clear in David's divine assertion that "God is making the American." The iteration of a "crucible" and "making" dramatically brings to light naturalization processes comprising state mechanisms that erase difference. On another level, this passage anticipates David's later refusal to kill the Baron despite "feuds and . . . vendettas," cementing the protagonist's allegiance to the United States.

The renunciation of past feuds manifest in David's declarations is steeped in the rhetorical structure of naturalization. In speech and action, David critiques the country of origin and praises the idealized principles of the country of settlement. Though not an "official" naturalized citizen, David strategically accesses naturalization requirements. Staunchly dedicated to the principles of the United States, willing to "pledge [his] heart" and life to protect his country, David is the ultimate immigrant patriot. He models sentimental understandings of U.S. citizenship and emerges as a model minority subject. David's dream—to write a symphony to America—represents, to quote from the official oath, a "work of national importance under civil direction."[18] Implicitly, within the dramatic narrative fabric of *The Melting-Pot* is an understanding that the United States is a nation-state of unfulfilled promise that accepts voluntarily amalgamated immigrant bodies.

Such romanticized national frames are further apparent in the following exchange between David and Mendel. After David's enthusiastic characterization of America as God's Crucible, Mendel responds: "I should have thought the American was made already—eighty millions of him." David replies, "Eighty millions! . . . Eighty millions! Over a continent! What, that cockleshell of a Britain has forty millions! No uncle, the real American has not yet arrived" (37). Emphasizing "arrival," David immediately and implicitly alludes to Ellis Island, a primary site for immigrants and immigration. Eschewing Anglo-Saxon whiteness in favor of Ellis Island heterogeneity, David sets aside Britain as a cockleshell, an island geographically and (by implication) politically inferior to the U.S. continent. The assertion that the "real American has not yet arrived" suggests that the immigrant-to-come provides a solution to the question of unrealized selfhood potential.

Alternatively, David's statement takes on self-referential importance vis-à-vis the play's ending. After all, it is not until the conclusion of the play that David, as a naturalized subject, "arrives" via citizenship. However, David's citizenship arrival is contingent on his ability to successfully declare—without interruption—his adherence to national ideals through a legible naturalization grammar. This allegiance pledge is abruptly interrupted by Mendel, who avers that the American has already been "made" as a consequence of geographic location. As evident in the previous passage, Mendel claims that Americanness is achieved through residence, that is, living in the United States. In so doing, Mendel becomes a cynical character witness to claims of David's declarations of wholesale U.S. exceptionalism. Mendel's skepticism anticipates in limited fashion similar anti-assimilationist sentiments that circumscribe pro-immigration movements. Mendel in effect collapses the space between an on-stage Americanization debate and off-stage immigration politics.

This alternative immigrant viewpoint is further expressed in act 2, scene 1. In the midst of patriotic reverie, David turns to an American flag, pledging:

> Flag of our Great Republic, Guardian of our homes, whose stars and stripes stand for Bravery, Purity, Truth, and Union, we salute thee. We, the natives of distant lands, who find [Half-sobbing.] rest under they folds, do pledge our hearts, our lives, our sacred honour to love and protect thee, our Country, and the liberty of our people forever. [He ends almost hysterically.] (56)

According to the stage direction, Mendel responds "soothingly," stressing to his nephew: "Quite right. But you needn't get so excited over it" (56). David's pledge to the "Flag of our Great Republic," a public declaration of affiliation and loyalty, intentionally evokes the indivisible politics of the "Pledge of Allegiance." Despite David's original subject position as a native of a "distant land," he eschews his citizenship past in favor of naturalized U.S. selfhood. Repudiating the country of origin and embracing the country of settlement, David legibly performs a naturalization oath, constructed through loyalty to dominant U.S. values.

Accordingly, David's belief in the nation makes him a vociferous patriot; unlike other white ethnic characters within *The Melting-Pot*'s imaginary (save for the Russian Vera), David's utterance occurs with no regional or ethnic accent. Out of context, it is unclear what David's ethnoreligious background is, reinforcing the play's larger focus on the viability of immigrants as successfully amalgamated sociopolitical subjects. Even so, Mendel's intervention—which initially "soothes" his overly emotional nephew—affectively undercuts David's oath of allegiance. In qualifying David's pledge, Mendel in effect puts a stop to it. Hence, Mendel's obstructionist intervention disallows the completion of a naturalization process as performed by David. Such avuncular interruptions persist until the conclusion of the play. It is only through Mendel's absence that David is able to successfully perform a naturalization oath without interruption. Reminiscent of a Bahktinian dialogic frame, wherein utterances are relationally configured within a given text, Mendel's subversive role is resolved when he does not occupy the same stage space.[19]

In a different yet related instance, the native-born Davenport, Vera's baron father, and Vera's Russian stepmother threaten the couple's voluntary love match and David's culturally embedded naturalization. To reiterate and expand a previous point, Davenport reintroduces Old World politics by funding the baron and baroness's trip to the United States. Responsible for the loss of David's family in Russia, the baron (and his wife) embody anti-Semitic politics and interconnected Old World values. In contrast, David is effectively a product of New World rebirth, which is reconfirmed by David's refusal to seek revenge against the baron. The tension between Old and New World dynamics (as articulated through characterization and plot) engenders a reconciled transnational dialectic. Thus *The Melting-Pot* is a play marked by a series of negotiations: between Old World and New, the past and the present, successive and different generations, religious practice and cultural dynamics. The older generation (inclusive of uncles, grandparents, mothers, and fathers) is partially dismissed to make way for the new generation (personified by Vera and David) intent on reproducing American subjects.

However, the memory of the past—and Vera's connection to that past—proves a final personal impediment for the protagonist. Indeed, the resolution of this past importantly determines whether or not the play is a comedy or tragedy. Given *The Melting-Pot*'s emphasis on U.S.-based reconciliation, the play's paradoxical relationship to transnational affiliations understandably addresses the less-than-desirable potential of immigrant bifurcation. Taken together, David and Vera's love match analogously speaks to processes of U.S. citizenship. Indeed, if naturalization affords the immigrant subject an alternative relationship to the nation-state, then *The Melting-Pot* extends this sensibility to the affective realm. Fittingly, Vera and David's relationship is "doomed to fail" in the Old World because of "age-old" conflict. In contrast, the New World marriage between Jew and gentile is able to succeed precisely because of the ability to remake oneself through naturalized frames.

The final moments of *The Melting-Pot* confirm this naturalized reading. Relying on a narrative of progression and succession, the final act mobilizes the dominant notion that the immigrant subject must shed transnational affiliations (such as the traumatic memory of the pogroms) to fully "become" American. As David admits to Vera:

> I preached of God's crucible, this great new continent that could melt up all race-differences and vendettas, that could purge and re-create and God tried me with his supremest [sic] test. He gave me

> a heritage from the Old World, hate and vengeance and blood, and said, "Cast it all into my Crucible." And I said, "Even thy Crucible cannot melt this hate, cannot drink up this blood." And so I sat crooning over the dead past, gloating over the old blood-stains—I, the apostle of America, the prophet of the God of our children. (193)

Such naturalized rhetoric, which comprises both repudiation and declaration, is repeatedly used in the play. In turn, this frame functions as an index upon which to measure the national loyalties of other characters in the play. Central to David's argument about U.S. superiority is the issue of reconciliation. Suggestive of putting to rest old debts, feuds, and prejudices, reconciliation becomes one of the primary solutions to the "immigrant question" and the "great ethnic question." Negotiable differences include a priori religious affiliation, country-of-origin conflicts (such as that between the Baron and David), or generational differences (for example, between Vera and her father or Mendel and David). Therefore, within its dramatic imaginary, *The Melting-Pot* promotes U.S.-centric models of geographic, historic, and cultural reconciliation.

Though not exact, David's final speech coheres with the spirit and grammar of the U.S. naturalization oath. The connection between dramatic and political performance is concretized in *The Melting-Pot*'s final scene. David pointedly asks Vera, "what is the glory of Rome and Jerusalem where all nations and races come to worship and look back, compared with the glory of America, where all races and nations come to labour and look forward?" (199). Not only does David emphasize the "glory of America"; he also renounces two geopolitical locations—Rome and Jerusalem. As a site, Rome calls forth a reading of Christian secular empire. In contrast, Jerusalem brings to mind a Judaic location and Judeo-Christian conflict. "America's glory"—constructed through "all races and nations"—is cemented in *The Melting-Pot*'s concluding stage directions:

> [An instant's solemn pause. The sunset is swiftly fading, and the vast panorama is suffused with a more restful twilight, to which the many-gleaming lights of the town add to the tender poetry of the night. Far back, like a lonely, guiding star, twinkles over the darkening water the torch of the Statue of Liberty. From below comes the softened sound of voices and instruments joining in "My Country 'tis of Thee." The curtain falls slowly.] (199)

The temporal setting for David's final American pledge of allegiance—the

Fourth of July—and the use of patriotic props as scenic backdrops (such as the Statue of Liberty), verifies the play's foci on affective and political citizenships. At the same time, the "softened sound of voices" who join in the performance of "My Country 'tis of Thee" attests to the performative dimension of citizenship. Indeed, David and Vera's theatrical declaration of love for each other and for country gives way to the collective, polyvocal performance of patriotism, or "country love."

Fittingly, the territorialization of immigrant transcendence and selfhood coincided with Zangwill's political agenda as a British Jewish writer. As Maurice Wohlgelernter reminds us, Zangwill was a "novelist, playwright, poet, essayist, polemicist, Zionist, Territorialist, pacifist, suffragist, and staunch advocate of a universal religion" invested in mainstream late nineteenth-century and twentieth-century thought about the creation of a Jewish homeland.[20] In his work, Zangwill consistently explored the viability of a Zionist state and the feasibility of a territorialist agenda. He founded the Jewish Territorialist Movement, which was dedicated to the creation of Jewish state wherever geographically and politically possible. In particular, Zangwill's *Children of the Ghetto: A Study of a Peculiar People* (1907) makes visible Jewish alienation through marginalized frames (as a minority in London) and displacement due to the absence of a politically identifiable homeland. Performed the following year, *The Melting-Pot* continues *Children of the Ghetto*'s contemplation of territorial citizenship, and emerges from Zangwill's own admission that after Territorialism, "America is the best solution to the Jewish question."[20]

The Melting-Pot predictably constructs a homeland through idealized American frames, which allegedly allow modes of religious tolerance and routes to political freedom unavailable in the Old World. Within this milieu, *The Melting-Pot*'s Jewish characters (David, Mendel, and Frau Quixano) need not convert to become Americans (a liberating dimension apparent in the original 1790 law). Rather, the United States becomes a seemingly ideal asylum for Jewish immigrants who wish to maintain their religious affiliations without Old World anti-Semitism and prejudice. England is not an option for the play's setting, despite Zangwill's own nation-state affiliation. After all, as David asserts, the "cockleshell" England was "not in the making" and represents an "old civilization stamped with the seal of creed." (97). Instead, "the new secular Republic" (the United States) is configured as a "promised land."

In contrast, *The Melting-Pot*'s Christian characters are more likely to convert. To reiterate, Kathleen (the Irish maid) is at once skeptical of

Jewish practice and critical of its tenets. All the same, through David's proselytizing, Kathleen's outlook on the "Jewish question" shifts. In the end, it is the Catholic Kathleen who reminds Mendel and David of religious holidays (e.g., Purim); in fact, Kathleen is the only character who actively assists Frau Quixano in the ritual rehearsal of Jewish tradition. Analogously, the Christian Vera voluntarily accepts her future husband's faith, vociferously defending her love choice to those who doubt its validity (her baron father, her baroness stepmother, the American, Davenport, and first-generation Jewish immigrant Mendel). To be sure, in act 3, after an argument with the baron over the "necessity" of pogroms, she tells David, "I come to you, and I say in the words of Ruth, thy people shall be my people and thy God my God!" (165). Like the biblical Ruth who expresses this sentiment to her mother-in-law, Vera will without a doubt follow David into his community. The connection between this parable and the Old Testament moreover proves her commitment to wholeheartedly accept and embody her intended husband's history and faith.

The prevalence of immigrant characters in Zangwill's play underscores the critical characterization of Quincy Davenport, the sole native-born American. Paradoxically, in terms of *The Melting-Pot*'s patriotic rhetoric, Quincy Davenport is in fact politically and culturally the least American. Davenport brings the Old World quite literally into the New World with his self-interested financial sponsorship of Vera's parents and Herr Pappelmeister's orchestra. Situating Old World culture in a superior position, Davenport denounces his country of origin—the United States—in favor of European preferences. In so doing, Davenport (through affective declarations and affinities) becomes a denaturalized subject. Conversely, *The Melting-Pot*'s characterizations of first-generation David and Vera are legibly "more American" because their connection to naturalization frames, which marries voluntary romantic desire to patriotic aspiration. Not coincidentally, the strategic deployment of immigrant bodies in the service of U.S. nationhood anticipates contemporary Jewish American Mary Antin's 1912 autobiographical assertion that the immigrant is more American than her/his native-born counterpart precisely because of an unfailing belief in the U.S. exceptional mythos.[21]

At its initial Washington, D.C., premiere, early reviews situated the sentimental Zangwill alongside his more famous contemporaries—European realists Henrik Ibsen and George Bernard Shaw. To some critics, *The Melting-Pot* was politically abhorrent because of its mention of "racial fusion" as a solution to unassimilability.[22] Such a "racial" answer was unacceptable to nativists, yet it also collided with racist politics apparent in Jim Crow law and anti-Chinese exclusion policy. The contemporaneous reading of problematic racial fusion undermines *The Melting-Pot*'s primary love match between Jew and gentile. It is also potentially at play in the last act of the play, wherein David tells Vera:

> It is the fires of God round His Crucible. . . . There she lies, the great Melting-Pot—listen! Can't you hear the bubbling? There gapes her mouth [He points East.]—the harbour where a thousand mammoth feeders come from the ends of the world to pour in their human freight. Ah, what a stirring and a seething! Celt and Latin, Slav and Teuton, Greek and Syrian, black and yellow. . . . (199)

Zangwill very much takes to task turn-of-the-century racialized anxieties about the immigrant body. In the play's imaginary, the Celt and Latin, Slav and Teuton, Greek and Syrian, black and yellow, are equal human freight, ingredients for the stirring and seething melting pot. On another level, *The Melting-Pot* makes apparent a simultaneous naturalized solution to the "immigrant question," "Chinese question," and "Negro question." Nevertheless, the endurance of racist policy and practice dramatically illustrates that such a naturalized solution was neither hegemonically practicable nor state-sanctioned. Undeniably, ethnicity and race still served as the bases for naturalization denials, restrictive immigration policy, and segregation.

At the very least, *The Melting-Pot* touches upon the tension between imagined U.S. exceptionalism and real racist practice. *The Melting-Pot* therefore tapped into what Benedict Anderson famously observed as a set of sociopolitical "imagined realities" which foreground turn-of-the-century patriotic and nationalistic discourses. As Anderson asserts, such "realities" included "nation-states, republican institutions, common citizenships, popular sovereignty, national flags, and anthems . . . and the liquidation of their conceptual opposites: dynastic empires, monarchical institutions, absolutisms, subjecthoods, inherited nobilities, serfdoms, ghettos, and so forth."[23] Although Anderson's characterization moves beyond the purview of the singular U.S. nation-state, such national signifiers are nevertheless reminiscent of *The Melting-Pot*'s deployment of patriotic symbols. The play's reliance on polar opposites (such as the baron and Vera) and identifiable national images (the American flag and the Statue of Liberty) illuminate Anderson's assertion that citizenship is "imagined" through national symbols that make possible "the liquidation of their conceptual opposites." Simultaneous to the construction of rhetorical and structural state-authorized apparatuses (institutions, citizenship, anthems, allegiances, and naturalization oaths), Anderson underscores what is elided, eliminated, and revised in the process of turn-of-the-century selfhood and nationhood.

Certainly, the history of slavery and the persistence of Jim Crow, the decimation of Native peoples, and anti-Asian immigration acts make less possible an unproblematic narrative of democratic achievement. And, as continuing politics make clear, the amnesia around these histories is complicit to the construction of imperial nationhood reliant on supremacist logics, civilizing impulses, and "benevolent" assimilation. Correspondingly, as Joe Kraus argues, the play (a combination love story, symphony, melodrama, and slapstick comedy) was performed in front of an American audience that was "renegotiating the aesthetic conventions of theater as one means of articulating what it meant to be American at all."[24] Such enthusiastic reception by one of the architects of American imperialism, Theodore Roosevelt, was consistent with the play's pro-American stance and a casting of the United States as a uniquely "kind" imperial power.

Still, if the play's tolerant logics did not match up to contemporary domestic policy, then neither did Zangwill's dedication to Roosevelt adequately address the brutality of U.S. empire. Regardless of President McKinley's assurance that the "mission of the United States [in the Philippines was] one of benevolent assimilation," the bloodiness of the Philippine-American War (1899–1902)—in which more than 200,000 Filipinos died—largely suggests that "the policy of benevolence" rested on violence.[25] Significantly, the ruptures between the articulation of U.S. imperial power and the reality of it in Asia would occur time and again in the twentieth century, as U.S. foreign policy would repeatedly make not "new Americans" but new refugees.

Returning to the Source: The Cold War and Chin Y. Lee's *The Flower Drum Song*

On January 12, 1950, U.S. Secretary of State Dean Acheson delivered his "Speech on the Far East," wherein he addressed the hot-button issue of communist China. Acheson at once acknowledged the heterogeneity of "the peoples of Asia," who were "so incredibly diverse and their problems are so incredibly diverse that how could anyone, even the most utter charlatan, believe that he had a uniform policy." Despite the recognition of "incredible diversity," Acheson still advocated a uniform foreign policy of containment. Modifying turn-of-the-century notions of benevolent assimilation to fit more comfortably with cold war realpolitik, Acheson firmly proclaimed:

> there is a new day which has dawned in Asia. It is a day in which the Asian peoples are on their own, and know it, and intend to continue on their own. It is a day in which old relationships between east and west are gone, relationships which at their worst were exploitations, and which at their best were paternalism. That relationship is over, and the the relationship of east and west must now be in the Far East one of mutual respect and helpfulness. We are their friends. Others are their friends. We and those others are willing to help, but we can help only where we are wanted and only where the conditions of help are really sensible and possible.[26]

Acheson's speech accentuates what other critics and historians note was a profound sense of U.S. loss following the "fall of China" in 1949. Dependent on discursive friendship and voluntary affiliation, Acheson's address calls attention to patterns of paternalistic exploitation in U.S. foreign policy. Indicating that the United States must recognize that "Asian peoples are on their own," Acheson opens the interventionist door with the politically charged mention of "willingness." Acheson explains that Asian peoples can be helped "only where the conditions . . . are really sensible and possible." Such conditions—built on U.S. willingness to intervene and the compliance of the Asian nation-state—euphemistically obscure imperial logics in a manner similar (but not identical) to the fin-de-siècle U.S. project in the Philippines.

If Acheson addressed Asia through U.S. foreign policy, then Senator Pat McCarran continued the cold war fight on domestic soil. That same year, the Democratic senator from Nevada was chief sponsor and architect of the Internal Security Act, which established the Subversive Activities Control Board. Intended to police domestic communist threats, the Subversive Activities Control Board would, in theory, register suspicious "red" organizations and individuals. Though no organizations (including the Communist Party of the United States) faced negative outcomes as a consequence of registration, the act nevertheless mobilized nascent cold war anxieties through congressional law. Although the Internal Security Act was symbolically important, given the milieu of the postwar period, more recognized was the Nevada senator's cosponsorship with Democratic Senator Francis Walter of Pennsylvania of the 1952 McCarran-Walter Act.

A landmark moment in U.S. naturalization history, the McCarran-Walter Act removed racial requirements for naturalized citizenship. Even though Chinese and South Asian immigrants were granted access to naturalized citizenship in 1943, to cement the pro-Ally relations between China and India during the Second World War, other groups such as Japanese immigrants were denied access because of Supreme Court precedent. At least on the surface, the McCarran-Walter Act enabled first-generation Asian immigrants to gain en masse naturalized citizenship for the first time since *In re Ah Yup* (1879), *Ozawa v. United States* (1922), and *United States v. Thind* (1923). But even with seemingly progressive racial moves, the act nonetheless was steeped in cold war politics.

Above all, the McCarran-Walter Act's continued reliance on nation-state quotas, the strategic use of exclusionary provisions for those affiliated with communism abroad, and the at-will deportation of allegedly communist alien bodies corresponded to the politics of the Internal Security Act. Following the successful passage of the McCarran-Walter Act, the Nevada senator opined:

> I believe that this nation is the last hope of Western civilization and if this oasis of the world shall be overrun, perverted, contaminated, or destroyed, then the last flickering light of humanity will be extinguished. I take no issue with those who would praise the contributions which have been made to our society by people of many races, of varied creeds and colors. America is indeed a joining together of many streams which go to form a mighty river which we call the American way. However, we have in the United States today hard-core, indigestible blocs which have not become integrated into the American way of life, but which, on the contrary, are its deadly enemies. Today, as never before, untold millions are storming our gates for admission and those gates are cracking under the strain. The solution of the problems of Europe and Asia will not come through a transplanting of those problems en masse to the United States.[27]

Drawing on Theodore Roosevelt's aforementioned declaration of "good faith" assimilability, McCarran cautions against the "transplanting of . . . problems en masse to the United States." For these reasons, the rhetoric and sentiment behind the mid-century senator's policy echoes the conditional "benevolent assimilation" offered by McKinley and his successor.

Analogously, the connection between early and mid century occurs through a divergent reading of Chin Y. Lee's *The Flower Drum Song*. Chiefly, while Zangwill's *The Melting-Pot* brokered a solution to contemporaneous anxieties about the Jewish immigrant, Lee's *Flower Drum Song*, on the surface, performed an analogous function for extant Asian immigration. It was published at a time when Asia, as a geographically complex location, was the focus of cold war initiatives abroad, and central to mid-century debates was the question of whether Asian subjects could (or, equally important, would) repudiate communism in favor of democratic rule. As Asian immigrants arrived on U.S. shores and Asian Americans were more demographically visible, turn-of-the-century questions about "assimilability" persisted. Within this conflicted cold war context, Lee's novel produces a destabilizing reading of a Chinese/Chinese American identity that undermines an emergent, sociologically driven, model minoritization. At stake in Lee's novel is not necessarily a solution to the "immigrant question" but rather an examination of its political and racial problems. Key to this exploration is the novel's focus on the refugee, a potent emblem of dislocation.

Correspondingly, *The Flower Drum Song*'s emphasis on dislocation as a primary theme and mode of characterization is foreshadowed in the opening paragraph of the novel. The unidentified, omniscient narrator observes:

> To the casual tourist, Grant Avenue is Chinatown, just another colorful street in San Francisco; to the overseas Chinese, Grant Avenue is their showcase, their livelihood; to the refugees from the mainland, Grant Avenue is Canton. . . . The Chinese theatres, the porridge restaurants, the teahouses, the newspapers, the food, the herbs . . . all provide an atmosphere that makes a refugee wonder whether he is really in a foreign land. And yet, in this familiar atmosphere, he struggles and faces many problems that are sometimes totally unfamiliar.[28]

The setting for the novel—San Francisco's Chinatown—is introduced as a foreign space that is "here and there." Revising Frank Norris's turn-of-the-century tripartite characterization of Chinatown, Lee expresses a markedly different reading of three distinct modalities. Specifically, to the "casual tourist" (an assumed outsider), Chinatown is a domestically foreign location, noteworthy as just "another colorful street in San Francisco." To overseas Chinese immigrants, Grant Avenue, Chinatown's main thoroughfare, is home, a space for their livelihood. For the stateless refugee—Chinatown's most recent arrival—the neighborhood embodies "Canton," an alienated site. And, as *The Flower Drum Song* progresses, Chinatown emerges as a contradictory location. Lee's Chinatown both engenders U.S. alienation and enables Old World nostalgia. Consequently, *The Flower Drum Song's* Chinatown setting becomes a global location where capital and individuals travel across borders. The novel's characters carry multiple global allegiances that work in alienating tandem with generational differences, fomenting further conflict and discord. To be sure, Chinatown is a largely denaturalized place wherein citizenship is both a contested and an illusive goal.

The Flower Drum Song's novelistic subversion of Americanization as an ultimate selfhood goal for Asian immigrants operates in direct opposition to its comedic, more well-known musical version. Indubitably, the more popular stage adaptation of the work—Richard Rodgers and Oscar Hammerstein's *The Flower Drum Song*—strategically downplayed refugee dynamics, stressing instead sympathetic assimilationist themes. Accordingly, the musical attempts to represent the viability of Asian immigrant "Americanization" for U.S. audiences. *The Flower Drum Song* musical follows patriarch Master Wang, his sister-in-law (Auntie Liang), and two sons. Whereas *The Melting-Pot* novel drew heavily from a Romeo and Juliet plot, *The Flower Drum Song* musical employs *A Midsummer Night's Dream* narrative twists.

Principally, nightclub owner Sammy Wong is betrothed to Mei-Li through an arranged marriage.[29] This involuntary love match is necessarily complicated by Sammy's romantic relationship with Linda Low, his featured nightclub singer. Meanwhile, Mei-Li develops an amorous interest in Wang Ta, Master Wang's eldest son. However, Wang Ta is initially infatuated with Linda Low. In turn, Linda Low is in love with Sammy. When she finds out about the arranged marriage, Linda begins a relationship with Wang Ta as an act of romantic revenge.

Through a series of mishaps and misunderstandings, the musical's characters eventually and successfully achieve voluntary romantic love. Mei-Li weds Wang Ta, and Sammy Wong marries Linda Low. The matrimonial plots that dominate the musical foreground an equally important naturalizing narrative. Explicitly, such couple combinations are naturalized according to sentimental American tenets and values. The undocumented, working-class Mei-Li fruitfully pursues a relationship with the Americanized Wang Ta, who is firmly middle class. Their eventual marriage potentially grants Mei-Li American citizenship and substantiates "classless" nationhood claims. Likewise, Sammy is able to domesticate—or tame—the ever-flirtatious Linda through marriage, fulfilling his male role within an identifiable 1950s patriarchal order.

Beyond romantic frames, these naturalization impulses are evident in the musical's characterization of the recently naturalized Aunt Liang, who celebrates her citizenship exam success at a gala held at Master Wang's house. The scene's featured song, "Chop Suey," is a polyvocal production involving Aunt Liang and other Chinese/Chinese American characters. As Master Wang's house is naturalized as a setting for Aunt Liang's U.S. citizenship, so do the song's lyrics naturalize the performers. Constitutive of U.S. pop cultural allusions (to celebrities, American-produced commodities, and hula hoops), American selfhood is constructed through mid-century U.S. consumption. Metaphorically, the song's title and lyrical accentuation of consumerism underscores Aunt Liang's new American self, who (like chop suey) is a "Chinese" commodity naturalized to suit American palates and tastes. And so, the musical version of *The Flower Drum Song* puts forth a dominant set of citizenship values, accents, and emphases.

Although Rodgers and Hammerstein's musical surely pays homage to Lee's 1957 novel, it is a liberal, not strict, adaptation. The comic tone of the musical is largely absent in Lee's version (as is Sammy Wong). Another principal character in the musical—Linda Low—is named "Linda Tung" and occupies a minor role *The Flower Drum Song* novel. While the musical Linda Lowe achieves heteronormative validation by the play's end, Lee's Linda Tung is dismissed as a superficial, materialistic fraud relatively early in the novel. Interestingly, two of these characteristics—Linda's superficiality and materialism—become pro-American attributes in *The Flower Drum* Song's theatrical and cinematic versions. What is more, central to Linda Low's success is her access to sexual capital. On the contrary, such sexual capital proves a liability for Linda Tung, whose alleged sexual promiscuity ostracizes (and denaturalizes) her from Chinatown.

Naturalization and Alienations: Refugees and *The Flower Drum Song*

Such revised characterizations are not limited to Linda Tung/Linda Low. Like her musical counterpart (Auntie Liang), Madam Tang is the most enthusiastic would-be patriot in the original *Flower Drum Song*. In the novel, Madam Tang constantly rehearses U.S. citizenship class lessons to prepare for a future naturalization exam. A devotee of U.S. traditions and ideologies, Madam Tang represents an idealized selfhood solution for Chinese refugees and immigrants. As the narrator reveals,

> For two years Madam Tang had been attending the American citizenship class at the Marina Adult School. She had no idea when the Immigration Service would write to her asking her to go to the preliminary hearing; Madam Tien, one of her closest friends, had waited six years before such a letter reached her. However, Madam Tang kept hoping and studying, memorizing every word of the American Constitution. (29–30)

Madam Tang's affective affiliation to the United States, manifest in her devoted study of the Constitution, is left largely unrequited and unacknowledged. Having "no idea when the Immigration Service would write to her" and emphasizing hope, the narrator brings to light an uncertain dimension to Madam Tang's quest for selfhood. This uncertainty remains unresolved by the novel's conclusion, which lacks the musical's "Chop Suey" celebration of naturalization. Implicitly, the cold war politics at play in the McCarran-Walter Act obstruct Madam Tang's naturalization. Undeniably, Madam Tang's previous political affiliation as a Chinese subject and current status as a refugee paradoxically make her both a threat and a welcome addition vis-à-vis cold war policies of containment.

In contrast, Madam Tang's brother-in-law, Master Wang (Wang Chi-Yang), is bonded to an older generation of Chinese immigrants who in fact remember a pre-Communist Chinese tradition. Such traditional proclivities are evident in Master Wang's initial reluctance to use Western banks, his distrust of Western medicine, and his insistence that his sons not become "too Americanized." For example, early in the novel, Madam Tang and Master Wang debate the pros and cons of using American banks after news of a robbery has hit the Chinatown papers. Madam Tang contends:

> My sister's husband . . . the American government is a democratic government; it is for the people and by the people, with three principles of the Constitution which are liberty, equality, and justice. You just cannot order the government to send you two soldiers to guard your house day and night as though you were a feudal lord. This is not China. You had better get that idea out of your mind. Besides, the American government has three departments: the

> legislative, the executive, and the judicial. All you can do is ask the police department of the Executive Department to catch the thief. (33–34)

Madam Tang's insistence that her brother-in-law adjust to an American sensibility consists of equal parts naturalization oath and citizenship test. Nonetheless, as the unidentified narrator previously averred, Madam Tang has spent the last two years attending the American citizenship class. It remains unclear as to how long she will have to wait for her preliminary citizenship hearing. As the novel later makes clear, though a model citizenship candidate, Madam Tang occupies the same political category as Master Wang. Indeed, both are de facto transnational refugees who lack nation-state certainty. Correspondingly, Master Wang's meditations about his place within Chinatown and the United States—which reinforce a "lost" sensibility"—occupy the same contemplative plane as Madam Tang's never-scheduled naturalization exam.

Notwithstanding Madam Tang's devotion to U.S. selfhood principles, she still adheres to Old World class biases. Explicitly, Madam Tang initially rejects Wang Ta's decision to marry the undocumented "peasant" Mei-Li, signaling disdain for working-class subjects regardless of "countrywoman" status. However, like Mei-Li, Madam Tang is ultimately a refugee who must contend with U.S. immigration law. Hence, *The Flower Drum Song*'s principal players are haunted by the specter of immigration policy and U.S. racial schemas. Such policies threaten the domestic imaginary. For example, when the patriarch Master Wang decides that his eldest son Wang Ta must marry, he turns to the possibility of an arranged marriage via a "picture bride." However, such a marital path is largely closed due to immigration policy prohibition and bureaucratic red tape. Even *The Flower Drum Song's* most dedicated U.S. advocate (Madam Tang) admits that such policies ensure that when Wang Ta's bride "arrives in this country, it is about time for her to die." As Madam Tang reminds, "To apply for an immigration quota, it takes about ten years; to wait for Wang Ta to become a citizen, it takes five years, and by the time he is permitted to bring his wife over, it will take another five years. Again ten years" (158).

When Master Wang threatens to deport Mei-Li and her father due to a false theft allegation, Wang Ta states, "we are all refugees from the Mainland China" (235). This assertion by Wang Ta to his father reminds the reader of Americanized Wang Ta's origin as a Chinese-born subject. Globally, the declaration necessarily brings to the fore diasporic histories that persist even with intergenerational temporalities and semi-naturalized plots. Accessing a collective identity forged through loss, Wang Ta attempts to make cohesive the experiences of Chinese/Americans in the novel. Nonetheless, Master Wang's silencing response to his son—"Hold your tongue!"—militates against such pan-Chinese classifications.

With Wang Ta's collective articulation that "we are all refugees," the novel at best offers an ambiguous resolution to the dilemma of transnational identities. Conversely, *The Flower Drum Song* (as novel) critically identifies the dilemma that faces the Chinese refugee. Such a figure is forcibly relocated, involuntarily classified as perpetual foreigner/model U.S. citizen, and occupies a tenuous ethnoracial, extrastatal position. Equally, *The Flower Drum Song* explores the degree to which mid-century Chinese Americans are faced with similar but by no means identical senses of dislocation. Wang Ta, the eldest son and protagonist, is at odds with his second-generation Chinese American identity. Such struggle ostensibly occurs in relation to his father's more traditional ways. Yet, it is Wang Ta's hyphenated identity that makes less certain his filial location as Chinese *or* American. As Chinese refugees, Mei-Li and her father embody a possible solution to Wang Ta's identity crisis. To that end, Mei-Li and her father (as recently arrived migrants) are more immediately connected to the country of origin, in this case, mainland China.

Correspondingly, Mei-Li and her father from the outset represent holders of Old World tradition, and this status carries cultural capital for both Master Wang and Wang Ta. To be sure, Wang Ta is initially smitten with Mei-Li's Chineseness. Still, it is Mei-Li's willingness to transnationally combine Chinese and U.S. practices that ultimately makes her a suitable love match. As *The Flower Drum Song* comes to an end and Mei-Li's undocumented status is made public, the two decide to marry in the face of ostensibly insurmountable class differences without full parental support.This lack of parental support in effect renders Wang Ta and Mei-Li "refugees" vis-à-vis familial affiliation. This choice forces the couple to leave Chinatown, further reinforcing a reading of refugee frames. In so doing, the novel's plot complicates a simplistic reading of affiliation (such as what it means to live in the United States) through its focus on refugees who, despite relocation, are diasporically, nostalgically, and transnationally connected to the country of origin.[30] Rather than offer a naturalized solution like Zangwill, Lee instead focuses on the failure of U.S. citizenship to concretize selfhood and belonging.

As *The Flower Drum Song* draws to an end, Master Wang's family is in disarray. Besides Wang Ta's exilic marriage, Master Wang's youngest son (an avid consumer of U.S. popular culture) is missing by novel's conclusion. The reason for his absence—that he is playing baseball with his Americanized friends—highlights his naturalization, wherein he privileges U.S. sport and pop culture. This naturalization and Wang Ta's marriage-driven departure foreground the novel's somber tone, which mourns—and does not celebrate—acts of Americanization such as voluntary love matches and baseball. *The Flower Drum Song* concludes with a rather dystopian U.S. vision. Within this loss-oriented milieu, the United States ceases to be an asylum refugee site and instead is the stage for disruption and alienation. Indeed, this dystopian perspective is made plain through *The Flower Drum Song*'s patriarch, Master Wang.

Seemingly an ancillary character, Master Wang is nevertheless the first figure introduced and the last discussed. As the opening pages of *The Flower Drum Song* reveal, Master Wang "escaped the mainland of China five years ago" as a result of the Communist takeover of the late 1940s (5). Although ethnically Chinese, Master Wang is still alienated in San Francisco's Chinatown community. This alienation is immediately confirmed following the Grant Avenue description, which sets the stage for Master Wang's introduction. A Chinatown refugee, Master Wang speaks in a "Hunan dialect, which neither a Northerner nor a Cantonese can understand. . . . His working knowledge of the English language was limited to two words: 'yes' and 'no'" (4). Though the patriarch "loved to walk on Grant Avenue," he would not venture further than Bush Street, which he considers "no longer Chinatown but a foreign territory" (5–6).

Similarly, Master Wang "seldom went farther to Kearny, for he regarded it as a Filipino town and had no desire to go there" (7). Primarily limited to his home and Grant Avenue, Master Wang is thus a voluntarily and involuntarily *contained* subject. Despite his alienated cultural position, Master Wang and his family lead an economically comfortable existence in Chinatown. Undeniably, the novel's love plot (involving Wang Ta) and intergenerational conflict between father and son dominate *The Flower Drum Song*'s imaginary. Further, Madam Tang's naturalization attempts form a substantial side story. Nonetheless, Master Wang's alienated contemplations constitute a significant part of the novel. For example, *The Flower Drum Song*'s pace relies on Master Wang's periodic walks through Chinatown.

Master Wang's Chinatown strolls are largely punctuated by acts of consumption, which include the perusal of Chinatown commodities, exchanges with Chinatown business owners, and restaurant scenes. In fact, Master Wang is not the only Chinatown pedestrian. All *The*

Flower Drum Song's characters enact similar pedestrian acts. Still, what differentiates Master Wang's walks from the others is the emphasis on affective belonging. In particular, Master Wang does not simply walk through Chinatown. Rather, Master Wang engages in nostalgic reverie and consumption. Accordingly, such excursions make apparent Master Wang's allegiance to (and disassociation from) mainland China, his country of origin.

Master Wang's immigrant consumer acts substantiate this reading. The narrator relates that Master Wang subscribes to all the Chinatown newspapers. Significantly, Master Wang reads them while sitting "comfortably in his rattan chair." These newspapers connect the refugee father to the politics of Chinatown and those of mainland China. The chair, purchased through order in Chinatown, collapses the space between the United States and China. The newspaper headlines prompt anti-communist commentaries. In line with an ideal cold war politics, Master Wang's dislike of communism makes him seem to be the willing democracy convert. Even so, Lee qualifies this dislike, making impossible a cold war/Master Wang alliance. To that end, the narrator stresses that Master Wang's anti-communist stance is born out of a pro-Chinese, prerevolutionary affiliation. Indeed, Master Wang is not a cold war stalwart but instead a refugee victim of a political ideology that "destroyed Chinese traditions and turned the Chinese order upside down" (7).

If material objects such as the rattan chair speak to a precommunist Chinese past, then Master Wang turns to capitalistic practices (consumption) to fulfill his "home country" nostalgia. Though unintentional, such consumption foments a superficial link to mid-century U.S. selfhood. At stake in cold war articulations was the successful deployment of democracy and capitalism in claims of U.S. superiority. Hence, what separated the American from his communist counterpart was the ability to not only vote but also buy. Nonetheless, Master Wang's purchasing power lacks naturalization impulse. Instead, Master Wang's purchases—which are imported from China and remind him of his former home—attest to the patriarch's desire to remain in some ways unassimilable.

On another level, such consumer desires make visible Master Wang's transnational and largely unresolved citizenship. Though geographically "at home" in the United States, the patriarch resides in Chinatown, an alienated site. Though Master Wang speaks an unintelligible Hunan dialect, Master Wang temporarily finds cultural asylum through material means (that is, Chinatown objects). Master Wang's home, decorated with "Chinese paintings and couplet scrolls, furnished with uncomfortable but expensive teakwood tables and chairs," provisionally assuages the patriarch's sense of being in a foreign land.[31] Nevertheless, such objects do not permanently relocate Master Wang to the country of origin. As Master Wang admits to his herbalist, he lives in a "foreign house . . . equipped with foreign contrivances and boilers supplying steam heat day and night" inhabited by "children born in a foreign land" (72). Fittingly, these imported commodities function as metaphors for Master Wang's own sense of being an imported (and not assimilated) subject.

Master Wang's tenuous (but all the same persistent) desire to "return" is also evident in his socioeconomic practices. As previously mentioned, the patriarch initially refuses to deposit his money in a Western bank because of the American strangers who work there. Even so, Master Wang (following a robbery) is forced to change his position. This forcible shift—like the commodities he buys—coincides with the involuntary choices made by refugees. Perhaps most telling is the Western suit Master Wang wears in a fleeting attempt to naturalize his appearance following the robbery. The narrator remarks:

> He acted very stiff that day. He felt uncomfortable in the foreign suit. The trousers seemed too tight; the open collar of the coat made him feel naked and cold, as though the front part of the clothes had been torn away in an accident. And when he lifted his arms, the sleeves seemed to pull them down; furthermore, the heavy shoulder pads bothered him, making him feel as if someone was putting his arm around his shoulders. After that day, he packed the foreign suit at the bottom of his trunk and never wanted to wear it again. (57)

The narrator's detailed description focuses largely on Master Wang's affective relationship to the suit. Uncomfortable, tight, and foreign, the suit makes Master Wang feel as though someone was putting his arm around his shoulders, an apt metaphor for cold war containment. The suit's inability to fulfill its ostensible function—as clothing that provides warmth—is at once reminiscent of Abraham Cahan's *David Levinksy* and its mention of "ill comport." Moreover, the suit's ill fit underscores Master Wang's uncomfortable and incongruous position as a Chinese refugee in the United States. Like the suit,which is unnatural, cold, and bothersome, Master Wang's relationship to the nation is largely contested. The patriarch's inability to wear the suit matches his failure to put on a convincing American citizenship performance.

Such ill-fits continue into *The Flower Drum Song*'s final pages. Throughout the novel, Master Wang suffers from a persistent cough, furthering a reading of "ill comport." At last, Master Wang yields, and the final scene of the novel involves his trip to a Western hospital. This decision is in some ways the most alienated and abject. As the narrator notes, Master Wang "was now deserting his herb doctor, his best friend, and the only man in Chinatown with whom he could happily associate." And, as Master Wang makes his way to the clinic, he resigns himself to "the world of the younger generation" (244). As a member of the "older generation," he is by his own admission obsolete. Despite the dominance of intergenerational conflict, it is this specific change in consumption, not a clearly stated shift in values, that signals Master Wang's partial—yet forced—naturalization. Ironically yet appropriately, Master Wang turns away from the more "natural" elements of herbal medicine. Consistent with *The Flower Drum Song*'s narrative structure, this decision does not render an unproblematic, facile solution. Indeed, Master Wang's "resignation" underscores an involuntary dimension to his visit that is consistent with his refugee status.

Still the novel offers—at its end—a transnational although brief glimmer of hope for the patriarch. Master Wang spies the hospital sign, which interrupts thoughts of resignation. The sign, "hanging under the red-tiled pagoda roof . . . [was] well-written . . . the product of years of patient practice in the Sung School." Master Wang then "looked at the revolving door, braced himself a little, took a deep breath, mounted the marble steps, and entered the building" (245). Though "Western," the hospital nevertheless carries Old World markers such as the Chinese characters and the pagoda architecture. Architecturally, the hospital represents a transnational blending, which brings together local and global. Its façade reminds Master Wang of his country of origin, yet it houses country-of-settlement medical practices. Though imperfect (the characters on the sign are "lacking strength in some strokes"), the hospital remains multifaceted and multilayered space (245). The "transnational" hospital provides a partial solution to Master Wang's dilemma of belonging.

In the face of its potential as a solution, this ending nonetheless leaves open the roots of Master Wang's citizenship problem: the dissolution of his family, his continued Chinatown outsiderness, and his refugee status. Given the back-and-forth nature of Master Wang's acculturation attempts, it is difficult to ascertain whether this "final" decision will last. With no epilogue, it remains unclear whether his newfound sense of belonging is temporary or permanent. Indeed, as the narrator asserts, Master Wang "was the one who also hated change and always dreamed of going back to the old village in China, to die in China, and be buried in a good coffin, with numerous offspring visiting his grave every spring, making offerings and burning incense for him" (243).

As Robert G. Lee argues, in *The Flower Drum Song* musical, "the theme of an ethnic generation gap is substituted for the interrogation of racial exclusion that organizes the novel."[32] Without a doubt, Lee's original work is less concerned with romantic possibility and unimpeded access to U.S. citizenship than is the stage version. Instead, *The Flower Drum Song* is a somber novel made unstable precisely because of unresolved intergenerational conflict (emblematic of affective belonging) and exclusionary immigration policy. Though *Aiiieeeee!* editors Frank Chin, Jeffrey Paul Chan, Lawson Inada, and Shawn Wong comment that Lee's novel emerges from "whiteness, not . . . Chinese America" and comes "from a white tradition of Chinese novelty literature," a close reading of character and plot makes possible an alternative consideration of narrative rupture, discontent, and racialization.[33]

In fact, *The Flower Drum Song* novel is not so much about achieving whiteness as it is concerned with negotiating Chineseness in a racialized imaginary. But though divergent in plot and characterization, the novel and musical versions of *The Flower Drum Song* do converge on the ways in which Asian immigrants and Asian Americans were constructed through shifting frames of ethnicity and foreign policy. In particular, the emphasis on assimilation in the stage version assuaged contemporaneous dominant-held anxieties about the very viability of an Asian American citizenry in a postwar domestic imaginary. Correspondingly, this comforting narrative of assimilation carried currency on the world stage. Certainly, as U.S. empire extended its reach into Korea, Vietnam, Cambodia, and Laos, the model minoritization of Asian Americans at home was revised abroad through cold war characterizations of would-be democracies threatened by the march of a Soviet/Chinese "red menace."[34]

Israel Zangwill's *The Melting-Pot*, on the other hand, relies on a more stable (and progression-oriented) model minority characterization. In so doing, Zangwill's "comedy of Americanization" anticipates naturalized categories of ideal subjects who could easily be deployed in the service of both U.S. foreign policy and claims of exceptionalism. Such utopian projections operate in stark contrast to Lee's *The Flower Drum Song*, which refuses to naturalize the Asian immigrant experience. Written in the "hopeful" glow of the McCarran-Walter Act, *The Flower Drum Song* nevertheless forces a reading of how U.S. immigration policy is necessarily restrictive. Further, Lee's cold war novel refuses a celebratory ending for its refugee characters in a manner that acknowledges the limitation of U.S. foreign policy. Presciently, the "drama of Americanization" that dominates the novel's plot and characterization provocatively anticipates more dystopian readings of U.S. citizenship. Such dystopian readings privilege limitation over possibility, favor cold war imperialism over benevolent assimilation, and make visible the continued exclusionary nature of both whiteness and citizenship.

3 / Utopian and Dystopian Citizenships: Visions and Revisions of the "Promised Land"

I have chosen to read the story of '76 as a chapter in sacred history; to set Thomas Jefferson in a class with Moses, and Washington with Joshua; to regard the American nation as the custodian of a scared trust, and American citizenship as a holy order, with laws and duties derived from the Declaration.

—MARY ANTIN

A postethnic perspective denies neither history nor biology—nor the need for affiliations—but it does deny that history and biology provide a set of clear orders for the affiliations we are to make.

—DAVID HOLLINGER

As the 1912 presidential campaign moved into full swing, the "party of Lincoln" faced a crisis of divisive proportions. On the national stage, the conservative probusiness agenda of Republican incumbent William Howard Taft was pitted against the reform-minded antitrust philosophy of former president Theodore Roosevelt, also a Republican. In an election typified by bitter political discord, a failed assassination attempt, and a melodramatic nomination at the Republican National Convention, campaign debates were admittedly less spectacular.[1] Marked not so much by fireworks as by differences of administrative opinion, such party-line disagreements—forged on the "crucible" of what role government would take in the coming decade—converged on the terrain of immigration policy.

In particular, Republican and Democratic Party candidates actively sought constituencies of both native and foreign-born. After all, between 1881 and 1920, an estimated 23.5 million immigrants (particularly from eastern and southern Europe) migrated to the United States, making it the largest immigration wave until the passage of the 1965 Immigration and Nationality Act.[2] As urban spaces became more crowded, as industrialization moved at breakneck speed, and as demands for cheap labor rose, those seeking the nation's highest office were necessarily obliged to opine about the "making of new Americans" through law, practice, and custom.

Correspondingly, the sitting Republican president vowed to veto any legislation that carried literacy requirements for new immigrants. Former president and well-known Zangwill supporter Theodore Roosevelt, the Republican Party "Bull Moose" candidate, followed suit. Relying on Progressive-era connections to Hull House founder Jane Addams, a staunch advocate of immigrant resettlement and open-door immigration policies, Roosevelt reiterated time and again his commitment to amalgamated immigrant selves and melting pots.[3] Even Democratic Party candidate Woodrow Wilson, a former Princeton University president and current New Jersey governor, was forced to revise past nativist ruminations to meet the demands of a voting immigrant populace.

Indeed, a decade prior, Wilson had ruefully proclaimed that masses of southern and eastern European immigrants threatened to overrun superior northern European stock.[4] However, by 1912, Wilson assured his audience that:

> Some people have expressed a fear that there is too much immigration. I have the least uneasiness as to the new arrivals all being gripped as we have been gripped. The vast majority who come to our shores come on their own initiative and have some understanding as to what they want and a definite object in view. . . . The country should be divested of all prejudices. . . . We are all Americans when we vote.[5]

Explicitly addressing the question of citizenship—that "we are all Americans when we vote"—Wilson's amended immigration outlook purposefully echoed that of his Republican counterparts. Unintentionally, Wilson also brought to light the naturalized legal treatment of eastern and southern European immigrants. Unlike their Asian counterparts, such subjects were (in spite of racial stereotype) considered "white" under naturalization law, hence eligible to cast a ballot.

This is not to suggest that eastern and southern European immigrants were universally welcomed into the U.S. body politic. The rise of the Immigration Restriction League, an anti-immigrant lobby begun in 1894, increased congressional demands for literacy requirements, and public calls for immigration quotas undermine characterizations of a progressive era in immigration politics. That same year, Socialist Party candidate Eugene V. Debs chose a decidedly different answer to the "immigrant question" from those of the major party presidential contenders.

Conscious of his constituency of domestic, native-born, working-class laborers, Debs publicly and vociferously opposed unrestricted immigration.[6] As historian Matthew Frye Jacobson observes, the perennial Socialist candidate was a long-standing nativist who pejoratively declared in 1891 that "the Dago works for small pay and lives far more like a savage or wild beast than the Chinese."[7]

Given that the "Chinese problem" was resolved through exclusionary legislation, the Socialist candidate's comparative statement gestures toward a need for similar policies against other "less desirable" groups. Consequently, Debs (despite his own political marginalization as a socialist) was in step with contemporaneous scholars and conservative politicians who advocated "closed-door" answers to the "immigration problem." Such solutions would be implemented in the latter part of the 1910s and into the 1920s, as seen in the successful passage of three restrictive immigration acts: the 1917 Asiatic Barred Zone Act, the 1921 Emergency Quota Act, and 1924 Johnson-Reed Immigration Act. Nonetheless, as Israel Zangwill's *The Melting-Pot* makes clear, such nativist calls and exclusionary politics did not go culturally unanswered.

Besides, Zangwill was certainly not alone in his pro-immigrant stance. Almost a decade before the 1908 *The Melting-Pot* premiere, the British author wrote the foreword to Mary Antin's *From Plotzk to Boston* (1899). A collection of letters authored by an eleven-year-old Antin (1881–1949), *From Plotzk to Boston* was originally written in Yiddish and later translated, in the published version, into English. In the foreword, Zangwill averred: "Mary Antin's vivid description of all she and her dear ones went through enables us to see with our own eyes how the invasion of America appears to the impecunious invader. It is thus 'a human document' of considerable value, as well as a promissory note of future performance."[8] Given Antin's later literary success, Zangwill's early praise proved prophetic. Notable for its autobiographical, first-person immigrant perspective, *From Plotzk to Boston* would lay the narrative groundwork for Antin's most famous memoir, the bestselling *The Promised Land* (1912).

Like Zangwill's *The Melting-Pot*, Mary Antin's *The Promised Land* (and, to a lesser extent, *From Plotzk to Boston*) confronted characterizations of immigrant inferiority founded on perceived inassimilability. Specifically, *The Promised Land*'s foci on faith, individual success, and Americanization struck the same chord hit by Zangwill's play. Conflating Old Testament stories of exodus with U.S. master narratives of equality and naturalized American acceptances, Antin's well-received bildungsroman strategically situated the immigrant as a viable candidate for citizenship, like *The Melting-Pot*'s David Quixano and Vera Revendal. What is more, whereas Zangwill's multicharacter "comedy of Americanization" relied on naturalized monologues, Antin's memoir deployed a decidedly narrower, protagonist-driven focus.

Set in Russia and the United States, *The Promised Land* is composed of episodes that reinforce the protagonist's allegiance to dominant U.S. values. In so doing, the immigrant memoir makes full use of uninterrupted naturalized performances emblematized in literary declarations of renunciation and acceptance. Paradoxically, such performances are temporarily threatened by a dialectical tension between the Old World immigrant and New World citizen, and between family and self. In the end, however, Antin's memoir chiefly settles on an ideal vision of U.S. citizenship. Correspondingly, *The Promised Land* imagines a utopian turn-of-the-twentieth-century citizenship reminiscent of *The Melting-Pot*. On another level, the memoir is both productive and reproductive in scope. Expressly, Antin produces U.S. citizenship through naturalized acts; in the process, Antin reproduces (for the reader) the naturalization process.

In contrast, *The Promised Land*'s intertextual successor, Gish Jen's *Mona in the Promised Land* (1994) closely corresponds to the dystopian content to C. Y. Lee's *The Flower Drum Song*.[9] With titular and plot allusions to Antin's narrative, Jen's fictional bildungsroman nevertheless diverges from Antin's "hopeful" memoir. Rather than stressing promise, *Mona in the Promised Land* emphasizes the racialized limitations of U.S. citizenship. Set within a volatile mid-century backdrop, Jen places her protagonist in a problematic "promised land." Revising Antin's journey from Russian Jewish subject to American citizen, Jen's fictional "sequel" features a Chinese American citizen who wants to convert to Judaism. The protagonist's desire to "switch" sets in motion a dystopian story of denaturalization. Undermining the "voluntary" mythos of American exceptionalism, Jen's protagonist Mona must contend with rigid U.S. logics of race, gender, and nation.

Rising Tides and Immigration Problems: Pathological Ethnicities

The racial and gendered logics that circumscribe *Mona and the Promised Land* were most forcefully articulated in the first two decades of the twentieth century.[10] Concomitantly, such logics necessarily impacted Antin's contemporaneous *In the Promised Land*. For example, Socialist candidate Eugene V. Debs's 1912 nativist platform reverberated with the restrictionist treatise of Jeremiah W. Jenks and W. Jett Lauck, *The Immigration Problem* (1911). Jenks in particular was very much politically connected to the "immigrant question." The Cornell professor of economics was an influential member of the congressional Commission on Immigration (the Dillingham Commission).[11] Formed in 1907, the Commission on Immigration was charged with the task of policy planning and data collection. By 1911, the commission concluded that eastern and southern European immigrants posed an inassimilable national threat. For that alleged reason, the Dillingham Commission encouraged a two-pronged approach to stem the tide of undesirable immigration: quota-based restrictions (to bar would-be immigrants) and literacy requirements (for those foreign-born living in the United States).

The commission's findings are revealed in *The Immigration Problem*.[12] Armed with the prefatory claim that they "were not advocates but interpreters of fact," *The Immigration Problem*'s authors introduced an "objective" matrix to evaluate immigrant citizenship viability. Different immigrant groups were analyzed in the following categories: degrees of mental defect, assimilability, poverty statistics, and literacy rates. Notwithstanding "factual interpretation," *The Immigration Problem* incontrovertibly anticipated more expansive racist (and eugenicist) arguments at play in Madison Grant's influential *The Passing of the Great Race* (1916).[13] Taken together, *The Immigration Problem* and Grant's subsequent sounding of the Anglo-Saxon alarm highlight the centrality of immigration in public discourse.

The primacy of immigration debate in U.S. sociopolitical imaginary was confirmed in a 1912 *New York Times* review of *The Immigration Problem*. Titled "Does the Pot Melt It?", the article carried the equally interrogative byline, "Can the Immigration into this Country Be Assimilated?—It Could Be Once, but Can It Now?" According to the review's unnamed critic, "there is probably no question of domestic policy that has been more debated or less understood than that of immigration."[14] Without a doubt, the *New York Times* reviewer corroborated pessimistic immigration forecasts. Simultaneously, he confronted claims of long-standing "melting-pot" nationhood. Regardless of the review's avowed purpose (to evaluate the text's strengths and weaknesses), "Does the Pot Melt It?" echoed and expanded *The Immigration Problem*'s cautionary argument against the continued importation of adulterated American "stock."

Explicitly, "Does the Pot Melt It?" begins with an immigration concession of a priori assimilation success. To that end, the review begrudgingly acknowledges that the United States had been an immigrant (albeit "Anglo-Saxon") nation. Still, the critic commends Jenks and Lauck for their "convincing" derailment of an immigrant-focused teleology. *The Immigration Problem* and the *New York Times* review deconstruct this misguided "melting pot" nationhood. In so doing, both authors and critic alike rely on a "past is *not* present" understanding of immigration. Accordingly, past immigration patterns are characterized by easily naturalized bodies. In contrast, the present tide of immigration consists of "probationary white" subjects who defy facile naturalization because of non-Anglo-Saxon diversity. Surely, as the review's title and content suggest, these "too-foreign" ingredients threaten to "melt" the very foundation of U.S. nationhood.

Extending the "melted pot" metaphor further, a question of resources is integral to this pro-restriction review. *The Immigration Problem*'s authors—the aforementioned Jenks and Lauck, "an expert upon industrial and economic questions"—argue for restriction through a "scientific" consideration of labor competition, supply management, and education. At the same time, *The Immigration Problem*'s authors and *New York Times* critic alike repeatedly return to ethnicity and race. Critical to *The Immigration Problem*'s nativist accusations of "resource depletion" is a restriction justified through the "diseased" delineation of social, racial, and ethnic valences. In turn, such "ethnic pathologies" (as gleaned from Jenks and Lauck) precipitate a potential national calamity.

Asserting that newly arrived immigrants are largely illiterate, "acquire English very slowly—often not at all," and chiefly consist of "nomadic" males, the critic's recapitulation of *The Immigration Problem*'s main points explicitly evaluates citizenship promise through naturalization prerequisites (such as the ability to read and write English, and residency requirements).[15] Implicitly, a central anxiety about U.S. selfhood materializes. Distinctively, the *New York Times* critic admits that though past immigration "has laid the foundations of our National greatness," the "new and alien flood" effectively reduces these previous contributions "to an almost negligible quantity."[16] This "immigrant question"—or threat —is articulated through a pathologized critical questioning of present open-door policies that inadequately address the "condition" (or disease) at hand. To be sure, the questioning of immigrant policy necessarily relies on the newly interpolated turn-of-the-century immigrant subject. Consequently, the altered, interpolated immigrant is a corrosive body that threatens to melt the very "pot" of U.S. nationhood.

Inassimilable and "deficient," this pathogenic immigrant body is the source of U.S. contamination and potential pandemic (or national) obliteration. The nation's health, discernible in the reproduction of citizens, thus depends on naturalization processes that distinguish the "nomad" from the permanent settler, delineate the educated over the illiterate, and establish the racially welcome from the racial other.[17] Reduced to an "alien flood," the reviewer's characterization of the turn-of-the-century immigration wave strategically attaches the recently arrived immigrant to national disaster.

Regarding Jewish immigration, Jenkins and Lauck initially take to task anti-Semitism abroad with the eugenicist declaration of Jewish "mental superiority." Nevertheless, Jenkins and Lauck stress that unfettered access to the United States by Jewish immigrants carries the likely potential of introducing another "race problem" and will inevitably foment further ethno-racial tension (416). This pessimistic future vision is indubitably built on multiple contagions. Concurrently, the immigrant is the embodiment of an "American nightmare" inclusive of ethnoracial inferiority and further racial strife. It is this dystopian projection that necessitates and anticipates restrictionist policy and ruling. From nation-state quotas to barred zones, from whiteness cases and Supreme Court rulings, the opening decades of the twentieth century fused dominant understandings of U.S. selfhood to immigration discourse and practice.

Situated within this dystopian backdrop, Mary Antin's *The Promised Land* provides a significant textual counterpoint to fears of an impending "alien flood." Within this politicized context, Antin's memoir insists that immigrants are not only viable citizens but—most important—are willing and able to assimilate. Emphasizing sameness and dismissing religious affiliation in favor of patriotic devotion, *The Promised Land* begins and concludes with "promise," connotative of both rhetorical act (that is, a pledge of allegiance) and an optimistic future. Indeed, the pronouncement of utopian selfhood, wherein the United States is cast as an idealized and transcendent citizenship space, the rehabilitation of immigrants as healthy U.S. bodies, and the recuperative power of naturalization principally dictate Antin's principally hopeful autobiographical project.

Articulating "My Country": Mary Antin's *The Promised Land*

> *No reverberatory effect of the great war has caused American public opinion more solicitude than the failure of the "melting-pot." The discovery of diverse nationalistic feelings among our great alien population has come to most people as an intense shock. It has brought out the unpleasant inconsistencies of our traditional beliefs. We have had to watch hard-hearted old Brahmins virtuously indignant at the spectacle of the immigrant refusing to be melted, while they jeer at patriots like Mary Antin who write about our "forefathers."*
>
> —RANDOLPH BOURNE

If Israel Zangwill's *The Melting-Pot* successfully recuperated amalgamation as a catchall metaphor for early-century immigrant experiences, then Mary Antin's *The Promised Land* performed an analogous but more specific function through memoir. The "comedy of Americanization" that characterizes Zangwill's play, which partially accessed a *Romeo and Juliet* storyline to imagine an immigrant-centric sameness in the United States, is missing from Antin's project. Instead, the "journey *to* Americanization" dominates *The Promised Land*'s plot. Correspondingly, *The Promised Land*'s protagonist is an immigrant author willfully made into an American. Equally divided between narratives about the country of origin (Russia) and stories set in the country of settlement (the United States), Antin's girlhood narrative of "becoming American" formalistically echoes the naturalization process.

The Promised Land opens with Antin's declaration that "I was born" and "I have lived," calling to mind the a priori dimensions of naturalization repudiation.[18] To be sure, Antin's birth location in Russia foregrounds the legal need to naturalize. Simultaneously, this opening proclamation reflects and anticipates Antin's naturalization. In this vein, the proclamation of being "made over" implicitly signals the completion of the naturalization process. Concomitantly, *The Promised Land*'s initial projections foreshadow what follows: Antin recounts the experiences in the Russian pale (under threat of pogrom) that justify her family's flight to America; she then enumerates her journey from Polotsk, Russia, to the United States. *The Promised Land* concludes with Antin's pronouncement of "true arrival" via acculturation and naturalization in her newfound Boston home.

Notwithstanding the literary seamlessness of Antin's naturalization, the author's declaration of U.S. selfhood was unquestionably contested in the public sphere. Irrespective of the author's declaration of a Boston "homecoming," as Randolph Bourne makes clear in the opening paragraph of "Trans-National America" (1916), "old Brahmins" (like Jeremiah W. Jenks and W. Jett Lauck) nonetheless "jeer at patriots like Mary Antin who write about our "'forefathers.'"[19] Bourne brings to light the contradictory dimensions of nativism with his observation that these same individuals remain "virtuously indignant at the spectacle of the immigrant refusing to be melted."[20] Positioned between these two poles of nativist thought, Antin's *The Promised Land* tactically opts to highlight a recognizable naturalization process. Through such a trajectory, Antin as immigrant subject voluntarily selects U.S. citizenship over less defined transnational affiliation. The protagonist repudiates Russian practices in favor of U.S. politics. In similar fashion, Antin consistently privileges secular faith over orthodox Jewish practice, therefore engendering a de facto cultural naturalization that matches her newfound political selfhood.

A Progressive-era immigrant rights activist, Antin purposefully structures the immigrant experience as an intimately "American experience" rooted in an overt naturalization agenda. Drawing on dominant notions of exceptionalism and past conceptualizations of the United States as an *e pluribus unum* place of possibility and space of religious freedom, Antin manipulates her coming-of-age narrative to address nativist concerns of inassimilability and unpatriotic affiliation. As such, Antin as a character is an ideal would-be U.S. citizen who skillfully negotiates the terrain of American personhood and enthusiastically embraces cultural practices in "her country." The exuberance of Antin's national pledge is unmistakable in exclamatory remarks about the possibilities at hand in the United States.

Tellingly, the pogroms that threatened familial dynamics in Antin's native Russia are juxtaposed with tolerant classroom spaces that afford the newly arrived Antin and her family equal access to public space and education. The superstitions constitutive of family practice in her native Russia give way to more "rational" capitalistic exchanges involving hard work and eventual reward. And, in the face of her initial location in Russia as a disenfranchised peasant, Antin ends her memoir with the empowered assertion that in America she is an "heir . . . awaiting maturity. I was a princess waiting to be led to the throne."[21] The reliance on regal characterizations reinforces a reading of the memoir through utopian frames, wherein a priori class affiliations are rendered meaningless in a space of unbounded socioeconomic opportunity.

Formalistically reminiscent of Zangwill's *The Melting-Pot*, *The Promised Land* is composed of public oaths to the United States. As the memoir progresses, each declaration brings to light Antin's evolving "American character." This identity, revealed through acts of learning, is largely forged in institutional places like the classroom. It is here where the first-generation immigrant Antin encounters U.S. history, studies English, and, most important, articulates (through writing) her patriotic connection to the nation. Like Benjamin Franklin, Antin uses memoir as a means to map her self-made Americanness. In so doing, she in effect composes a readily intelligible nation-state affiliation that underscores Antin's seriousness as a "student of American letters."

What is more, Antin's naturalized self-revision is most evident in her negotiation of language and acquisition of dominant U.S. narratives. The evolution of Antin's legibility via the nation becomes clear in an episode involving a school assignment. Assigned to write a piece celebrating George Washington's birthday, Antin composes a prize-winning poem. Asked by her teacher to publicly recite it, Antin admits, "My pronunciation was faulty, my declamation flat." Still, the protagonist quickly interjects: "But I had the courage of my convictions. I was face to face with twoscore Fellow Citizens, in clean blouses and extra frills. I must tell them what George Washington had done for their country—for our country—for me" (194). The inclusion of "fellow citizens," the mention of Washington (a founding father), and the rhetorical conflation of "their country" and "our country" reinforce Antin's declaration that she too is a citizen. The recitation, "repeated by request" on the part of the teacher and received by students with "applause [that] was equally prolonged at each repetition," cements a successful reading of Antin's poetic patriotism, which resembles in form and function a partial naturalization oath.

Central to Antin's citizenship process is literacy, entrenched in her ability to read U.S. sociocultural cues; understand official, historical U.S. narratives; and write to American citizens. Reflective of such citizenship epiphanies, Antin professes:

> What more could America give a child? . . . As I read how the patriots planned the Revolution, and the women gave their sons to die in battle, and the heroes led them to victory, and the rejoicing people set up the Republic, it dawned on me gradually what was meant by *my country*. . . . For the Country was for all the Citizens, and I *was a Citizen*. And when we stood up to sing "America," I shouted the words with all my might. I was in very earnest proclaiming to the world my love for my newfound country. (190–191)

Included in a chapter entitled, "My Country," Antin's connection to national identity commences with an act of literacy (reading) and concludes with the patriotic vocalization of "America the Beautiful." The use of an ownership pronoun (my) and the deployment of affective allegiance (apparent in Antin's declaration of "love") confirm her previous avowal of citizenship. In so doing, Antin's fuses affect to patriotic performance. This fused performance, staged in the public space of a classroom, enables a de facto naturalization oath. Correspondingly, the first-generation child immigrant claims "her newfound country" through an allegiance to American history (that is, Washington) and the U.S. nation. On another level, Antin's articulation of U.S. nationhood occurs through sequential means (from "Revolution" to "Republic," from colonial subject to citizen of the United States). Taken together, the "poem episode" calls forth analogous immigrant teleologies wherein the foreign-born eventually becomes an "American."

The chapters that precede "My Country" furnish the necessary repudiation of the country of origin required for naturalization. The characterization of Russia as a totalitarian, discriminatory dystopia (placed in stark utopian contrast to "America") provides the compulsory binaried repudiation/declaration grammar. In the same chapter, Antin challenges the belief that immigrant bodies cannot be made into "American" stock. Militating against pathogenic immigrant discourses, Antin contends, "The public school has done its best for us foreigners, and for the country, when it has made us into good Americans" (224). The repetition of "constructed" language—observable in the use of "made" in the memoir—makes clear Antin's conviction that immigrants can in fact be molded into good Americans despite their beginning location as foreigners. Indeed, the public school becomes an important site of "making," for it not only engenders the production of good Americans but manufactures citizens for the good (or health) of the country.

Antin as a legitimate and legitimated American subject is strengthened in the concluding moments of the memoir. The author maintains:

> Having traced the way an immigrant child may take from the ship through the public schools, passed on from hand to hand by the ready teachers; through free libraries and lecture halls, inspired by every occasion of civic consciousness; dragging through the slums the weight of private disadvantage, but heartened for the effort by public opportunity; welcomed at a hundred open doors of instruction, initiated with pomp and splendor and flags unfurled; seeking, in American minds, the American way, and finding it in the

> thoughts of the noble,—striving against the odds of foreign birth and poverty, and winning. . . . I lived very much as my American schoolmates lived, having overcome my foreign idiosyncrasies. (360)

Antin carefully lists the educational means that enable her journey from immigrant child to assimilated U.S. subject. From the ship to public schools, from free libraries to lecture halls, Antin has (up to this point in the memoir) benefited from "a hundred open doors of instruction." Intentionally, Antin's motif of open doors within *The Promised Land* speaks directly to the author's desired vision of a comparable open immigration policy. Celebrating the "American way," Antin has "won" against the "odds of foreign birth." Regardless of odds (a term indicative of a relationship to chance), Antin stresses that her success occurs as a result of purposeful action. Having taken full advantage of "free" U.S. resources, Antin has, in good faith, overcome "foreign idiosyncrasies" in the service of wholesale citizenship.

This faith, constitutive of Antin's repudiation of the foreign in favor of the domestic, resembles a mode of civic consciousness that potentially overcomes foreign affect and poverty. In this regard, Antin is not only a triumphant American citizen but also the embodiment of capitalistic virtue, reflected in individual gain and profit. Less explicit, but just as important, is Antin's calculated and qualified dismissal of family frames. Within *The Promised Land*'s imaginary, Antin's mother and father must work to sustain the family. This need to work extends to her oldest sister Frieda, who must drop out of school to supplement the household income. Antin briefly acknowledges the realities of working-class, first-generation immigrant subjectivity, yet does not offer much in terms of an analysis of sociopolitical dynamics such as discrimination and potentially disruptive class politics. A sustained reading of uneven, exploitative labor politics would force a less noble U.S. narrative.

In its place, Antin articulates a stark dichotomy between her father's socioeconomic agendas and her politicized project of "self-making." Whereas her "father had come to America to make a living," Antin "had come to America to see a new world, and I followed my own ends with the utmost assiduity; only, as I ran out to explore, I would look back to see if my house were in order behind me—if my family still kept its head above water" (197). Positioned within a larger history of American letters, Antin's desire to see a new world intersects with recognizable, idealized U.S. tropes of adventure, individual discovery, and revision through education. In opposition, Antin's father is interested in an alternative form of "making." Unable to affectively divorce himself from the country of origin, Antin's father speaks "imperfect English" and is marked by a "Jewish appearance" (201). Antin's father, a "marked" character, is invested in a decidedly different U.S. promise, primarily one of economic gain.

Nonetheless, what connects father to daughter, individual to community, and self to family is the issue of citizenship affiliation. Written decades before the geopolitical formation of Israel in 1948, the Jewish immigrant Antin is effectually stateless. This statelessness alternatively informs Antin's characterization of the United States as the promised land—a geographically specific location of religious tolerance that grants the author (and by extension, her family) a heretofore elusive nation-state affiliation. Hence, Antin's aforementioned pledge of allegiance relies on both the "discovery" of her country and her newfound status as a viable citizen. As Antin declares,

> I strained to hear, through closed doors, some neighboring class rehearsing "The Star-Spangled Banner." If the doors happened to open, and the chorus broke out . . . delicious tremors ran up and down my spine, and I was faint with suppressed enthusiasm. . . . Where had been my country until now? What flag had I loved? What heroes had worshipped? . . . Well I knew that Polotzk was not my country. It was *goluth*—exile. (226)

Emblematic of a Jewish diasporic condition, Antin's repeated questions about location—"where" and "what"—bring to light concerns over geographic certainty and nation-state affiliation. To Antin, Polotzk is not a homeland place but rather a banishment site (*goluth*). Lost without a flag, bereft of heroes, and lacking access to a national past, Antin's statelessness is most apparent through the absence of civic participation and state-recognized belonging. The United States allows Antin to be a citizen and becomes a space that makes available a definite cultural, political, and historical location. At the same time, the multifaceted opportunities afforded to Antin and her family in the United States enable multiple points of access to "utopian promise." Therefore, "America" as an identifiable promised land affords the protagonist a heretofore untenable citizenship. For Antin's family, "America" offers economic gain without anti-Semitic impediment.

Still, the use of "exile" to instantiate Antin's political statelessness deliberately calls into question the "homeland." After all, Antin and her family (as discriminated subjects) are economically and politically forced out of the country of their birth to settle in the United States. Antin leaves what initially seems to be a homeland space (the place of birth) for "the promised land." Consequently, the mention of exile paradoxically highlights and destabilizes a traditional understanding of countries of origin and settlement. Antin reverses this trajectory so that the United States, as a promised land, ultimately becomes (analogously to Israel Zangwill's *The Melting-Pot*) a viable homeland for Jewish subjects.

Accordingly, Polotzk as configured location is a "land of exile," a "non-homeland." Antin's discursive subversion of homeland dynamics implicitly counters anti-immigration advocates who argue that immigrants are perpetually bound by country of origin affiliations, prejudices, and politics. Instead, Antin emphasizes the lack of such allegiances due to intolerable and stateless politics in the assumed homeland. Though Russia is Antin's country of origin, it is characterized largely through an "anti-home" discourse. Hence, without sanctuary from nation-state persecution and without access to religious freedom, Antin accesses a useable, American Puritanical past. Antin situates the Jewish immigrant alongside the Puritan forefather, the archetypical model immigrant subject, who (according to the tenets of national myth) faced similar persecution.

At the same time, mindful of New World anti-Semitic prejudices, Antin distances herself from a solely religious affiliation and opts instead to privilege a secular citizenship. Antin writes that "the story of the Exodus was not history to me in the sense that the story of the American Revolution was. It was like a glorious myth, a belief in which had the effect of cutting me off from the actual world, by linking me with a world of phantoms" (226). In this instance, Antin eschews a foundational Jewish narrative in favor of a complementary U.S. script, forging an identifiable disconnect between the "actual world" of U.S. politics and the biblical "phantom world." Correspondingly, in the coming-of-age narrative that principally marks *The Promised Land*, revised religious metaphors of selfhood accommodate a secular conversion to U.S. citizenship. As literary critic Evelyn Salz compellingly observes, "the biblical title of the autobiography sets the stage for the chapter headings: 'The Tree of Knowledge,' 'The Exodus,' 'Manna,' and 'The Burning Bush.'"[22]

Yet the secularist, naturalized focus of Antin's text uneasily coexists with the author's own conflicted imagining of the immigrant past alongside a seemingly inevitable American present. From the start, Antin confesses, "It is painful to be consciously of two worlds. The Wandering Jew in me seeks forgetfulness. I am not afraid to live on and on, if only I do not have to remember too much. A long past vividly remembered is like a garment that clings to your limbs when you would run. And I have thought of a charm that should release me from the folds of my clinging past" (6). Reminiscent of Abraham Cahan's authorial articulation of "ill comport," Antin's admission that it is "painful to be consciously of two worlds" is initially constructed through a tension between remembrance and forgetfulness. Predicated on a duality, Antin briefly interrupts her celebratory account of Americanization with an affective nod toward the painful. And, "a long past vividly remembered" takes the form of a restrictive garment. The raiment metaphor fittingly illustrates Antin's larger project of shedding past identities in favor of new affiliations.

In addition, the "charm" that should release the author from the fold of a clinging past carries a double meaning. Connotative of liberation and freedom, "release" can be read as an ulterior authorial motive conditionally reliant on the successful deliverance from Russian pogroms and anti-Semitism. Alternatively, writing functions as a cathartic act for Antin, who effectively renders her life story in the language of her country of adoption. In so doing, the memoir as completed text becomes a charm or emblem of Antin's successful journey to and acculturation within a utopian promised land. In this manner, Antin's larger political project (wherein she implicitly and explicitly advocates for the unimpeded and unrestricted inclusion of immigrants through autobiographical claims of assimilation) supplants the Plymouth Rock narrative of citizenship. As important, such naturalized strategies attempt to answer the "immigrant question" that marked turn-of-the-century domestic discourse and foreign policy.

Still, even with Antin's activist literary agenda (indicative of utopian nationhood), the dystopian tone and argument apparent in "Does the Pot Melt It?" would forcefully resurface a dozen years later during congressional immigration policy deliberations. Reminiscent of previous anti-immigrant arguments about resources, "melted pots," and citizenship stock, South Carolina Senator Ellison DuRant Smith, influenced by Madison Grant's *The Passing of the Great Race*, declared on April 9, 1924, that:

> the time has arrived when we should shut the door. We have been called the melting pot of the world. We had an experience just a few years ago, during the great World War, when it looked as though we had allowed influences to enter our borders that were about to melt the pot in place of us being the melting pot. I think that we have

> sufficient stock in America now for us to shut the door, Americanize what we have, and save the resources of America for the natural increase of our population.[23]

In the shadow of Jeremiah W. Jenks and W. Jett Lauck's *The Immigration Problem*, Smith's 1924 insistent appeal to "shut the door" and "Americanize what we have" was not so much new as it was congressionally forceful. Indeed, Smith's "closed door" order was part of a much longer anti-immigrant discourse built on the exclusion of undesirable subjects, the regulation of foreign bodies, and the maintenance of Anglo-Saxon whiteness.

And, like *The Immigration Problem*, central to Smith's demand for closed-door immigration policies is a belief in the fragility of U.S. nationhood in the face of immigrant threat. A little more than a decade in the making, the turn-of-the-century solution to the "immigrant problem" would favor nativist politics. In particular, such a vision for U.S. immigration policy met restrictive fruition in 1924 with the passage of the Johnson-Reed Act. Reducing the number of immigrants through a quota system based on 2 percent of that nationality in 1890, the act had a profound impact on southern European and eastern European immigration. Because most southern and eastern European immigrants arrived after this date, the number of individuals from these locations was greatly reduced.[24] Despite Mary Antin's autobiographical interpellation, pro-immigrant politics would largely be erased in the 1920s. In a decade that witnessed the passage of the Emergency Quota Act, *Ozawa*, and *Thind*, the Johnson-Reed Immigration Act was incontrovertibly in line with an increasingly narrow ethnoracial vision of U.S. selfhood, which would persist until the 1965 Immigration and Nationality Act.

Open Door Polices, Civil Rights Agendas, and Cold War Logics: The Hart-Cellar Immigration Act

Four decades after the passage of the Johnson-Reed Act, immigration policy would once again find a national audience. Amid the rise of the civil rights movement, with Supreme Court rulings, marches, and sit-ins on the domestic political stage, the racialized dimensions of immigration became an undeniable impediment to U.S. superpower claims of tolerance, equality, and democracy. As Democratic California Representative and immigration policy reformer Philip Burton opined on August 25, 1965, "Just as we sought to eliminate discrimination in our land through the Civil Rights Act, today we seek by phasing out the national origins quota system to eliminate discrimination in immigration to this nation composed of the descendents of immigrants."[25] If, as Burton argues, the Civil Rights Act eliminated "discrimination in our land" for American subjects, then a concomitant immigration reform—without racial requirements and nation-state quotas—would potentially perform an analogous function on would-be American subjects: immigrants.

Beside the undeniable impact of the civil rights movement on contemporaneous immigration reform, equally important was the ever-increasing military role of the U.S. on the world stage. To be sure, the heating up of cold war foreign policies at mid-century (in Korea, Vietnam, and Southeast Asia) further substantiated the need to reconcile notions of democratic virtue domestically and abroad. If the United States as democratic superpower was worth its weight in ideological gold, then state-authorized discrimination policies, evident in Jim Crow segregation, publically sanctioned biases, and ethnically based immigration restrictions, could neither be sustained nor tolerated. Therefore, understood through increasingly "common sense" civil rights, the political language around mid-1960s immigration policy intersected with cold war initiatives abroad.

Moreover, this "common sense" was constructed through a liberal reading of human rights through universal means. For example, overt discriminatory policies made glaringly apparent asymmetrical power relations that impeded not only basic rights but capitalistic enterprise. It therefore made "common sense" that such abuses of power potentially threatened—through state-authorized hypocrisy—cold war claims of U.S. superiority over Soviet Union totalitarian abuses of human rights. This interrelated reading of civil rights and immigration policy is evident in President Johnson's vehement assertion in 1966 that previous immigration restrictions violated "the basic principle of American democracy—the principle that values and rewards each man on the basis of his merit as a man. It has been un-American in the highest sense, because it has been untrue to the faith that brought thousands to these shores before we were a country."[26] Appropriately, Johnson's vociferous disavowal of past policy occurred in the most iconic immigration venue—at the base of the Statue of Liberty. Further, the setting for Johnson's "declaration of immigration" makes more noticeable the implied revival of immigrant activist Mary Antin's turn-of-the-century open-door claims that the United States was, at heart, a nation founded by immigrants and through immigration.

In the face of coherences between civil rights, cold war logics, and immigration policy, supporters of the bill—including Massachusetts senator Edward Kennedy—found it necessary to assuage fears that such legislation would "flood our cities with immigrants" nor would it "upset the ethnic mix of our society."[27] At stake in debates over the impact of the reform was the ever-present "Asian question." For instance, Secretary of State Dean Rusk, when questioned specifically by reporters about Indian immigration, averred: "Based on the best information we can get . . . there might be, say, 8,000 immigrants from India in the next five years."[28] Republican Senator Hiram Fong of Hawaii, answering a similar query, maintained that "Asians represent six-tenths of 1 percent of the population of the United States. . . . The people from that part of the world will never reach 1 percent of the population."[29] Within the context of contemporaneous U.S. foreign policy, which was increasingly entrenched in cold war excursions in Asia, and in light of past immigration policy that explicitly excluded Asian bodies, declarations against the rise of a "yellow peril" bespeak the continued currency of anti-Asian sentiment. In turn, this anti-Asian sentiment underscores the ongoing immigration preference for white bodies within the larger U.S. body politic.

Despite such anxieties, roughly two months after the Voting Rights Act became a legislative reality, on October 3, 1965, President Lyndon Johnson signed the Hart-Cellar Immigration Bill into law. Known widely as the Immigration and Nationality Act, the Hart-Cellar Act eliminated the restrictionist nation-state quotas that had haunted immigration policy for more than half of the twentieth century. Legislatively linked to the removal of racial requirements in the 1952 McCarran-Walter Act, the 1965 Immigration and Nationality Act would introduce a new era of U.S. immigration policy. Eschewing national origin quotas in favor of hemispheric designations (170,000 from the Eastern Hemisphere and 120,000 from the Western Hemisphere), the law abolished the final governmental vestige of ethnoracial bias from codified U.S. immigration policy. In addition, the act included seven preferences that categorically organized would-be immigrants to the United States:

> 1) Unmarried children under 21 years of age of U.S. citizens; 2) Spouses and unmarried children of permanent residents; 3) Professionals, scientists, and artists "of exceptional ability"; 4) Married children over 21 years of age and their spouses and children of U.S. citizens; 5) Siblings and their spouses and children of U.S. citizens;

6) Workers in occupations with labor shortages; and 7) Political refugees.[30]

Privileging open-door access over closed-door prohibition, the 1965 Hart-Cellar Act signaled a paradigmatic shift in national thinking about the immigrant body with regard to family frames. Contrary to previous nativist anti-family agendas, the Immigration and Nationality Act implicitly characterized newly arrived immigrants as family members (parents, spouses, and children). Correspondingly, middle-class heteronormative familial structures became a prominent basis for legitimate and legitimated access to the United States.

Couched by the executive and legislative branches simply as an initiative that reconciled U.S. democratic virtue and U.S. immigration policy, the Hart-Cellar Act was, at its inception, symbolically envisioned. The symbolic intent of the immigration act is apparent in President Johnson's pronouncement on October 3 that "This bill we sign today is not a revolutionary bill. It does not affect the lives of millions. It will not structure the shape of daily lives."[31]

Notwithstanding symbolic intent and presidential declaration, the 1965 Immigration and Nationality Act would enable the mass migration of Asian and Latin American immigrants to the United States.[32] As such, the bill engendered a revolutionary demographic shift. According to sociologist Pyong Gap Min, between 1965 and 2002, 8.3 million Asian immigrants became permanent residents, a number that represents 34 percent of total immigrants.[33] As demographic scholar C. N. Le notes, between 1971 and 2002, an estimated 7,331,500 Asian immigrants came to the United States.[34] In fact, the 1965 Immigration and Nationality Act heralded the second largest, most racially diverse tide of immigration in the twentieth century. Between 1901 and 1920, 88 percent of immigrants were from European nation-states, 4 percent were from Asian nation-states, and 3 percent were from Latin America. However, as the twentieth century came to a close, the ethnic affiliations that marked the opening decades were overturned. Between 1980 and 1993, 39 percent of immigrants came from Asia, 43 percent from Latin America and the Caribbean, and only 13 percent hailed from Europe.[35]

For these reasons, irrespective of the seemingly apropos location of Johnson's immigration declaration at the Statue of Liberty (which was in sight of Ellis Island), a more suitable place for such presidential cogitation would have been San Francisco's Angel Island. The question of Asian bodies within the U.S. body politic carried the potential to derail immigration reform, yet contradictorily Asian Americans (and by extension, Asian immigrants) were cast as "model minorities." Read as a group that both overcame discrimination and achieved socioeconomic success, Asians and Asian Americans became at mid-century promissory subjects in "the promised land." Such utopian tropes, reflective of "promise" and inclusive of these subjects, necessarily undergird Gish Jen's *Mona in the Promised Land*, a second-generation bildungsroman that follows the eponymous Asian American protagonist's journey from adolescence to adulthood.

Whereas Mary Antin's *The Promised Land* directly spoke to the contemporary calls for closed immigration and the policing of immigrant Jewish bodies, Gish Jen's intertextual response retrospectively addresses the legacy of the civil rights movement, the assimilation of Jewish Americans within the larger body politic, and the 1965 Immigration and Nationality Act. In tandem, the removal of ethnic markers and the inclusion of political refugees suggest a nascent, civil rights-era inspired colorblindness at the level of immigration policy. If, as the Reverend Martin Luther King, Jr. so famously argued, Americans should be judged by the "content of their character" and not the "color of their skin," then the Hart-Cellar Act assumed a similar logic in judging immigrants not by the "nation of origin" but instead by the "content of their labor" and familial capital. The dichotomy between "skin" and "character" (alongside the growing emergence of Asian bodies on the U.S. demographic scene) foreground considerations of ethnicity, religion, and race in *Mona in the Promised Land*, a novel that makes apparent the limitations of U.S. selfhood vis-à-vis claims of unbounded possibility.

Returning to the "Promised Land": Gish Jen's *Mona in the Promised Land*

Mona in the Promised Land is a sequel to Gish Jen's first novel, *Typical American* (1991), which thematically and intertextually anticipates its successor.[36] *Typical American* opens with the unidentified narrator's declaration that what follows is "an American story: Before he was a thinker, or a doer, or an engineer, much less an imagineer like his self-made-millionaire friend Grover Ding, Ralph Chang was just a small boy in China, struggling to grow up his father's son."[37] The unidentified narrator's insistence that the ensuing tale is an American story is corroborated through a tongue-in-check enumeration of U.S. myths. Such myths—apparent in assertions of self-made-millionaires, doers, and Disney-inspired "imagineers"—are deconstructed through failure and folly. Ralph, an engineering graduate student who eventually becomes a tenured professor, fails in his attempt to access a legibly capitalistic American dream through restaurant ownership.

Opting to abandon the stability of academe in favor of running a fried chicken establishment, Ralph's food venture structurally fails. Built on an unstable foundation, the restaurant literally collapses like a house of cards (or, given concomitant familial disintegration, like Edgar Allan Poe's "Fall of the House of Usher"). Ralph's willingness to seek less stable economic futures is predicated on Grover Ding, a con artist whose guidance Ralph mistakenly follows. The failure of economic success is matched by the dissolution of the familial, marked by his wife Helen's affair with Grover and his sister Theresa's decision to leave Ralph and Helen's home. Hence, the novel's "hopeful" opening gives way to a pessimistic conclusion, wherein utopian tropes of success are displaced by dystopian plots of failure. The revelation and exploration of dystopian, undesirable elements within the terrain of U.S. sociopolitics is intimately tied to a decidedly "anti-Antin" immigrant narrative that in turn foreshadows Jen's later novel.

Central to *Typical American*'s plot and characterization is the first-generation Chinese immigrant who, on the one hand, struggles with U.S. cultural practices and politics. On the other hand, as the narrator observes, the same immigrant subject must also struggle to "grow up his [Chinese] father's son," implicitly reminding the reader of the country of origin (China). The emphasis on first-generation dynamics is evident in *Typical American*'s preoccupation with adaptation to life in the United States. Ralph and Helen (along with Ralph's sister Theresa) negotiate the New World through Old World frames, and naturalize, to varying degrees, through consumption and capitalist enterprise into dominant 1950s "American" values.[38] To the first-generation protagonists in *Typical American*, being American becomes an unstable identity constitutive of equal parts frustrated economic desire and cultural loss. The term "typical American" is at first deployed by Ralph, Helen, and Theresa as a catch-all phrase for unwanted "country-of-settlement" traits (e.g., laziness, ignorance, lack of clear conviction). As the novel progresses, each character, to varying degrees becomes a "typical American" disconnected from filial loyalty and Chinese tradition.

In *Mona in the Promised Land*, Jen's protagonist remains even more distant (generationally, historically, and geographically) from filial obligation and Chinese tradition. However, even with coherences apparent in conflicts between and among characters, the focus on the country of origin is largely eschewed in favor of a contemplation of second-generation Americanness in the country of settlement, the United States. Vital to Jen's second novel is the issue of not only arriving in the "promised land" but living within its social, cultural, and political borders. At the same time, the typicality afforded American existence in Jen's first novel is expanded to encompass other U.S. myths of individual freedom, agency, and choice. As such, *Mona in the Promised Land* displaces an outsider, first-generation immigrant perspective in relation to the possibilities embedded in U.S. nationhood in favor of a contemplation of the limitations that inevitably accompany racially circumscribed U.S. selfhood. In *Mona in the Promised Land*, the reader is given a protagonist who is perpetually becoming American. To use Antin's language, Mona is "made over and over." The second-generation Chinese American Mona attempts to incorporate identities that are not (drawing on cultural critic David Hollinger's observations in the epigraph above) biologically determined. Mona's "identity performances" as a Jewish Chinese American subject are frustrated by ancillary characters, who make "unnatural" and "illegible" Mona's ethnoreligious shift.

In *Mona in the Promised Land*'s opening pages, the Changs are reintroduced to the reader as a "nice Chinese family—father, mother, two born-here girls."[39] The unidentified narrator establishes from the outset an intergenerational immigrant dynamic. The two "born-here girls"—Mona and her older sister Callie—are described as second-generation Chinese Americans with Americanized birth names who speak English as their first language. In contrast, the parental Changs—Ralph and Helen—are first-generation immigrants with Americanized "adult" names.[40] Ralph and Helen speak Chinese in a Shanghai dialect, remind their children of the way things "were in China," and embody values that emphasize family affiliations over all other associations. Unlike their American progeny, the parental Changs are characterized by their declarative adherence to "old country" Chinese roots.

Additionally, the first-generation Chineseness that permeates the opening chapters of the novel operates as a necessary basis for Mona's eventual ethno-religious shift. In *Mona in the Promised Land*, the protagonist replaces this Chinese affiliation in favor of a Jewish subject position. This switch in turn foregrounds intergenerational, parental, and ethnic conflicts that constitute the bulk of the narrative. The "remaking" of Mona is embedded in the negotiation of past identity modifiers as a second-generation Chinese American. The resultant grammar—replete with revision, deletion, and addition—further speaks to the protagonist's being "born again and again." The fluidity afforded Mona's identity is matched by the unstable politics at the novel's forefront. The unidentified omniscient narrator supplements prefatory comments about the familial Chang unit with the evocative declaration that "it's only 1968; the blushing dawn of ethnic awareness has yet to pink up their inky suburban night" (3). The temporal setting of the novel, which begins in 1968 and ends "some years later" in the early 1980s, encompasses a period that witnessed both the rise of the ethnic revival and the emergence of multiculturalism in American discourse.

Accordingly, notwithstanding the novel's preoccupation with U.S. ethnoracial frameworks and "promised land" dimensions, as significant are the accompanying geopolitical imaginaries which circumscribe the novel's temporal frame. The year the novel begins (1968) is made more meaningful in light of U.S. foreign policy, the establishment of ethnic studies, and the rise of the Asian American movement. Within the realm of U.S. geopolitics, the success of the 1968 North Vietnamese Tet offensive and the public outcry over the My Lai massacre effectively undermined hawk-oriented political avowals that the United States was winning in the cold war Southeast Asian front. Protests over the war became increasingly vociferous, evident in the late-summer riots that overwhelmed headlines about the 1968 Democratic National Convention in Chicago. Shifting from the antiwar movement to the civil rights movement, the largest student strike in U.S. history was staged in 1968 at San Francisco State College, wherein students of color and community activists (via the Third World Liberation Front) sought substantial representation in higher education curricula and hiring. This strike, along with similar initiatives at University of California-Berkeley, is credited with the development and institutionalization of ethnic studies.[41] In hindsight, the strike represents a foundational moment for the Asian American movement, committed to deconstructing traditional hierarchies of racial power and U.S. foreign policy in Asia.

Moving from the historical to the literary, in *Mona in the Promised Land*, the protagonist's sister Callie (appropriately named to recall the West Coast student strikes) becomes the standard bearer for this movement in the sense that she becomes increasingly more invested in ethnic studies and ethnic pride as the novel progresses. The rise of "ethnicity" in public discourse belies the unidentified narrator's initial claim that the ensuing story of the Changs commences before "the blushing dawn of ethnic awareness." Instead, ethnic awareness, inclusive of solidarities among third-world peoples and people of color, had given way in 1968 to less timid (or "blushing") politics. Therefore, the novel is firmly situated within the fabric of largely monolithic ethnic awareness. At the same time, the monolithic dimension of ethnic consciousness is made unstable by Mona's insistence on taking on multiple forms of ethnic awareness. The implicit negotiation of politics through the narrator's omission establishes an implicit template for the rest of the novel, which is manifest to varying degrees in *Mona in the Promised Land*'s plot, further deconstructing the claim of a "blushing dawn" via its preoccupation with ethnic (inclusive of Jewish) consciousness.

What is more, Jen anachronistically (with regard to the 1960s and 1970s setting for the novel) and contradictorily brings to the fore a 1990s postethnic awareness mediated through late twentieth-century colorblindness. David Hollinger's notion of "postethnic," suggestive of a mode or time after ethnicity, signals a philosophical turn toward the voluntary over the socially or biologically determined. Mona's ethnoreligious shift is further construed (and to some extent made possible) through the protagonist's understanding of American identity as inherently flexible and performative in scope. When asked whether she is American, Mona responds, "Sure I'm American. . . . Everybody who's born here is American, and also people who convert from what they were before. You could become American. . . . You only have to learn some rules and speeches" (14). Mona's inclusive answer—that not only "everybody who's born here is American" but also "people who convert from what they were before"—characterizes citizenship through natural-born subjectivities and naturalized performances. The learning of some rules and speeches is a direct nod toward basic requirements of naturalized citizenship. In addition, the deployment of conversion (as a legible citizenship frame) echoes Antin's literary "remaking" project and foreshadows Mona's religious conversion to Judaism.

In the face of Mona's confident citizenship assertion, the novel fails to fully engender a liberating postethnic affiliation. As is evident from the parental Changs' at times tenuous relationship with country-of-origin practices (coupled with the unwillingness of other characters to acknowledge the viability of the protagonist's "shift"), *Mona in the Promised Land* underscores the ongoing rigidity of ethnicity as a marker of citizenship. Consequently, the thematic outcome of Mona's journey from Chinese American to Chinese Jewish American is that identities are never fully deconstructed, negotiated, or dismissed. The "natural" elements of citizenship give way to "denaturalized" discussions of legibility. On another level, the multisited dimensions of identity deconstruction, coupled with the illegibility of the protagonist's identity via other characters in *Mona in the Promised Land*, makes less available a utopian reading of the novel wherein absolute freedom, equality, and choice are universally afforded "American" subjects. In doing so, Jen constructs a dystopian imaginary in which the United States is a place not of gain but of loss, a location marked not by possibility but by limitation, and a country still invested in monolithic articulations of identity regardless of the passage of open-door immigration laws and civil rights legislation.

The unstable nature of citizenship is apparent in symbolic ethnic moments which come to typify the parental Changs.[42] These symbolic ethnic episodes are obscured by the introduction of transnational adaptation, wherein Chinese traditions are revised according to "American" palates. Such transnational revision fails to articulate a lasting multicultural coexistence between the country of origin and the country of settlement. In an early Thanksgiving scene, the unidentified narrator divulges the fact that Helen stuffs the turkey with "stir-fried rice stuffing." The narrator buttresses this observation with the acknowledgment of a peculiar culinary practice: Ralph carves it with "a knife and chopsticks." When asked by a non-Chinese American friend if carving a turkey in this manner corresponds to a "Chinese tradition," Ralph "nods gravely." The Chang patriarch replies, "This is the Chinese tradition when we cannot find the big fork" (41). The joke relies on the inflexible ethnoracial assumption that chopsticks are for the "Chinese" Ralph more "natural" than forks, notwithstanding his status as a first-generation Chinese American. His alleged admission that chopsticks are used when "we cannot find the big fork" inadvertently speaks to a "state of nature" to which Ralph returns. Ralph's response, reliant on an ethnically inspired punch line, acknowledges the assumption and subverts it to comic effect.

Taken together, the question about "Chinese tradition" and Ralph's joke highlight a stereotypical economy wherein commodities and food practices corroborate dominant understandings of citizenship. Regardless of Ralph's humorous retort, the scene bespeaks a perpetual foreigner characterization. Accordingly, the fork embodies U.S. affiliation and the chopsticks signify Chinese nationality. Similarly, Helen's stir-fried rice stuffing makes foreign the "American" turkey. The ensuing culinary mixture does not engender a "melting pot" amalgamation of flavors or practices.[43] Rather, the stir-fried rice stuffing remains a distinct ingredient that can be named and isolated, in a manner reminiscent of a cold war policy of containment. Ironically and perhaps intentionally, the holiday setting for the meal—Thanksgiving—brings to mind a legible immigrant-centric moment. After all, Thanksgiving ostensibly celebrates the arrival of the "first" immigrants—Pilgrims—to what would become the United States. Within this context, the first-generation Changs are historically relevant U.S. immigrant subjects. Still, Ralph and Helen attempt to manipulate the Thanksgiving tradition so that it becomes a "Chinese American tradition," which superficially symbolizes a bicultural layering. This bicultural layering dissolves via the non-Chinese/American character's response, which militates against a successful reading of the Chang Thanksgiving as unproblematically "American." In turn, the failure of comprehensibility by an outside viewer brings to light the failure of seamless amalgamation.

In another culinary instance, Helen's duck recipe, "Peking duck, Westchester style," involves "soaking the duck overnight in Pepsi Cola" (186). The secret American ingredient (Pepsi Cola) from the outset recalls a traditional immigrant narrative of assimilation. The duck, a food commodity that (within the novel) embodies Chineseness, is invaded by an American product. This invasion, akin to U.S. foreign policy, metaphorically complements the previous Thanksgiving example. The juxtaposition of two geographic locales, Peking and Westchester, seemingly signals a transnational sensibility that embodies the country of origin and the country of settlement. The division of locales into East and West addresses not only existing immigration policy (the partitioning of Eastern and Western hemispheres) but gestures toward a disaggregated citizenship status. In spite of the "Westchester" ingredient, the dish still maintains its Chineseness. Collectively, each culinary instance underscores the persistence of Chineseness, which necessarily militates against a reading of wholesale assimilation. Further, the doggedness of previous affiliations makes plain a specific citizenship economy wherein identities are fluid and fixed.

The interplay between cultures—embodied by the mixture and manipulation of ingredients—does not lead to amalgamation or fusion. Instead, such interplay concludes without a "melting pot" utopian resolution. Hence, the parental Changs remain as ethnically marked as their food practices. Further, they are bifurcated according to a transnational frame that delineates the country of origin from the country of settlement. This bifurcation extends into the realm of child rearing, and a constant parental refrain is "in China, children listen to parents." Despite the paradoxical literary fact that "everywhere else is America," the unidentified narrator and protagonist both note that in the Chang house "it's China." As literary critic Begona Simal Gonzalez maintains, "Helen and Ralph can make concessions and adapt, but they cannot stop being Chinese, or let that happen to their daughters."[44] At first glance, Ralph and Helen seem to voluntarily affiliate themselves with this Chinese sensibility, to the extent that their speech acts and culinary performances make visible this location. However, this reading of voluntary ethnicity is made less certain because it is increasingly less accessible due to temporal and geographic distance from China.

The failure to access a "usable" cultural past converges at the level of memory. In particular, Helen's maternal role in the intergenerational transmission of cultural memory is obfuscated because she can no longer recall specific details or practices from the country of origin. Helen admits to her daughter Mona "that China was such a long time ago, a lot of things she can hardly remember. She said sometimes she has trouble remembering her characters, that sometimes she'll be writing along, and all of a sudden she won't be sure how the strokes go" (7). Emphasizing time alongside geographic distance ("China was such a long time ago"), Helen underscores the historical and geographic challenges that impede immigrant memory. As a result of this memory failure, Helen is unable to model her Chinese citizenship through the act of writing in the face of voluntary desire. Jen offers an unclear resolution to this cultural dilemma. When Mona asks what she does when this happens, Helen replies, "Oh, I just make a little sloppy" (7). Helen confesses to a "sloppiness" that potentially undermines her authority as a Chinese subject and confirms her position as a liminal Chinese American subject. The improvised writing performance echoes culinary slippages that occur in the kitchen. Additionally, the instability of identity at the maternal level foreshadows the protagonist's subsequent attempt to revise her own affiliations (to shift from a Chinese American to a Jewish Chinese American), with varying degrees of success and failure.

Returning to the opening pages of *Mona in the Promised Land*, the unidentified narrator maintains that the Changs are "the New Jews, after all, a model minority and Great American Success. They know they belong in the promised land" (3). The mention of their status as New Jews, along with their location in the promised land, reinforces an intertextual reading of Jen's novel alongside Antin's memoir. The characterization of the Changs as the New Jews occurs alongside the narrator's assertion that they are both a "model minority and a Great American Success," highlighting their model minoritization through a dominant U.S.

ethnoracial and capitalistic schema. Cast as the New Jews, the Changs implicitly share an immigrant consciousness analogous to probationary Jewish whiteness. Yet, as the New Jews (and not the new Italians, new Irish, or new Germans), the Changs are situated within a longer history of discrimination, contested assimilation, and middleman classification. Though a Great American Success as New Jews, the Changs potentially occupy a "stranger" status in the promised land.

Furthermore, the characterization of the Changs as Asian American model minority subjects who are in effect the New Jews is immediately undermined by the narrator's interrogative aside. What follows the observation that the Changs "know they belong in the promised land" is the evocative question, "Or do they?" (3). The concomitant uncertainty (afforded by the question) pushes an alternative reading of self-determinism concerning the Changs. Their classification as the New Jews or as a model minority may not, as the omniscient narrator suggests, necessarily reflect a Chang-centric classification. Instead, such a characterization is predicated on a dominant reading of Asian Americans as "model minority" immigrant subjects who are read according to U.S. ethnoracial logics.

Still, Ralph and Helen consider themselves Chinese, making little or no mention of their position in the American sociopolitical imaginary as either the New Jews or as a model minority. Therefore, the narrator's articulation of the Changs' political position relies on a dominant-driven reading divorced from a self-determined voluntary affiliation. Reflective of a sociological group framework, the casting of the Changs as New Jews contradicts individual familial interactions, which stress Chineseness over Americanness and privilege a reading of Jewishness not as a voluntary but racial category of difference.

The narrator's discussion of New Jews anticipates the major plotline in the novel, which involves the titular protagonist's conversion to and subsequent experiences as a Jewish subject. At stake in Mona's desire to "become Jewish" is the issue of legibility. If Mona's switch is to be deemed fully successful, her conversion to Judaism must engender legitimate readings of her identity outside the biological rubric of racial categorization. Such a reading, suggestive of identity literacy, relies on a two-part performance wherein Mona is a convincing Jewish American subject who is also able to transcend her Chinese Americanness. Nevertheless, impeding her wholesale identity revision is the inability of those around her to forget or dismiss dominant readings of ethnicity and race. As the omniscient narrator relates, "Mona tries to imagine what it would be like to forget she's Chinese, which is easy and hard. It is easy because by her lonesome she in fact often does. Out in the world of other people, though, Mona has people like Miss Feeble to keep the subject shiny. So here's the question: Does the fact that Mona remembers all too well who she is make her more Jewish than, say, Barbara Gugelstein?" (32). Mona's ability to forget she's Chinese is easy "by her lonesome" in part because she considers herself American, especially when juxtaposed with her parents' practices and values. Further, Mona's focus on remembering is attached to her understanding of Judaism as a religion focused on cultural and historical memory. All the same, "out in the world of other people," Mona's Chineseness overwhelms her Americanness, and remains a "shiny" unavoidable subject.

The "shininess" of the protagonist's ethnicity is brought into focus via Mona's best friend, Barbara Gugelstein, a Jewish American, who is not forced to contend with a sociobiological reading of her identity. Mona's comparison of "selves" (with regard to Barbara) signals a reading of whiteness through voluntary affiliation that is available to some and not all. As a category of power, a social construct, and racial mode, whiteness offers a flexible citizenship inaccessible to individuals of color, including Mona. Whereas Barbara can seemingly travel back and forth from Jewish to non-Jewish, Mona is not provided similar movement between Chinese and non-Chinese. As Andrew Furman argues, the liminality of Jewish identity (apparent in the characterization of Mona's friends, who are predominantly Jewish) makes necessary a reading of probationary whiteness. On the one hand, the ability to "switch" from Jew to WASP (White Anglo-Saxon Protestant) and back again at their convenience affords a flexible affiliation largely unavailable to Mona as a Chinese American.[45] On the other hand, this flexibility is not fully afforded the racialized Chinese American protagonist, who is able to convert but must contend with those who doubt her "true conversion."

Racially read, Mona must also deal with her ethnic status as second-generation immigrant subject. As the narrator reveals:

> one day she [Miss Feeble] asks Mona if she is really Chinese. This is while Miss Feeble pushes desks around, arranging them in a horseshoe. . . . "Of course I'm Chinese," Mona says, helping out. "I'm Chinese American." . . . "And your parents?" continues Miss Feeble, pushing. "They're Chinese too?" "Of course," Mona says. "They're *immigrants*." She knows as she says this, they naturally never use that word on themselves. They think it means people who try to

> bring live chickens on buses and don't own real suitcases. . . . All the same, it works on Miss Feeble. . . . "Ah." she repeats the holy word. "Immigrants." It is as if Mona has cut a little window into the fence of a construction site. Sure enough, there it is, the big crane. (27–28)

At first, what prompts Miss Feeble's ethnic question is the protagonist's active class participation. In contrast to a stereotyped Asian American femininity through submissive frames, Mona repeatedly raises her hand, to the point Miss Feeble tells her "to give someone else a chance to talk" (27). Though seemingly minor, Miss Feeble's inquiry makes obvious an economy of stereotype that casts Asian American female subject as shy and silent. Hence, Mona's ethnoracial "authenticity" as Chinese is predicated on a dominant reading of Asian American difference.

Additionally, Mona's response—that she is Chinese *and* Chinese American—subverts another stereotypical notion that Asian Americans are not truly citizens of the U.S. nation-state but instead perpetual foreigners. Notwithstanding Mona's intervention, Miss Feeble willfully ignores Mona's Americanness and instead privileges her Chinese ethnicity. Miss Feeble's racial reading echoes analogous but divergent interpretations of the parental Changs. Moreover, Miss Feeble's subsequent inquiries about Mona's parents fit neatly into a larger discussion of immigrant subjectivity apropos established U.S. myths and tropes. The mythologizing of the immigrant body is most manifest in the understanding of "immigrants" as a "holy word." Reflective of the conceptualization that United States is a "nation of immigrants," the utopian and hopeful foregrounds Miss Feeble's response. The implied emphasis on the "utopian" strategically dismisses the very real dystopian history of nativism which effectively turned "the promised land" into a space of regulation, discrimination, and limitation for immigrants, Chinese and otherwise.

Whereas Mary Antin likened her literary naturalization to conversion, Mona Chang draws upon her American citizenship to justify her subsequent religious conversion to Judaism. Even with the revision, Mona's conversion takes on the repuditive and declarative processes of nation-state naturalization. As the omniscient narrator conveys,

> Rabbi Horowitz assigns so many books that Mona feels like she started on a mud bath, only to end up on a mud swim. . . . Still, she slogs through. A lot she knows already. All about the holidays, for example, and what is a mitzvah—namely a good deed. Also what is rachmones, namely a type of mercy every human should extend to others

> but sometimes doesn't. That part is easy and fun.... Then there are the new parts Mona likes—all the big ancient stories of blood and gore and guile. Rabbi Horowitz makes her glad she never had to put up with those stiffs the Egyptians—what do you expect from people who wore so much eye makeup—or wander around the desert for forty years. She feels concerned for those ten lost tribes of Israel. She wishes she'd been around for the liberation by the Persians and the era of the Great Prophets.... What a down-to-earth religion this is! It's not like Catholicism, with people electing to get crucified upside down, as if right side up wasn't bad enough. (35)

The acquisition of a new vocabulary (or grammar), allegiance to the Jewish faith, and the renunciation of her past religious affiliation in favor of Judaism hearken back to the primary tenets of state-authorized naturalization. Mona denounces Catholicism, dismissing it as a not "down-to-earth" religion marked by "people electing to get crucified upside down."

What is more, the gerund form of "elect," suggestive of an ongoing process of choice, unintentionally emphasizes Mona's voluntary decision to eschew Catholicism (and by extension, Chineseness) in favor of Judaism and its "ancient stories of blood and gore and guile." Requiring historical and cultural immersion, Mona's conversion is, at the level of practice, embedded in naturalization. The naturalizing impulse is attributable to the predominantly Jewish American Scarshill neighborhood Mona calls "home," wherein the Chinese Catholic Changs are an ethnic and religious minority. Thus, Mona's conversion into the dominant ethno-religious community of Scarshill gestures toward a naturalized analysis.

At first, Mona's desire to convert is predicated on the aforementioned best friend, Barbara Gugelstein. Barbara's mother, a second-generation Jewish American, rediscovers her Jewish heritage, which influences her daughter's "return" to ethnicity. The impulsive, sudden nature of Barbara's rediscovery (in no doubt influenced by the civil rights movement) is apparent in her pronouncement of ethnic awareness to the protagonist and her family. Barbara marches into the Chang family restaurant, a pancake house, and abruptly "announces that she's Jewish." Mona's response is tellingly underwhelmed: "Now, this is news. And what were you before?" (30). Mona's question is partially rooted in a comprehension of identity via natural-born affiliation. As such, she initially cannot understand the gravity or scope of Barbara's declaration. Mona further attributes logics of biological determinism to Barbara's announcement in her sardonic reminder of what she was "before." Therefore, to Mona, Barbara's reclamation of this identity is rendered unremarkable given her best friend's ethno-racial background. Barbara doesn't answer Mona's question, but begins to play a ram's horn, which is "for making new beginnings. Which I am now doing and which you should do too" (31). Mona eventually takes up Barbara's challenge to be "remade," and embarks on what she calls "a new chapter of their [Barbara's and Mona's] lives."

As the novel progresses, both characters undergo an identity rebirth. Ironically, Barbara is "reborn" a Jewish American, an identity she already had "biologically" but not culturally. In contrast, Mona remakes herself in more revolutionary fashion. She commences her conversion by attending the neighborhood temple and discussing the possibility of her conversion with Rabbi Horowitz, an unorthodox, nontraditional Jewish leader who "looks like a Hasid turned rock star . . . and he doesn't mind being called Rabbi H., or the Big R.H., or even Rabbit H. He is young enough to sit cross-legged; he listens to Crosby, Stills and Nash; he plays the harmonica. He doesn't insist that anyone learn Hebrew, much as he'd like to encourage it" (33). Even though a relatively liberal figure politically (he is "anti-Vietnam, and also pro things like letting the kids wear what they want at confirmation, including bare feet"), Rabbi Horowitz is initially unwilling to accept Mona's desire to convert, wary about "a sixteen year old choosing her own faith" (33). Irrespective of Rabbi Horowitz's eventual "conversion" to Mona's decision, his initial reluctance foreshadows similar doubts about the efficacy of the protagonist's "switch."

Historically, culturally, and politically rooted in Judaism as a practiced religion, Mona's allegiance to faith is built on a legible conversion process, reliant on acts of literacy (reading, writing, and comprehending) and convincing performances. Within *Mona in the Promised Land*'s imaginary, conversion underscores the unidirectional nature of naturalization. With a rhetorical rigidity mirrored in practice, conversion as naturalization engenders movement away from one modality to another. However, conversion (and by proxy, naturalization) does not accommodate a reverse trajectory. As Mona ponders, "it's okay to turn into a Jew, but not turn out of one?" (35). Mona's question acknowledges that Jewish subjects are both born and made, yet once one converts, one cannot "turn out." Similarly, for the naturalized subject, once "made" American, that same subject cannot necessarily—after repudiation—return to a pre-American subject position.

In spite of such fixity, the cultural, political, and social dimensions that foreground Mona's repudiation via conversion are initially unclear. Specifically, rather than Mona's apriori religious affiliation (which is Catholic), what primarily dominates the narrative is a repudiation of the protagonist's Chineseness. Indeed, Mona's conversion, which mirrors the affective political dynamics of naturalization, muddles the boundaries between religion and ethnicity. Additionally, the uncertainty of boundaries reinforces the historic racialization of Jewish immigrants and Jewish Americans. Alternatively, Mona's lack of substantive awareness about Chinese history is situated adjacent to her ever-growing knowledge of Jewish history.

To Mona, the Chinese, and by extension Chinese immigrants and Chinese Americans, have not "always been the oppressed. They used to be oppressors, and that makes them, as a minority, rank amateurs" (36). Missing is a sustained consideration of colonialism, Chinese history, and contestations over Chinese immigration, with regard to prohibition and exclusion. Mona's unawareness of her ethnic lineage highlights an intergenerational conflict between parent and child that converges on cultural memory. The absence of knowledge makes more legible Mona's "Americanness," which in turn can be read through a "blank slate" sensibility.

Conflict and this blank slate characterization foreground Mona's relationship with a Japanese exchange student Sherman, whom she invites to her house. While there, Sherman draws a Japanese flag, prompting an angry reaction in Mona's mother Helen. Helen tells Mona that "World War II was in China too," stressing the Nanking Massacre, wherein an estimated 369,366 Chinese civilians and prisoners of war were slaughtered by the invading troops. Between December 1937 and March 1938, approximately 80,000 women and girls were raped, many of whom were then mutilated or murdered.[46] Though the narrator largely omits the specific exchange between mother and daughter, the discussion is forcefully implied via Mona's confused response: "What Napkin Massacre?" (15).

Mona fails to hear her mother's historical intervention, which quickly transforms into a further refusal to believe her mother's account. Mona asks, "Are you sure? In school, they said the War was about putting the Jews in ovens" (15). Even in this instance, Mona privileges Jewish victimhood, betraying a specific historic solidarity with regard to Jewish, and not Chinese, Americans. To Mona, being Jewish is a more concretized identity, with an expansive history and a clearly defined religious doctrine. In *Mona in the Promised Land*, Jewishness within a U.S. context affords Mona an elusive probationary American identity that ostensibly is liberated from racial expectation. As the narrator observes: "The

Changs don't have their friends' instincts, or reflexes. They don't have their ready alert. They don't have their friends' institutions, or their ways of reminding themselves who they are, that they may not be lulled by a day in the sun. Prescriptions and rituals, holidays and recipes, songs. The Jews have books, they have games, they have tchotchkes. They have catalogs. And soon, G-d willing, so will [she]" (38). Without ways of reminding themselves who they are, the Changs as Chinese/Chinese Americans lack a legible, distinct, or instinctual culture. The Changs' lack of ways of reminding themselves who they are recalls Helen's inability to remember Chinese characters. Mona conflates cultural practice and commodity, for the Changs lack books, games, and tchotchkes, and catalogs. The appearance of legible "Jewish" commodities is juxtaposed with the absence of Chinese cultural artifacts, which speaks to the relative assimilation of Jewish Americans versus that of Chinese Americans in the larger U.S. body politic, despite model minority classifications.

Evident in the improvisation of Chinese customs and practices, the Changs (at least according to Mona) lack prescriptions and rituals, holidays and recipes, songs. As illustrated by Helen and Mona's discussion of Nanking, Mona's refusal to hear her mother's history contributes to this lack. The isolation Mona feels as a Chinese American occurs because Asian Americans, despite model minoritization, are still largely absent within the larger U.S. body politic. Regardless of the passage of the 1965 Immigration and Nationality Act, which would undeniably make more real Asian immigration, the novel's focus on the second-generation immigrant subject necessarily brings to the fore the experiences of a native-born American subject who remains alienated. Divorced from Chinese history, language, and culture, Mona is thus an unformed citizen notwithstanding a clear U.S. nation-state affiliation.

The definite perimeters of U.S. citizenship are discussed, negotiated, and challenged within the novel. Despite Mona's strategic deployment of personhood, apparent in her assertion that to be "American means being whatever you want" and that she "happened to pick being Jewish," family members, friends, and acquaintances fail to accept this articulation of selfhood. For example, Mona's mother Helen disputes this claim, stressing that "American [is] not Jewish." After Mona asserts her ethno-religious shift and her "American right" to do so, Helen asks, "Who knows? Tomorrow you'll come home and tell me you want to be black" (49). Unlike her second-generation daughter, Helen reads Jewishness not as voluntary but as biologically determined, underlining in the process past racial categories. Mona counters, stating, "How can I turn black?

That's a race, not a religion" (49). In the face of Mona's intervention, Helen's initial reaction draws attention to what will become the most potent impediment to Mona's utopian—or liberated—sense of voluntary selfhood. Within this more dystopian setting, postethnic frames are rendered nonviable, for they are illegible due to racial categories.

At the same time, the mother/daughter discussion reconfirms the restrictive valences of racial categorization. Mona's response—that "black" is a race—makes apparent the limitations of voluntary affiliation. Though Mona attempts to "correct" her mother's racialized assumption about Jewishness, she still conforms to U.S. ethnoracial logics that characterize blackness as a race and is thus involuntary. Appropriately, then, the most vehement criticism of Mona's switch emerges from Alfred, an African American cook at the Chang family restaurant. Jen deliberately uses Alfred's ethnoracial identity to test Mona's assertion that as an American one can switch. A follower of Black Nationalism, Alfred is close friends with "Luther the Race Man, Big Benson, Ray, and Professor Estimator" (197). True to the novel's temporal form, each character (to varying degrees) reflects the emergent Black Nationalist and Black Power movements of the later 1960s and early 1970s. For example, Alfred's colleague Luther is characterized as a "race man" whose theme "goes race, race, race. Luther attends rallies, and returns blowing black" (198). Invested in black pride, Luther, Big Benson, Ray, Professor Estimator, and Alfred occupy a spectrum of civil rights–era ethnic awareness and racial consciousness. The setting for this multiracial conglomeration—Camp Gugelstein—initially resembles a utopian hippie commune, replete with acoustic guitars and all the trappings of communal living.

Regardless of the possibility of kindred ethnic moments between Alfred and Mona, Alfred frustrates Mona's attempt at self-determination. When Barbara states that Mona is Jewish, Alfred incredulously replies, "Jewish? . . . You expect me to believe that? Uh uh. Not until you grow your nose, baby" (136). Alfred, like Mona's mother, phenotypically deconstructs Mona's ethnoreligious shift. The signifier of both Jewishness and Mona's non-Jewishness (and by proxy her Chineseness) centers on the nose. The "nose" as a site of racial signification becomes more meaningful in its contrast to Barbara's story. Prior to Barbara's reclamation of Jewishness, Mona's best friend undergoes rhinoplasty because of her mother's then disidentification with her Jewish identity. The initial phenotypic dimensions behind Alfred's disbelieving response underscore a biological racial determination. In turn, such biologically informed racial readings give way to a more cogent critique of voluntary affiliation.

Alfred proclaims: "We're never going to be Jewish, see, even if we grow our nose like Miss Mona here is planning to do. . . . And, nobody is calling us Wasp, man, and nobody is forgetting we're a minority, and if we don't mind our manners, we're like as not to end up doing time in a concrete hotel. We're black, see. We're *Negroes*" (136). Alfred's declaration that "we're never going to be Jewish" occurs through a reading of Jewishness via whiteness. Whiteness, initially evident through "noses," is reinforced at the semantic level through the use of term WASP. Concurrently, Alfred's blackness is antithetically situated. Stressing to Mona that "nobody is forgetting we're a minority," Alfred directly accesses Mona's Asian American position as a "model minority." Like Jewish Americans, Asian Americans occupy a probationary white status, which affords a "forgetting" of a dominant negative reading of difference.

The asymmetrical power relations that undergird racial formation in the United States ultimately undermine a utopian postethnic consideration of voluntary affiliation.[47] At stake in Alfred's claim that "we're Negroes" is a lengthy history of oppression that continues to persist in the face of civil rights–oriented legislation and claims. In turn, Alfred's declaration necessarily forces a decidedly dystopian reading of the United States through rubrics of discrimination, limitation, and intolerance. Consequently, the citizenship foundation for Mona's "switch" is effectively deconstructed through Alfred, who is not afforded the opportunity of identity shift irrespective of his American affiliation.[48] Unwilling to read Mona as Jewish, prohibited from accessing democratic virtue on the basis of race, and unable to engage in U.S. "promised land" nation building, Alfred destabilizes notions of U.S. exceptionalism.

Additionally, Albert's interpellation of Mona's "switch" potently brings to light the rigidity of racial and class-oriented formations. Albert's class position—as a working-class subject—calls to mind the paternal Antin's situatedness within a larger U.S. socioeconomic frame. Mona's upper-middle-class socioeconomic position affords her the necessary leisure time to convert. And, notwithstanding moments of frustration, made visible through incidents of doubt involving ancillary characters, Mona's conversion is eventually accepted. In the final moments of the novel, which take place well after the discussion between Albert and Mona, readers are introduced to the protagonist's daughter. Racially Caucasian and Asian, ethnically Jewish and Chinese, with a last name of "Changowitz," Mona's progeny embodies her mother's desire toward multiplicity. In a moment that leaves the door open for more postethnic switches, the narrator asks, "For what else would be the favorite cuisine of a child part Jewish, part Chinese, barely off breast milk? But of course, Italian" (303).

All the same, even with the "open door" nature of *Mona in the Promised Land*'s ending, the threshold remains closed to Albert. Unlike Mona, Albert must contend with economic forces, which in the novel are made more perilous with the loss of his job at the Chang restaurant following unsubstantiated claims of theft. Such claims are racially motivated, making Albert the victim of stereotyped racial profiling. Hence, his ability to "purchase" whiteness—which in turn leads to access to identity flexibility—is thus doubly prohibited on the grounds of race and class.

As the only character not able to "switch," Alfred most pointedly highlights the failure of a postethnic schema. In *Postethnic America* (1995), David Hollinger argues that one *ought* to be able to make "Haley's choice," which is predicated on author Alex Haley's ethnoracial background as Irish and African American. Accordingly, Hollinger maintains that Haley, and other individuals of color, should be granted the voluntary opportunity to affiliate with one identity over another. Nonetheless, what Hollinger argues as a "should" or "ought" is made unfeasible in a novel circumscribed by sociopolitical racial binaries and classed delineations.

If Mary Antin's literary intent was to "write herself" into the larger U.S. narrative, Jen attempts, through Mona, to fictionally imagine an alternative U.S. narrative wherein "switches" are in the end recognized. And, central to the ethnic, racial, and religious discussions that dominate the novel's imaginary is the issue of "literacy." The multiple literacy tests that Mona must endure highlight the precarious nature of a narrative concerned with experiences in the promised land. In *Mona in the Promised Land*, following the accusation of Alfred's theft, Camp Gugelstein falls into dissolution, an experiment that largely fails when confronted by race. Similarly, Mona's "switch"—in the face of its eventual legibility—faces constant threat of dissolution precisely because of the protagonist's racial identity. What begins as a novel invested in the possibilities offered in the promised land ends with the unavoidable confirmation of limitation. In this regard, *Mona in the Promised Land's* dystopian structure addresses the failure of the civil rights movement to engender systemic racial change and acknowledges the problematic model minoritization of Asian Americans within a proscribed hierarchy.

4 / Reading and Writing America: Bharati Mukherjee's *Jasmine* and Eva Hoffman's *Lost in Translation*

At ten in the morning on a Monday I arrived in New York City. There were scores of policemen swinging heavy nightsticks, but none of them pounced on me at the bottom of the escalator. They were, indeed, watching. A black man in shredded pants asked me for a handout. Beggars in New York! I felt I'd come to America too late. I felt cheated.

—BHARATI MUKHERJEE, *JASMINE*

The America of [Mary Antin's] time gave her certain categories within which to see herself—a belief in self-improvement, in perfectability of the species, in moral uplift. . . . And what is the shape of my story, the story my time tells me to tell? A hundred years ago, I might have written a success story, without much self-doubt or equivocation. A hundred years ago, I might have felt the benefits of a steady, self-assured ego, the sturdy energy of forward movement, and the excitement of being swept up into a greater national purpose. But I have come to a different America.

—EVA HOFFMAN, *LOST IN TRANSLATION*

At 9:28 p.m. on July 3, 1986, President Ronald Reagan addressed an exuberant crowd assembled on New York's Governors Island. At the president's side was First Lady Nancy Reagan (an Empire State native), festively clothed in red and white. Standing behind a podium emblazoned with the presidential seal, the former California governor wore subdued navy blue. A glitzy blue-white backdrop completed the American flag tableau. Irrefutably, the president and the First Lady were executive actors in a televised event, held in honor of the Statue of Liberty. Aptly named Liberty Weekend (and labeled "The Party of the Century" by New York mayor Ed Koch), the ABC-produced spectacle was meant to observe Lady Liberty's one hundredth birthday and unveil her recent $86 million makeover. Part patriotic celebration, part opportunistic profit, the celebration was indubitably marked by commodified commemoration.[1]

From Lady Liberty-themed tobacco and charcoal briquettes to beach towels and dry-roasted peanuts, the statue's symbolic function as immigrant shrine at times spoke more to free markets than democratic freedom. But despite such commodity-driven fanfare, the statue's symbolic function as immigrant emblem remained front and center. Fittingly, Lady Liberty had, a century earlier, traveled 3,600 trans-Atlantic miles from her native France to the United States. Incontrovertibly, as the telegenic fortieth president averred: "Miss Liberty, like the many millions she's welcomed to these shores, is of foreign birth, the gift of workers, farmers, and shopkeepers and children who donated hundreds of thousands of francs to send her here."[2]

The statue's journey mirrored the contemporaneous exodus of almost twelve million European immigrants, including the likes of Abraham Cahan and Mary Antin. "Miss Liberty" would also bear symbolic witness to multiple mid- and late-century migrations, as East Asian, South Asian, and Southeast Asian immigrants arrived en masse to U.S. shores. Their journeys to the "promised land" were chiefly enabled by legislative routes. In particular, the 1965 Hart-Cellar Act, the 1975 Indochinese Migration/Refugee Assistance Act, and the 1980 Refugee Act facilitated a profound demographic shift, comprised of Koreans, Indians, Chinese, Vietnamese, Cambodians, and Laotians seeking economic opportunity, educational access, and cold war "asylum" due to failed U.S. foreign policy.

Such immigrant bodies—joined by migrants from Latin America, Puerto Rico, the Caribbean, and refugees from eastern Europe—would constitute the majority of New York City's population growth in the 1980s and 1990s. Following a decade of deindustrialization, stagflation, and white flight, the "Crossroads of the World" had suffered a 13.8 percent drop in population.[3] However, by 1990, *The New York Times* noted that "immigration remade much of the city. . . . New Yorkers born abroad constituted a majority of residents in the five [boroughs]."[4] In 2000, 35.9 percent of the city's population would be foreign-born, speaking 170 different languages. By century's end, English was not the primary language in almost half of all New York City households, linguistically confirming the city's status as a global hub.[5]

Amid this post-1965 multiethnic, polyvocal, multicultural imaginary, Reagan's "Lady Liberty" comments anachronistically call attention to a late-century transnational current of bodies and capital. Concentrated on foreign-born benevolence and foreign-dollar kindness (manifest in diplomatic declarations of "welcome," acknowledgments of "gifts," and recognition of "donations"), Reagan's remarks nonetheless engender an affective, immigrant narrative. Such oft-accessed sentimentality is emblematized by Miss Liberty who—in true beacon fashion—projects an idealized, open-door America. Simultaneously, Reagan's mention of "hundreds of thousands of francs," recalling the statue's past and mindful of its recent multimillion dollar restoration, locates the "mother of exiles" within the confines of a two-sided economy.

In particular, Reagan's Statue of Liberty is both "immigrant" and "commodity," a foreign-funded body deployed in the exceptional service of U.S. nationhood. Such labor is forged through the strategic omission of exclusionary immigration politics, built on a narrative of nostalgic timelessness. Correspondingly, Lady Liberty—and by extension immigrant writers—are cast as two sides of the same coin. To that end, the Statue of Liberty, as conceived by the fortieth president, is an eternal reminder of a maudlin immigrant past, carrying in the process the same "then and now" symbolic currency. Within this "foreign-born" triumphalism, Indian American Bharati Mukherjee and Polish Canadian/American Eva Hoffman seem ideal open-door subjects. A self-described "immigrant living in a continent of immigrants," Mukherjee as writer at once embraces her foreign-born past; analogously, Hoffman celebrates immigration as "a sort of location in itself."[6] As a matter of fact, Reagan makes no distinction between various waves of immigrants, representing them instead via quantity ("millions"). Therefore, Mukherjee and Hoffman become two out of "millions" ostensibly welcomed to U.S. shores.

Nonetheless, as the opening epigraphs make clear, Mukherjee and Hoffman write decidedly pessimistic narratives about the United States. On the one hand, such critical considerations reinscribe a temporal dimension to immigration. Mukherjee's protagonist Jasmine, an undocumented worker, laments that she has "come to America too late." Hoffman rues that she has "come to a different America" from that of her turn-of-the-twentieth-century Antin counterpart. Despite affective coherences, the cause for discontent varies between fictional protagonist and autobiographer. Jasmine's declaration of "lateness" is constructed through the policing of undocumented foreign bodies and dissolution of capitalist promise. Hoffman's anxiety is fixed to the elusive nature of self-definition in a hyphenated American landscape.

On the other hand, *Jasmine* and *Lost in Translation* register the tenor and outcome of contemporaneous immigration debates, which largely focused on illegality and bilingualism. A prime example can be found in an April 18, 1986, *New York Times* "Letter to the Editor" authored by

Chief Border Patrol Agent Alan E. Eliason of San Diego County. The agent warned readers of an unprecedented escalation in illegal migration, claiming that "apprehensions [of undocumented workers] have risen by an incredible 48 percent over the same period a year ago." Even more extreme, Eliason alleged that San Diego County was "encountering an average of one illegal alien every 35 seconds" and "we know that we're locating, at best, about half the flow of illegal entrants." Asking "Do we truly have to absorb the world's surplus populations until we become like the third-world countries from which they come: overpopulated, with our resources depleted and with massive unemployment?" Eliason then concluded with an all-too-familiar assertion of "a swelling [immigrant] flood."[7] Focused on resources, employment, and potential overpopulation, Eliason accesses a supply-side vocabulary wherein the United States' status as first-world country is threatened by third-world poverty and need.

A multicultural nativist, Eliason later "reported" in a April 21, 1986, *New York Times* article that "the number of would be immigrants from Central and South America, Korea, Hong Kong, the Middle East and other parts of the world was increasing even faster."[8] Eliason's admonition of an inevitable "brown" and "yellow" flood—or peril—was echoed by fellow San Diego County lawman John Duffy. In the same *New York Times* "exposé," Sheriff Duffy (in equally alarmist fashion) contended that "a third of the men arrested for rape in the county last year were illegal aliens" and that "aliens were involved in a third of the murders, either as killers or victims."[9] Focusing principally on criminality, Eliason and Duffy produce a reading of an uncontrolled alien flood that threatens the very foundations of family, community, and nation.

Nonetheless, Sheriff Duffy was not limited to the dystopic "alien" present. Indeed, the sheriff further opined: "Illegal aliens are gradually affecting the quality of life as we know it. Now we have to admit illegal aliens into our colleges, which means my grandchildren may not be granted entry because of an illegal alien, and they'll probably require her to be bilingual."[10] In so doing, Duffy wages an attack on post-1965 multiculturalism, which threatens "native-born" (and by implication "white") opportunity. Concomitantly, Duffy casts "illegal aliens" as both intergenerational menace and multivalent pollutants who "have to be admitted" to colleges (because of affirmative action) at the expense of Duffy's grandchildren. Further adding fuel to the nativist fire, "legitimate and legal" child bodies will "undeniably" be contaminated through forced multicultural bilingual education.

Duffy's focus on literacy and language make visible the means through which Bharati Mukherjee and Eva Hoffman read and write "America" through late 1980s immigration politics and conservative culture wars. Published in the aftermath of heated debates over undocumented workers, thousand-mile border fences, and bilingual education, Mukherjee's *Jasmine* (1989) and Eva Hoffman's *Lost in Translation* (1989) imagine (or write) two different "Americas." Each makes legible (or reads) an uncertain sociopolitical terrain that forcefully naturalizes foreign bodies. Concurrently, U.S. "promise" gives way to disappointment. Rather than "open arms," Mukherjee's protagonist is greeted by surveillance (e.g., the "scores of policemen" who "watch") and racialized poverty (emblematized by the African American beggar). Noting that a "black man in shredded pants" asks for a handout, Jasmine problematically recuperates Reagan's language vis-à-vis "welfare mothers" and anti-affirmative action claims. For Hoffman, immigrant success stories necessarily dissolve into narratives of self-doubt and equivocation.

If Mukherjee and Hoffman read a divisive politics in their writings about contestations over U.S. selfhood, *Jasmine* and *Lost in Translation* also call attention to a still unresolved immigrant imaginary in the face of recent immigration reform. Deemed a late twentieth-century solution to the "immigration problem," the 1986 Immigration Reform and Control Act (IRCA) was the legislative culmination of a five-year struggle. Sponsored by Wyoming Senator Alan K. Simpson (Republican) and Kentucky Representative Romano L. Mazzoli (Democrat), the bipartisan IRCA was touted by President Ronald Reagan. The fortieth president purposefully accessed the more "progressive" dimensions of the McCarran-Walter Act in his declaration that the IRCA was "the most comprehensive reform of our immigration laws since 1952."

Promising to curb undocumented immigration through employer sanctions and increased surveillance of work authorization forms (including the introduction of the I-9 form), the Simpson-Mazzoli Act also included concessions to agribusiness via temporary work visas. Through citizenship provisions, the 1986 Immigration Reform Act carried what proponents like Reagan repeatedly termed a "humanitarian" response to the impending citizenship crisis. Though not an open-door policy, the Immigration Reform and Control Act offered a hybrid "closed door/naturalization" solution. With economic penalties of $250 to $10,000 levied against employers who hired undocumented workers, the congressional sponsors of the act averred that the primary incentive for illegal immigration—job opportunities—would be eliminated.[11]

After five years as permanent residents, those individuals could apply for U.S. citizenship. Further, the law afforded immigrants who had resided "in an unlawful status" before January 1, 1982, legality or "amnesty." Defined as an act of pardon, this amnesty provision drew the most ire from antireform advocates, who claimed that immigrants who entered the country illegally were rewarded with U.S. citizenship. As per the Simpson-Mazzoli Act, undocumented immigrants would have one year to seek legal status. First, such individuals would become lawful temporary residents. After eighteen months, those temporary residents could become permanent residents, provided they demonstrate "a minimal understanding" of the English language and "some knowledge of the history and government of the United States."[12] On another level, the act was fixed to an alleged humanitarian understanding of the "immigration problem" which necessitated intervention, bureaucratization, and asylum.

Such humanitarianism is fundamentally founded on capitalist enterprise and alienation in *Jasmine* and *Lost in Translation.* To reiterate, Mukherjee and Hoffman construct immigrant stories set not in a promised land but within a "false promised" nation. Correspondingly, if *Jasmine*'s eponymous protagonist feels cheated, then Hoffman is analogously left wondering "what shape her story will take." Central to *Jasmine* and *Lost in Translation* is the means through which capitalist desire produces alienated identities vis-à-vis immigrant bodies. As Mukherjee's protagonist proclaims, "On the streets I saw only more greed, more people like myself. New York was an archipelago of ghettos seething with aliens."[13] Though Hoffman notes that "America. . . . has for us the old fabulous associations: streets paved with gold, the goose that laid the golden egg," she nonetheless is still "a Jew, an immigrant, half-Pole, half-American" who "suffer[s] from certain syndromes because she was fed on stories of war."[14]

Situated in the midst of U.S. exceptionalism and amnesty, *Jasmine* and *Lost in Translation* make visible a set of politicized exchanges that take economic form. And, in so doing, Mukherjee and Hoffman take on the economics of naturalization, which hinge on labor, cultural currency, and political cachet. For Mukherjee's *Jasmine*, the protagonist's labor as a dutiful spouse and caregiver determines her access to naturalized U.S. selfhood. In contrast, Hoffman's failure to adequately translate (despite her position as a writer) produces a composite, denaturalized identity. Not incidentally, such literary exchanges reflect a contemporaneous shift in immigration law that married together politics and economics. Indeed, the Simpson-Mazzoli Act—which ostensibly granted asylum to undocumented workers and strengthened extant border patrol provisions—transformed U.S. citizenship into commodity at the level of rhetoric and practice. As President Ronald Reagan proclaimed in response to the 1986 immigration reform, "Future generations will be thankful for our efforts to humanely regain control of our borders and thereby preserve the value of one of the most sacred possessions of our people, American citizenship."[15]

Regulation and Naturalization: Bharati Mukherjee's *Jasmine*

> *Last week on our favorite cable channel, Du and I saw twenty INS agents raid a lawn furniture factory in Texas. The man in charge of the raid called it a factory, but all it was a windowless shed the size of a two-car garage. . . . . A woman in a flowered dress said, "I don't think they're bad people, you know. It's just that there's too many of them. Yesterday I opened the front door to get the morning papers and there were three of them using my yard as a personal toilet."*
>
> —*JASMINE*, 22–23

In a September 10, 1989, *New York Times* review, Smith College professor Michael Gorra affirmed, "*Jasmine* stands as one of the most suggestive novels we have about what it is to become an American." Further, Gorra observed that Mukherjee's protagonist is an exile who "chooses to redefine [her experience through] immigration as the Indian-born Mukherjee herself has recently done in choosing to become an American citizen."[16] Gorra was not alone in his selfhood-oriented praise of Mukherjee's *Jasmine*. An unnamed *USA Today* critic concurred with Gorra's "national" reading, insisting that "Mukherjee forces us to see our country anew."[17] The most assimilationist evaluation of Mukherjee's novel came from the *Baltimore Sun*, which likewise contended that *Jasmine*, "the story of the transformation of an Indian girl, whose grandmother wants to marry her off at 11," turns out to be a triumphant narrative of "an American woman who finally thinks for herself."[18] A fantastical story about an Indian widow who comes to the United States, makes her way from Florida to New York to Iowa, and eventually (or "finally") becomes "American," *Jasmine* evocatively and troublingly uncovers asymmetrical global politics, second-wave feminisms, and established U.S. expansionist narratives.

To be sure, the unproblematic story of a "third world" subject made "first world" American—recurrent in mainstream appraisals of the novel—drew justified postcolonial critique. For example, Aijaz Ahmad and Gayatri Chakravorty Spivak deconstruct Mukherjee's past and present deployment of essentialized South Asian subjectivity in the service of a North American hegemonic nationalism and exaltation of assimilative American-ness.[19] Postcolonial critics take issue with the novel's largely uncontextualized conflict between Punjab Hindus and Sikhs, traditional gender roles, and superstitious scenes of all-too-familiar "third world backwardness." The regressive politics and practices of the country of origin operate in direct contrast to the novel's depictions of U.S. modernity and capitalist practices. Such modernity, constructed through scenes of urbanization and the protagonist's declarations of ordered (and often unimpeded) progress, set the problematic stage for Jasmine's exceptionalist transformation from a grief-stricken suicidal widow to an American "greedy with wants and reckless from hope" (214).

Such an exceptionalist transformation is rooted in Jasmine's naturalization in the novel. Though the novel is set in India and the United States, *Jasmine* begins with an Americanized Indian protagonist who tells the story of her journey from Indian peasant to middle-class U.S. subject. Retrospectively imagined, *Jasmine*'s achronological narrative structure mirrors the frenzied nature of the protagonist's multisited migrations, foreshadowed in the novel's opening epigraph on chaos theory.[20] Jasmine's penultimate identity as "Jane Ripplemeyer"—the twenty-four-year-old expectant mother and live-in partner of wheel chair–bound Iowan banker Bud Ripplemeyer (who was shot by a disgruntled bank customer upset about impending foreclosure)—frames the protagonist's past identities, Jyoti, Jasmine, Jazzy, and Jase. Admittedly the most "assimilated" name in the novel, "Jane Ripplemeyer" nonetheless structurally coheres with the protagonist's other identities. Taken together, the names make visible cartographies of geographic location and citizenship as an Indian, an American, and an Indian American.

Moreover, the novel's "name motif" draws attention to Jasmine's fixation on identity. This preoccupation—manifest in protagonist declarations of being American—marries filial desire with coming-of-age adulthood, which produces a revised nation-state affiliation. Though it is in many ways a prototypical American immigrant story, focused on rebirth and remaking, literary critic Patricia Chu rightly notes that Mukherjee draws from the genre power of the British bildungsroman, replete with negotiations of class and race. This reading is certainly apparent in the novel's plot and the protagonist's own allusions to Charlotte Brontë's *Jane Eyre*.[21] Mukherjee employs a colonial British frame that in turn gives way to an individualistic American story of freedom and self-actualization. Like Brontë's Jane, Mukherjee's Jasmine is a live-in governess (or "caretaker") for an American family; she looks after Taylor and Wylie Hayes's child, Duff, and she also cares for Bud Ripplemeyer after he is shot and paralyzed. As part of this Iowan "family unit," she also cares for Du, a Vietnamese male adolescent Bud sponsors.

Alternatively, the designation Jane Ripplemeyer and its very quotidian nature attest to the protagonist's initial location as a twenty-four-year-old narrator in America's heartland—Iowa. In contrast, the protagonist's concluding reclamation of the given name Jasmine underscores the protagonist's reconciliation of her past widowhood (in India) and her blossoming romantic present with Taylor (in the United States). A designation in both the country of origin and the country of settlement, the name Jasmine makes legible the movement of an Indian immigrant body into the United States. At the same time, the forename Jasmine concretizes the protagonist's newfound citizenship status as an "Indian American." All the same, Jasmine's seemingly name-driven embrace of transnational multiplicity is destablized by her actions in the novel.

Specifically, even if the name Jasmine indicates a transnational history, the character Jasmine is decidedly more invested in a national—and not transnational—citizenship project. Although she is a transnational due to immigration, Jane/Jasmine begins and ends the novel a transplanted American. Indeed, the name Jasmine—redolent of a plant native in tropical Old World locales—promulgates a reconsideration of the novel's closing moments. In particular, the protagonist's reclamation of this name underscores a successful U.S. transplantation through a fitting horticultural metaphor. It is through transplantation (born out of the uprooted experience of involuntary exile) that Jasmine paradoxically finds rootedness. Following suit, Jasmine equally engages the naturalization process, wherein she repudiates her former Indian identity in favor of Americanness.

Even so, a major impediment to Jasmine's "coming of age" as an immigrant-turned-American is her illegal immigrant status, which limits the protagonist's unimpeded access to the nation as state-authorized citizen. Jasmine's early admission that she was not only a "caretaker" but an "undocumented 'caregiver' during [her] years in Manhattan" underscores this obstructed subject position (34). Jasmine as undocumented worker faces possible regulation in a post-1986 Immigration Reform and Control Act state, a point made clear by the opening epigraph. Consequently, Jasmine's coming-of-age American story carries with it an added weight of illegitimacy. This illegitimacy is ultimately resolved through immigrant-focused (and naturalized) speech acts inherent in the rhetoric of naming. Therefore, insofar Mukherjee's novel is about "names," *Jasmine* is dominated by the act of naming, which offers agency through state-authorized complicity. Jasmine's illegality unfolds via a narrative of "amnesty" consistent with extant U.S. immigration law.

Born "Jyoti," the protagonist spends her childhood in the rural Indian village Hasnapur. Jyoti/Jasmine's future is foretold "lifetimes ago . . . under a banyan tree." The national tree of India, the banyan image reinforces not only Jyoti's birth location but her citizenship status. In the face of de jure citizenship, Jyoti/Jasmine will nevertheless encounter statelessness. According to the astrologer's vision which opens the novel, the seven-year-old Jyoti will live in "widowhood and exile" (1). From the outset, the protagonist is situated between spousal and national loss ("widowhood" and "exile"). It is Jyoti/Jasmine's foretold (and actualized) widowhood that prompts her exile. Further, the declaration of "lifetimes ago" presages the protagonist's many lives and names to come.

The first of these "adult" lives commences in India, when at fourteen Jyoti marries Prakash Vijh. Jyoti is renamed "Jasmine," signaling her heteronormative identity as wife. Simultaneously, Prakash's insistence that his wife have a name is presented within the novel as a progressive, nontraditional act. Prakash's articulation of a proper spousal name contradicts the more traditional practice of pronoun usage between husband and wife. Concomitantly, the protagonist's renaming coincides with her development into a resourceful woman who happily works alongside her husband. An electronics repairman, Prakash initially aspires to own a shop. Ostensibly interested in a spousal economic partnership (which speaks to a second-wave feminist concern about equality in the workplace), Prakash envisions the husband/wife owned and operated "Vijh and Vijh." This entrepreneurial desire is supplanted by Prakash's plan to study in the United States. Accepted by a university in Tampa, Florida, Prakash intends (as a student) to pursue the "American dream." This educational desire coincides with the post-1965 dreams of countless numbers of Asian immigrants, who came specifically to study in American universities.

Jasmine's prophesized widowhood begins at nineteen when Prakash is killed by a terrorist bomb, the victim of a militant Sikh attack. Now an Indian widow, Jasmine is forced to return to her childhood home and live with her mother. Electing to abandon this existence, Jasmine decides to travel to Tampa the aforementioned site of Prakash's "American dream." In Tampa Jasmine intends to honor her husband and commit *sati* (ritual suicide). In order to leave India, Jasmine must obtain forged citizenship papers. Therefore, her journey to the United States begins illegally, anticipating the undocumented subject position she will hold for the remainder of the novel.

As the protagonist "phantoms" her way "through three continents," the last leg of Jasmine's trip to the United States is aboard the *Gulf Shuttle*, a smuggling vessel that operates under the less illicit guise of a shrimper. The unlawful enterprise of the *Gulf Shuttle* reconfirms the "illegality" of Jasmine's journey to the United States. This undocumented status (configured through her own location as a transnational, border-crossing subject) connects Jasmine to a larger flow of "outcasts and deportees, strange pilgrims visiting outlandish shrines, landing at the end of tarmacs, ferried in old army trucks where we are roughly handled and taken to roped-off corners of waiting rooms where surly, barely wakened customs guards await their bribe" (90–91). Initially treated as an "outcast" because of her widow status and forged citizenship papers, Jasmine inhabits the same stateless space of "refugees and mercenaries and guest workers" who take "out for the hundredth time an aerogram promising a job or space to sleep" (90). Reliant on an underground economy wherein "barely wakened customs guards await their bribe," Jasmine is a citizenship outlaw. Outside the perimeters of the law and nation-state, Jasmine contemplates her own selfhood, provocatively asking, "What country? What continent?" (91).

Though an illegitimate subject, Jasmine reminds readers that such statelessness occurs for a reason. As the protagonist asserts, she and the other "deportees" are forced to seek transnational routes as a result of war and plague. Be that as it may, this illicit noncitizenship makes Jasmine an "unnatural" body within an imaginary of world borders and nation-state contours. Relegated to living "undercover," Jasmine, like the millions of immigrants, enters the country without the cover of law. However, unlike other immigrants and refugees, Jasmine's intended U.S. mission—to commemorate her husband through *sati*—unintentionally ameliorates such illegality. Contrasted with those who seek their fortunes and asylum in the U.S., Jasmine initially has no designs on the American dream. Instead, Jasmine yearns "to breathe free" through death and permanent closure.

Jasmine's search for sacred reconciliation through *sati* is made profanely untenable by Half Face, the *Gulf Shuttle's* captain. Half Face is aptly named, for he "lost an eye and ear and most of his cheek in a paddy field in Vietnam" (93). His service in the war—which comes at great physical and emotional cost—substantiates his status as a loyal U.S. subject. His literal "loss of face" echoes a national loss via the shame of the Vietnam War. He is thus the "monstrous" product of a disastrous U.S. foreign policy. However, his actions after the war—as a smuggler of immigrant bodies—make him a "traitor" vis-à-vis an increasingly regulated U.S. immigrant economy. If Half-Face's physicality bespeaks the failure of foreign policy, his current self-employment attests to a breakdown in U.S. domestic policy. After all, Half-Face makes a successful living smuggling human cargo. His ability to bring "undercover bodies" is in part predicated on the absence of adequate border controls. Half-Face highlights the inefficacy of contemporary immigration law. And Jasmine's successful migration to the United States confirms the porosity of U.S. borders.

Armed only with a suitcase filled with her husband's clothes and a university brochure, with no connections and with little means, Jasmine is forced to travel with Half-Face, who takes her to a remote motel. Half-Face's criminality as an immigrant smuggler is exacerbated by his subsequent rape of the young widow. In the motel bathroom, Jasmine contemplates the involuntary removal of her subjectivity as a traditional Indian woman and seizure of female agency. With knife in hand, Jasmine relates, "I extended my tongue, and sliced it. Hot blood dripped immediately in the sink" (105). This act of self-violence prefigures Jasmine's revenge killing of Half-Face.

Afterward, Jasmine reveals:

> I had not given even a day's survival in America a single thought. This was the place I had chosen to die, on the first day if possible. I would land, find Tampah, walking there if necessary, find the college grounds and check it against the brochure photo. . . . I had dreamed of arranging the suit and twigs. . . . I had protected this sari, and Prakash's suit, through it all. Then he [Half Face] touched it. He had put on the suit, touched my sari, my photographs, and Ganpati. (107–108)

The slicing of her tongue initially renders Jasmine speechless, yet her next action—the violent stabbing of Half-Face—speaks to a newfound sense of self (and renewed sense of survival) forged through sexual violence. Following the murder of her assailant, Jasmine decides not only to live but "live in *America*" (emphasis added)" (108).

As such, the protagonist elects to fulfill one of the requirements for naturalization via residency. This sets the stage for *Jasmine*'s preoccupation with American mythos through immigrant-turned-citizen revision. Jasmine further relates, "My body was merely the shell, soon to be discarded. Then I could be reborn, debts and sins all paid for. . . . With the first streaks of dawn, my first full American day, I walked out the front drive of the motel to the highway and began my journey, traveling light" (108). The protagonist's articulation of "rebirth" and reconciliation ("debts and sins all paid for") at once motions to the realization Jasmine no longer has to commit *sati* because the rape and subsequent revenge murder have effectively killed her former self. The double death that occurs—Half-Face and the former Indian widow Jasmine—buttresses the protagonist's claim that her past life is in fact a shel" that will soon be discarded.

Another reading surfaces when the enunciation of debt repayment is placed alongside extant U.S. immigration policy. Jasmine not only pays back the "debt and sin" of her previous life through the revenge killing of Half-Face. She also pays forward on the "sin" of immigrant illegality. A smuggler of human cargo, Half-Face is in direct violation of immigration law. As a sexual predator and smuggler, Half-Face endangers the moral sanctity of the nation and the political borders. If Jasmine initially arrives to the States an illegal immigrant, then the killing of Half-Face makes her a de facto border patrol guard, an unintentional "model" enforcer of INS policy. Within this immigrant-focused milieu, Jasmine's revenge is personally justifiable *and* sanctioned by the U.S. nation-state. In the process, Mukherjee naturalizes Jasmine's actions for a dominant U.S. readership.

For those reasons, *Jasmine* makes apparent a different type of "model minority" reading. Situated as Jasmine is "within a historical moment marked by popular apprehensions of a crisis in American identity attributed to the changes caused by the new immigration and ethnic separatism indentified with multiculturalism," Susan Koshy convincingly argues that Jasmine's relationships with American men in the novel make visible her sexual model minority status.[22] Maintaining that Jasmine is a "sexual model minority," Koshy observes that such an "affirmative discourse" masks "the psychological costs of assimilation that the text dare not name, but which erupts periodically in episodes of seemingly agentless violence."[23] Acknowledging Koshy's analysis of *Jasmine* through rubrics of sexual model minoritization and sexual naturalization, Jasmine's rape—a potent "episode of seemingly agentless violence"—nonetheless engenders a complementary examination of model minoritiziation.

In particular, this multivalent model minoritization is evident when fixed to a contemporary immigration policy increasingly focused on the regulation of employers and smugglers. Though Jasmine is denied agency through sexual violence, she nonetheless becomes an accidental agent of the state through her capital punishment of Half Face. This is not to suggest that Jasmine consistently assumes a border patrol agent position. Indeed, what follows destabilizes a uniform application of Jasmine as constant border patrol actor. Jasmine is rescued by Lillian Gordon, a sympathetic figure who provides undocumented immigrants refuge. Still, what separates Half-Face from Lillian is the question of exploitation. If the 1986 Simpson-Mazzoli Act intended to fine employers for exploiting undocumented labor, then Half-Face's sexual exploitation and immigrant profiteering make him the ultimate state villain.

In contrast, Lillian's status as a "mother of exiles" occurs without any money-making agenda. Still, as later revealed, Lillian Gordon is eventually "busted . . . for harboring undocumenteds, exploiting them (the prosecution said) for free cooking cleaning and yard work" (121). Therefore, the state has in effect "taken care of" Lillian Gordon and need not rely on outside actors like Jasmine. Unable to testify because of her "own delicate status," Jasmine writes a letter of support wherein she asserts that Lillian "represented to me the best in the American experience and the American character" (121). Hence, Lillian not only provides Jasmine asylum; like the statuary "mother of exiles," she emblematizes for the immigrant protagonist an idealized "America." What is more, Lillian is responsible for Jasmine's initiation into assimilation. Renamed "Jazzy," the protagonist learns from Lillian how to walk and dress "American" (118–119).

An assimilated subject (via "walk" and "dress"), Jazzy/Jasmine eventually journeys north to Queens, New York, where for five months she stays with her husband's acquaintance Professorji and his extended family. Within the confines of a predominantly Punjabi Flushing neighborhood, Jasmine confronts the borders of a "traditional" Indian community existence, which offer little access to employment outside the home. Jasmine again takes flight, this time to Manhattan, where she finds work as a live-in nanny for the abovementioned Taylor and Wylie. It is on the Upper West Side, away from the Indian affects of the Flushing neighborhood and the country of origin, where Jasmine declares: "I became an American in an apartment on Claremont Avenue across the street from Barnard College Dormitory" (145). Renamed Jase, the increasingly Americanized Jasmine discovers a heretofore unknown rootedness. According to Jase/Jasmine, "America may be fluid and built on flimsy, invisible lines of weak gravity, but I was a dense object. I had landed and was getting rooted" (159).

Central to Jase/Jasmine's newfound "rootedness" is her ability to "responsibly" negotiate a capitalist economy. At first, Jasmine's enthusiastic and excessive consumption of mail-order goods threatens her economic well-being. Spending her money on meaningless commodities, Jasmine initially succumbs to the lure of U.S. consumer culture. Nonetheless, with the help of her American "family," Jasmine regains control of her finances, which in turn gives rise to claims of being "landed and getting rooted." Jasmine proudly asserts, "I had controlled my spending and now sat on an account that was rapidly growing. Every day I was being paid for something new" (159). In the face of her illegal worker status, Jasmine is still committed to a conservative capitalistic ethic. Jasmine's model minority subjectivity is reified through "hard work" and "perseverance" in the face of adversity.

Furthermore, Jasmine's (unintentional but still legible) willingness to enact justice against an illegal alien smuggler makes her a border-conscious "model minority." This model minoritization is apparent in a scene with Taylor and Duff in Central Park. The idyllic and romantic tenor of the moment is interrupted by Jasmine's sighting of an Indian hot dog vendor. Jasmine tells Taylor, "That was the man who killed my husband. . . . He knows . . . he knows me. He knows I'm here" (167–168). When Taylor asks why she cannot go to the state authorities, Jasmine replies, "Don't you see that's impossible? I'm illegal here, he knows that. I can't come out and challenge him. I'm very exposed " (168). Notwithstanding Jasmine's initial unwillingness to confront the man responsible for her husband's death, the protagonist all the same enacts her revenge via immigration policy.

Expressly, after fleeing to Iowa, Jasmine confesses:

> Sukkhi, the New York vendor, pushes his hot dog cart through my head. I do not seek to forgive, and I have long let go of my plans for revenge. I can live with both impulses. I have even written an anonymous letter to the INS, suggesting they look into the status of a certain Sukhwinder Singh, who pushes a hot-dog cart in New York City. . . . I dream only of neutralizing harm, not absolute and permanent conquest. (180–181)

In reporting Sukkhi to the INS, Jasmine once again assumes the performative role of a border patrol agent. As an undocumented immigrant-turned-INS informant, Jasmine's desire to "neutralize" her husband's murderer is negotiated through state-authorized means. Jasmine's letter reveals not the crime Sukkhi has committed but rather pushes the authorities to evaluate his citizenship status. Therefore, it is through the state—and its deportation apparatus—that Jasmine attempts to avenge her husband's death. On another level, the Jasmine/Sukkhi episode links terrorism to illegal immigration. In so doing, *Jasmine* makes visible a transnational reconciliation to a particular Indian conflict. If Jasmine's first husband dies as a result of domestic Indian terrorism, the protagonist is able to avenge his death through domestic U.S. immigration policy, via INS notification. This reading confirms Jasmine's naturalization vis-à-vis amnesty. Though an undocumented worker, Jasmine is nonetheless a subject seeking asylum from country-of-origin politics emblematized by Sukkhi.

Taken together, Jasmine's journey northward and westward, her pioneering spirit in the face of uncertainty, and her rise from child bride to woman and mother (or coming-of-age story) make visible a "typical immigrant American" narrative. Simultaneously, the "typicality" of the South Asian immigrant-turned-American is complicated by Jasmine's transformation from rural Indian subject to transnational body to American citizen. It is her ability to perform a naturalized foreignness that makes Jasmine a true 1980s American heroine. After all, she successfully repudiates an undocumented sensibility and gains (through proxy) a de facto documented selfhood. Correspondingly, Jasmine's "naturalization" intersects with late twentieth-century politics. As Susan Koshy argues, *Jasmine* reflects "social and political changes within the United States [that] contributed toward the rearticulation of the meanings of Asian American femininity. The breakdown of overt racial barriers following civil rights struggles, the positioning of Asian Americans as model minorities, the valorization of multiculturalism, and the celebration of ethnic difference created a more varied terrain within which racial, sexual, and class differences produce the possibilities of Americanization."[23] Hence, *Jasmine* speaks to both the social rise of multiculturalism and the political changes inherent in a post-1986 Simpson-Mazzoli Act immigration imaginary. With heightened awareness of illegality and regulation, Jasmine's American identity is principally in conflict with her illegal subjectivity. Nevertheless, this illegal subjectivity—which positions her on the "wrong side" of immigration policy—is subverted by Jasmine's willingness to police other illicit bodies. In doing so, Jasmine as character (and *Jasmine* as narrative) draws attention to an alternate model minorityhood/citizenship born out of immigration regulation.

Denaturalizing English: U.S. English and Eva Hoffman's *Lost in Translation*

> *Who, among my peers, is sure of what is success and what is failure? Who would want to be sure? Who is sure of purposes, meanings, national goals? Perhaps a successful immigrant is an exaggerated version of the native. From now on, I'll be made, like a mosaic, of fragments—and my consciousness of them. It is only in that observing consciousness that I remain, after all, an immigrant.*
>
> —HOFFMAN, *LOST IN TRANSLATION*

If the 1986 Simpson-Mazzoli Act employed a "humanitarian" response to the impending immigration crisis, it necessarily deployed (as *Jasmine* illustrates) a regulatory agenda via border patrols and workplace surveillance. Simultaneously, the act reinscribed tenets of U.S. naturalization through its requirement of residency and a "minimal understanding of English." In particular, the legibility of immigrants as U.S. subjects is principally charted through the ability to "understand" (or *translate*) English. In contrast, Eva Hoffman's *Lost in Translation: A Life in a New Language* disrupts dominant, naturalized readings of "successful immigration." Rather than distinguish the "foreigner" from the "native," in the above passage Hoffman collapses the two categories. In line with Hoffman's interpellation, the immigrant becomes an exaggerated version of the native who nevertheless remains fragmented.

In this manner, Hoffman introduces an alternative reading of the immigrant body through multiplicity and paradox. Eschewing claims of multicultural nationhood such as U.S. melting-pot or Canadian mosaic, Hoffman instead lays linguistically bare the polyvocal routes through which citizenship is "made." As *Lost in Translation* repeatedly avows, the dominant rubric for immigrant "success," monoculturalism, is largely uncertain ("who is sure?") and ideologically driven ("purposes, meanings, national goals?"). Indeed, such rubrics for success undergird the foundations of a particular late-century culture war.

As the likes of Sheriff Duffy make plain, turn-of-the-twenty-first-century nativism concentrates on criminality or illegality and multilingualism. Explicitly, the anxiety over multilingualism (and multiculturalism) pits native speakers against the foreign-born. Articulating patriotism through "common language" proclamations, English-only movements relied, and continue to rely, on an "us" versus "them" binary.[24] To be sure, the rise of such English-only movements in the United States during the late 1980s and early 1990s reveal an unquestionably racialized politics.

Correspondingly, those "lost in translation" are cast as the primary antagonists in a national cultural narrative.

The most politically empowered organization in the movement was U.S. English, founded in 1983 by Dr. John Tanton, former director of the Sierra Club's population committee and Zero Population Growth, and Senator S. I. Hayakawa of California, who was also the president of San Francisco State College during the 1967–1968 student strikes. An advocacy group committed to making English the "official" national language, U.S. English initially seemed a valid, albeit conservative political group, with support from the likes of Walter Cronkite, Arnold Schwarzenegger, Saul Below, and Gore Vidal.[25] Its executive director, Linda Chavez, was a leading Republican who would eventually gain notoriety as a failed George W. Bush Secretary of Labor nominee. Ironically, within the context of 1980s "immigration illegality," Chavez at the time employed Guatemalan Marta Mercado, an undocumented domestic worker.

Even so, the organization's legitimacy was irrevocably undermined not by Chavez's employment practices, which were revealed in 2001, but by the publication of an internal memorandum. The memo, dated October 10, 1986, surfaced in 1988, just as Arizona voters were to decide on an English-only state referendum. In the memo, U.S. English cofounder John Tanton wrote:

> *Gobernar es poblar* translates "to govern is to populate." . . . In this society where the majority rules, does this hold? Will the present majority peaceably hand over its political power to a group that is simply more fertile? . . . Perhaps this is the first instance in which those with their pants up are going to get caught with those with their pants down! . . . As Whites see their power and control over their lives declining, will they simply go quietly into the night? Or will there be an explosion?[26]

A self-described Malthusian, Tanton begins his argument with Argentine political philosopher Juan Bautista Alberdi, who celebrates the role immigrants play in politics and nation building.[27] Alberdi's decidedly pro-immigrant stance through Tanton's cooptation turns sinister and morally corrupt, with allusions to uncontrolled sexuality and reproduction. Couched as a struggle between the "majority White" population and the unregulated, inferior "minority," Tanton's call to action makes visible the same reactionary politics as the abovementioned San Diego County officials. Accordingly, whiteness becomes a site of victimhood (that is, immigration has led to a decline in "power and control over their lives"). Analogously, "Whites" are cast as an essential political bloc to be mobilized via anti-immigrant, English-only action.

Incontrovertibly, Tanton's anxiety over immigrant bodies and reproduction accesses a century-long nativism, redolent of past and present racialized "peril" discourses. To that end, Tanton's appeal to "democratic virtue"—evident in his observation that the United States is a society in which the "majority rules"—is all the same constructed against a threatening minority presence. Despite the anti-immigrant currency of such pronouncements, the overtly racist nature of the Tanton memo did not sit well in a post-civil rights moment. The publication of the memo led to resignations by Cronkite and executive director Linda Chavez. Tanton himself resigned following the scandal, though he would resurface in 1994 as a founder of ProEnglish, which carried an identical English-only agenda.

Similarly, the cultural aims of U.S. English would also resurface. In February 1989, New York's Suffolk County was faced with an "official English" bill. The proposed initiative would eliminate bilingual county publications such as brochures and pamphlets. Additionally, the bill would reduce bilingual country jobs and prohibit the local Human Rights Commission from investigating English-only discrimination cases. The bill's supporters claimed the initiative would "speed the assimilation of immigrants into American society and curb a growing number of bilingual programs in county government."[28] Though the Suffolk County bill did not pass, it nonetheless illustrates a potent English-only trend. That same year, English-only initiatives were put on the ballot in seventeen states, including Florida, Arizona, and Colorado.

The English-only goal of "speedy assimilation" is incontestably undermined in Hoffman's *Lost in Translation.* As Katarzyna Marciniak maintains, though *Lost in Translation* "ends on a note of immigrant success, Eva's story questions conventional immigrant narratives of complete assimilation."[29] Significantly, Hoffman's linguistic interrogation opposes the very foundations of the U.S. English movement. As *Lost in Translation* elucidates, English acquisition does not lead to wholesale assimilation. Nor does linguistic naturalization resolve alien subjectivities and concomitant feelings of alienation. Taken together, Eva Hoffman's *Lost in Translation* situates the immigrant body within a conflicted cultural terrain, and maps, through migration and translation, the affective toll of relocation.

The child of Jewish Holocaust survivors, Hoffman is a postwar product born in 1946. From the outset, Hoffman examines her citizenship via Jewishness. As Hoffman insists, "being Jewish is something definite; it is something that I am." Still, this location is circumscribed by a lingering anti-Semitism, which is a "subject . . . [that] now [in the mid-1950s] comes up frequently" and represents "a darkness of the mind, a prejudice—rather than a deviation from moral principles" (32). Because of such virulent anti-Semitism, Hoffman's Jewishness (the site of her original citizenship) threatens her and her family's Polish selfhood. Consequently, Hoffman's family leaves Poland in 1959, when Hoffman is thirteen years old.[30] Such anti-Semitism foregrounds a reading of *Lost in Translation* through amnesty frames in a manner reminiscent of Mukherjee's *Jasmine*. Both Hoffman and Jasmine are victims of home country violence, potential and actualized.

This "immigration/refugee story" foregrounds *Lost in Translation*, and Hoffman reads her forced relocation primarily through language (as indicated by the memoir's title). Divided into three sections ("Paradise," "Exile," and "The New World"), *Lost in Translation* begins in Poland, which the author configures (or writes) as a "paradise" location. The family's relocation to Vancouver comprises the "exile" section, wherein Hoffman must learn to articulate selfhood through a non-native language, English. The final section—"The New World"—takes place in the United States (in Cambridge, Massachusetts, and New York City). Situated in the fabric of social, political, and personal change, Hoffman's memoir cartographically reproduces the emotional contours of the immigrant landscape.

Moreover, *Lost in Translation* brings to light the affective and linguistic dimensions of citizenship. Responding to fellow immigrant claims of "success" through assimilation, Hoffman observes:

> Theirs is an immigrant story, and that's the story of their lives that they accept. But perhaps, if they had the words to say just what they feel, something different might pour out, an elusive complaint of an elusive ailment. For insofar as meaning is interhuman and comes from the thickness of human connections and how richly you are known, these successful immigrants have lost some of their meaning. In their separateness and silence, their wisdom—what they used to know in an intimate way, on their skin—is stifled and dries up a little. (143)

Hoffman's analysis of "an immigrant story" connects citizenship, language, and affect. Indeed, such a stock immigrant story nevertheless fails to encompass elusive complaints and elusive ailments. This breakdown is due to the paucity of adequate language ("words to say just what they feel"). The "successful" immigrant falls short because intimate meaning is lost in dominant discourse, which for the most part is overdetermined to fit a naturalization end.

Equally, the ensuing assimilationist narrative is, above all, an essentialized tale that "stifles," lacking individual complexity and connection. The absence of difference speaks to the naturalization of "successful immigrant" narratives, which privilege *e pluribus unum* citizenships. In contrast, Hoffman's "immigrant story" reproduces an *ex uno plures* (out of one, many) selfhood. Despite her status as a Polish Jewish Canadian turned Polish Jewish Canadian American, Hoffman does not lose identities so much as she accretes affiliations and citizenships. Correspondingly, Hoffman becomes a self-inscribed transnational national. This reading of multiplicity is at once geographically configured. From Cracow to Vancouver, from Houston to Cambridge, from Boston to New York City, Hoffman's memoir undeniably crosses multiple national and state borders. In the process, *Lost in Translation* principally becomes a narrative of statelessness and unbounded selfhoods.

Repeatedly at stake in *Lost in Translation* is the inadequacy of language to concretize citizenship. Illustratively, Hoffman avers, "You can't transport human meanings whole from one culture to another any more than you can transliterate a text" (175). This failure to translate consumes Hoffman's memoir, which is likewise filled with moments of "linguistic inadequacy." Simultaneously, the critique of transliteration—to represent letters from one language directly into another—highlights the incomplete processes of cultural exchange. Focused on the failure of translation and transliteration, *Lost in Translation* necessarily challenges English-only movements that evaluate citizenship viability on the basis of monoculturalism. Hoffman further weakens claims of English superiority with the assertion that "English words don't hook on to anything" and that they "float in an uncertain space" (108). On one level, the lack of English "situatedness" mirrors Hoffman's immigrant identity, which analogously "floats in an uncertain space."

On another level, such linguistic instability (embodied by the claim that "English doesn't hook on to anything") denaturalizes the dominant language's position to mimetically and unilaterally inscribe nation-state affiliation. Though Hoffman can speak and write English, the physical act is unmatched by abstract meaning, which renders language an incomplete signifier of citizenship. Her negotiation with translation necessarily forces her "to write in the language of the present, even if it's not the language of self" (121). In *Lost in Translation*, such presentist language—necessarily fixed to a specific temporality—does not address the dynamic development of the immigrant body (or self) over time and space. For that reason, Hoffman's assertion that one cannot "transport human meanings" gestures toward a fluid, transnational selfhood.

What is more, the affective inertia of past immigrant selves is foreshadowed in the memoir's opening pages. As Hoffman recollects:

> We can't be leaving all this behind—but we are: I am thirteen years old, and we are emigrating. It's a notion of such crushing, definitive finality that to me might as well mean the end of the world. . . . I desperately want time to stop, to hold the ship still with the force of my will. I am suffering my first, severe attack of nostalgia, or *tesknota*—a word that adds to nostalgia the tonalities of sadness and longing. It is a feeling whose shades and degrees I'm destined to know intimately. (3)

From the outset, Hoffman subverts the expected immigrant narrative. Rather than embracing the New World, the thirteen-year-old Hoffman desperately wants to stop and hold the ship still. With affective mention of desperation, sadness, and longing, Hoffman's preemigrant account introduces an emotional intimacy that promptly establishes cost and loss. Though Hoffman's family leaves Poland "voluntarily," the introductory description produces a refugee discourse, evident in "desperate" acts to remain "in country." Besides, this intimacy is marked by "shades and degrees" and is best understand through sad nostalgia (*tesknota*), which lacks absolute definition in English. All things considered, Hoffman's account of departure militates against literal translation. Instead, this "parting" anecdote is figured through approximation of words and emotion.

Like the linguistic difficulties she encounters, Hoffman's transnational affect (embodied in *tesknota*) refuses complete naturalization. Despite the memoir's titular assertion that Hoffman is living a new life in a new language, the untranslatable is a palpable source of distress, trauma, and denaturalization. This particular failure of language conversion is immediately apparent in the memoir's "Exile" section. Spefically, Hoffman details a classroom interaction in which her Canadian teacher struggles with the protagonist's name. Unable to properly pronounce Hoffman's first name "Ewa" as "Eva," her teacher (a de facto representative of nation via public education) renames her "EH-vah." Similarly, Hoffman's sister Alina is renamed "Elaine." This "renaming" episode is an undeniable source of alienation for the autobiographical protagonist, who writes: “we walk to our seats, into a room of unknown faces, with names that make us strangers to ourselves” (105). Denaturalized through naming, Hoffman’s assertions of “strangeness” therefore reinforce a reading of the “foreign” in the face of assimilative speech act.

Ironically, the classroom as denaturalization site is briefly revised later in the memoir. As Hoffman learns to “live in a new language,” she nevertheless sees herself as a distinct protagonist in a larger “Americanization” performance (that is, the naturalization ceremony). Following the completion of her Harvard doctorate, Hoffman notes that “Like characters in a climactic scene of a comic opera summoned to deliver a furiously paced summation, the main figures of my personal mythology have all gathered in one place at the very point when, in effect, I receive the certificate of full Americanization. . . . Everything comes together, everything I love, as in the fantasies of my childhood; I am the sum of my parts” (226). Supplanting a “drama of Americanization” with a “comic opera” (calling to mind Gilbert and Sullivan light comedies), Hoffman relies on the main figures of her personal mythology. The episode’s crowning moment—the receipt of a diploma that resembles a certificate of full Americanization—brings everything together. The oldest university in the United States, Harvard as symbolic institution is imbued with “first immigrant” meaning embodied in Puritan emigrants from England. Established in 1636, Harvard predates U.S. nationhood, yet its connection to a Puritanical past makes it a national emblem of “city upon a hill” progress. Following suit, as a graduate whose institution was accepting of her, Hoffman is (at least for the moment) naturalized (226).

Nonetheless, this naturalization feeling is fleeting. In the end, Hoffman’s immigrant selfhood, the source of her inability to adequately translate, becomes her principal anchor in the New World. Hoffman’s story, overtly reminiscent of Mary Antin’s *The Promised Land*, takes a different direction via selfhood claims. If upon arriving at and assimilating in the United States, Antin was “born, remade, and born again,” Hoffman is not so much remade as she is amended. As the memoir progresses, Hoffman’s old identities ebb and flow, largely remaining fluid. The “back and forth” nature of Hoffman’s many selfhoods is deliberately suggestive of translation as an identifiable practice, which is similarly unfixed. Correspondingly, Hoffman repeatedly returns to the meaning of translation (the carrying across of meaning through language) as an ever incomplete process that still offers agency within the U.S. cultural landscape.

Moreover, instead of naturalization, Hoffman (unlike her *Jasmine* counterpart) privileges a priori and composite citizenships. Specifically, Hoffman's past identity as the daughter of Polish refugees affords her first-person access to citizenship rupture and selfhood eruption. Compelled to listen in order to learn to speak, Hoffman eschews one-sided forms of literacy. In their place, Hoffman offers the following observation: "It's difficult to tell the truth to another person. The self is a complicated mechanism, and to speak it forth honestly requires not only sincerity but the agility to catch insight on the wing and the artistry to give it accurate words. It also requires a listener who can catch our nuances as they fly by. Spoken truth shrivels when it falls on a tin ear" (279). To understand the self, and by extension selfhood, Hoffman stresses the need for multiple literacies. In order to understand the American (and, in the grander scheme, the human) experience, one must be willing to speak with sincerity but have the necessary agility to carefully render meaning. Thus, Hoffman advocates an in-depth practice that also requires a listener attuned to nuances. Such a position produces a reading of selves focused not on essentialized economies of understanding but two-sided literacy acts that involve both reading and listening.

Alternatively, emphasizing complexity in the face of immigration debates that privilege "English only" and strict regulation, Hoffman resists compartmentalization, classification, and containment. In the process, as Katarzyna Marciniak observes, Hoffman is chiefly invested not so much in state-sanctioned selfhood as self-determined "alienhood." This alienhood makes visible Hoffman's "textualization of the in-between space of resistance: resistance to a traditional notion of assmiliation that works to accept, but also absorb and flatten the exile; resistance to smoothing out the foreigner's otherness, and a defiance against the creation of a new proper subject that erases her past so that she can successfully function in a new community" (79). As well, Hoffman's assertion of an immigrant location is predicated on multiple citizenships. This composite selfhood is determined by history (that is, a forced relocation as a result of the Holocaust and its aftermath), by her religious affiliation as a Jew, her political Polish selfhood, and her linguistic acquisition of English. A multivalent cultural citizen, Hoffman simultaneously inhabits multiple linguistic spaces. In articulating her location vis-à-vis her immigrant identity, Hoffman declares allegiance to the many selfhoods contained within it. She is thus a denaturalized subject through Canada and the United States but nonetheless a world citizen (albeit bifurcated).

Finally, Hoffman's phenomenological explorations of English enable her to rethink not how Americans are "made" but instead how they are "unmade." In other words, Hoffman's unique location—reflecting a sense of not only living in two worlds but within multiple words and languages—produces a deconstructive reading of U.S. citizenship. Indeed, Hoffman remarks that her American friends:

> share so many assumptions that are quite invisible to them, precisely because they are shared. These are assumptions about the most fundamental human transactions, subcutaneous beliefs, which lie just below the stratum of political opinion or overt ideology: how much "space," physical or psychological, we need to give each other, how much "control" is desirable, about what is private and what is public. (210–211)

Configuring her American friends as a "readable" text, Hoffman enacts (to all intents and purposes) a translation of citizenship. Noting that their selfhood is constructed not on tangible characteristics but more abstract assumptions and "subcutaneous beliefs," Hoffman deconstructs the very tenets of naturalization as a learned process. When it is all said and done, Hoffman undercuts the communal power of naturalization, which does not necessarily lead to a shared citizenship or political kinship. To be sure, if naturalization is a state-authorized process, then the question of who can or cannot naturalize is determined not by sentimental declarations of faith but by constructed political opinion and overt ideology.

Indeed, it is between poles of public opinion, politics, and debates over immigration that *Jasmine* and *Lost in Translation* are largely circumscribed and contained. Correspondingly, U.S. citizenship thematically undergirds Bharati Mukherjee's novel and Eva Hoffman's memoir, which are structurally determined through the shifting terrain of present-day immigration policy. Accordingly situated within a space of mixed immigrant feelings, declarations of race and racism, and delimited by the ever-pressing state need to regulate immigration, *Jasmine* and *Lost in Translation* underscore a late twentieth-century unresolved tension. Such anxiety foregrounds, influences, and shapes 1980s and early 1990s characterizations of the nation through and against immigrant bodies.

Haunted by politics in the country of origin and marked by multiple border crossings, *Jasmine*'s protagonist and Hoffman's narrator self attempt to settle—through affect and naturalization—the pressing matter of U.S. selfhood. On another level, connotative of deciphering acts, comprehension moves, and strategies that foment readability, the question of citizenship legibility in *Jasmine* and *Lost in Translation* is negotiated through history, memory, speech, and grammar. Such an analysis provokes a reading of *Jasmine* as a text consumed with an unstable form of "remarkable Americanness" principally forged through the regulation of immigrant bodies. In Eva Hoffman's *Lost in Translation*, at stake is an unachievable "Americanness" that thematically undermines melting-pot utopianism. In related fashion, if Bharati Mukherjee's *Jasmine* highlights a national focus on illegality and immigrant bodies at the turn of the twenty-first century, then Eva Hoffman's *Lost in Translation: A Life in a New Language* examines the role of language in the making (and unmaking) of Americans.

In so doing, Hoffman's memoir further addresses contemporary immigrant-oriented debates that dominated late twentieth-century public discourse. As a result, *Jasmine* and *Lost in Translation* engender a totalizing reading of the cultural and political dimensions of late 1980s immigration policy. Illustratively, African American writer Alice Walker notes: "*Jasmine* begins to answer some of the questions I have had about the emotional landscape of recent immigrants to this country. This *is* a novel of great importance to any contemporary insight into ourselves as Americans in the midst of enormous social, political, and personal changes."[31] Walker's reading of Jasmine speaks not only to the shifting terrain of Americanness in the midst of enormous social, political, and personal changes, but to the question of the emotional landscape of recent immigrants. In turn, Walker concretizes the affective dimensions of U.S. selfhood, which are forged through the contested crucible of politics and culture.

Such affective dimensions were more than apparent in Reagan's Liberty Weekend remarks, which structure a patriotic love of country through immigrant emblem (the Statue of Liberty). However, such "structures of nationalistic feeling" were most embodied in a citizenship spectacle that followed Reagan's address. To be sure, this moment—which exists in the shadow of Lady Liberty's centennial celebration—brings into focus a late twentieth-century understanding of citizenship through repudiation and reclamation. Meant to recognize twelve "remarkable naturalized Americans," the subsequent Medal of Liberty ceremony worked in media-oriented conjunction with the statue's anniversary celebration. If the initial focus of Liberty Weekend was the reconstructed celebration of the statue's iconic immigrant status, then the recognition of "remarkable" naturalized bodies offers further proof that Americans are not only made but also fashioned into nation-building laborers. Conjured up by Liberty Weekend producer David L. Wolper, the Medal of Liberty was an award created specifically for the statue's centennial. Notwithstanding the medal's mass-media roots, the award was without a doubt state-authorized and state-sanctioned, with the Reagan administration responsible for the selection of recipients from the realm of politics and the fields of art, science, and culture.

Among those "remarkably recognized" was cold war/Nixon administration fixture Henry Kissinger, a Jewish subject whose family escaped Nazi Germany in 1938. Similarly, fellow German American Hanna Holborn Gray, the nation's first female university president, fled her country of origin when confronted with assured fascist persecution.[32] The legacy of Nazi rule is abundantly plain in the case of Medal of Liberty recipient Elie Wiesel, a Romanian Jewish Holocaust survivor and, like Kissinger, a Nobel Prize winner.[33] Kissinger, Gray, and Wiesel were joined by Jewish Americans Dr. Albert B. Sabin, inventor of the oral polio vaccine, who emigrated from Poland, and Itzhak Perlman, renowned Israeli American violin virtuoso. Panama-born Kenneth B. Clark, an African American psychologist most known for his role in conducting the doll tests used to dismantle "separate but equal" in *Brown v. Board of Education* (1954), was another Medal of Liberty beneficiary. Also present was Franklin R. Chang-Diaz, the first Hispanic astronaut, who originally hailed from Costa Rica. Two first-generation Chinese Americans and one former British subject were also recognized as "remarkable naturalized Americans": I. M Pei, respected architect, famed computer engineer/entrepreneur An Wang; and USO tour stalwart Bob Hope, a comedian/entertainer born in London, England.[34] The final recipient, Russian Jewish American composer Irving Berlin, who wrote "God Bless America," was unable to make it to the ceremony due to illness and was awarded his medal in absentia.[35]

The ethnic backgrounds of the twelve recipients did not go unnoticed by the always opinionated New York City Mayor Koch. As *Time* magazine reporter Richard Stengel sardonically notes, the mayor, "ever ready to leap to the defense of ethnicity," took issue with the absence of particular hyphenated Americans. Decrying the dearth of Irish and Italian recipients, Koch "denounced the awards as 'idiotic' and promptly decided to give out 87 medals of his own."[36] Despite Koch's tongue-in-cheek response to the Medal of Liberty award list, the selection of specific naturalized subjects makes more seriously discernible the conservative multicultural, model minority politics that characterized the Reagan administration and the 1980s. Tellingly missing from the roster of remarkable naturalized Americans were civil rights protestors, revolutionary activists, and 1960s radicals. Instead, what united the group of Medal of Liberty honorees was their presidentially legible faith in the nation, which implicitly precluded dramatic calls for systemic change. Certainly, their very naturalization—dependent on the state-authorized fulfillment of patriotic and residency requirements—politically signaled the voluntary repudiation by each "remarkable American" of past affiliations and their state-sanctioned commitment to U.S. principles.

In this regard, the Medal of Liberty recipients adhered to the president's consistent appeal to individual responsibility, undying belief in teleologies of racial progress, and dismissal of social welfare programs. The emphasis on individualism and discipline, a trademark position for the former New Deal advocate-turned-supply-side economist, was clear in a February 23, 1984, address to Asian and Pacific American leaders. President Reagan credited Asian Americans with helping to "preserve [the American] dream by living up to the bedrock values that make us a good and a worthy people." The president then clarified, averring, "I'm talking about principles that begin with the sacred worth of human life, religious faith, community spirit . . . tolerance, hard work, fiscal responsibility, cooperation, and love."[37]

In contrast to the model minoritization of Asian Americans, the fortieth president (whose administration was openly anti–affirmative action, dismissive of social welfare programs, and unabashedly supportive of South Africa during apartheid) publicly questioned the objectives of African American civil rights leaders who continued to push for social justice. In an oft-quoted statement, Reagan reportedly inquired, "Sometimes I wonder if they [civil rights activists] really mean what they say, because some of those leaders are doing very well leading organizations based on keeping alive the feeling that they're victims of prejudice."[38] In this instance, the affective feeling of prejudice is rendered rhetorically invalid through Reagan's question, which presupposes an uncertainty about "real" versus imagined meaning. In doing so, Reagan circulates a reading that civil rights leaders—and not actual systemic racism—are responsible for the perpetuation of victimhood. Reagan's questioning of prejudice is reminiscent of the 1960s political foundation for the Asian American model minority myth. Consistent with established model minority logics disseminated in mass press venues like the *New York Times* and *U.S. News and World Report*, Reagan's casting of "Asian American dream holders" versus histrionic African American activists makes irrefutably visible a divisive people-of-color politics and selective affirmations of probationary whiteness.

What is more, the inclusion of Jewish refugees and Asian immigrants in the Reagan administration-sanctioned Medal of Liberty ceremony equally highlights a conservative cold war model minoritization that reconfigures, revises, and celebrates narratives of U.S. domestic and foreign policy. Accordingly, the preponderance of individuals connected to World War II confirms a dominant U.S. narrative of the war as "the good fight." Additionally, the Medal of Liberty awardees from eastern Europe and Asia substantiate a correlative conservative narrative of the post–World War II era as "the good fight against communist totalitarianism."[39] With "remarkable Americans" from formerly fascist and communist nation-states (including China, Poland, and Romania), the Medal of Liberty ceremony implicitly underscores twentieth-century foreign policy triumphalism and simultaneously monumentalizes the "benevolent" success of cold war political conversion policies. Domestically, America's Jim Crow past—exemplified by Kenneth B. Clark's work and presence—is to varying degrees "reconciled" on stage, which presents an integrated body politic constitutive of naturalized citizens.

Most significant (given the focus on immigrants-turned-Americans), the problematic immigration policies of the twentieth century—with wide-ranging racialized immigration quotas, inclusive of nation-state preferences, and replete with racial citizenship requirements—were in "naturalized" fashion predictably omitted from the Liberty Weekend celebration.[40] As a consequence, the Medal of Liberty ceremony offers for public consumption embodied "solutions" to the very questions (the "women's question," the "Chinese question," the "great ethnic question," and the "immigrant question") that began and persisted throughout the twentieth century. And, for those reasons, the inclusion of Jewish and Asian American Medal of Liberty recipients publicly and politically instantiates an amended and euphemistic sense of U.S. nationhood reliant on a model minoritized tolerance. The Medal of Liberty beneficiaries are deemed remarkable because in large part they personified a nostalgic, open-door immigration past and a now unproblematic civil rights present.[41]

5 / Demarcating the Nation: Naturalizing Cold War Legacies and War on Terror Policies

Snow: Let me start basic here. Is the U.S. government becoming Big Brother?

Dinh: No, it is not. We are engaged in a full-frontal war against terrorism and we are fighting that war on two fronts, obviously. Abroad, our men and women are fighting bravely. But here, we are trying to fight the threat of terrorism by preventing and disrupting future terrorist activity. We are very careful in targeting our actions, our regulatory enforcement and preventative actions [will be] directed at terrorists. If you are a terrorist, you have every reason to fear the United States of America. But if you're a law-abiding citizen, you have every reason to be free from fear.

—VIET DINH, DECEMBER 8, 2001

On the one hand, the Cold War is gone; we don't have to worry about a Soviet Union with whom we are eyeball-to-eyeball, poised with weapons of mass destruction. On the other hand, we have a much more disorderly set of threats, much more networked, much more widely distributed, much more difficult to deter and, unfortunately, much better enabled to carry out acts of violence because of what modern technology affords in terms of weapons, in terms of the ability to operate over the Internet, and in terms of the means of travel around the globe and communication around the globe, literally in real time or less.

—MICHAEL CHERTOFF, APRIL 7, 2008

In early April 2001, an M-17 helicopter crashed into a mountain range south of Hanoi, killing all sixteen on board.[1] Of the sixteen-member team, seven were U.S. armed forces personnel. Its primary mission—the search for soldiers' remains—was part of a two-decade-long Vietnam War recovery program intended to facilitate closure for veteran's families.[2] Despite the war's traumatic resonance within U.S. national memory, the April 7 crash received scant media attention due to another event in the South China Sea. Six days prior to the Hanoi crash and 297 miles away, a U.S. Navy surveillance plane collided with a Chinese military jet over Hainan Island in the People's Republic of China.[3] Labeled in major media outlets as the "Hainan Island incident," the twenty-four-member American crew was summarily detained on a Chinese military base. For a tense eleven-day period, the recently installed George W. Bush administration and the People's Republic of China government traded accusations of espionage, contradictory claims to "international air space," and heated allegations about responsibility.

While the U.S. commander-in-chief technically apologized for the collision (with the president publicly expressing "regret" and "sorrow" to the wife of downed Chinese fighter pilot Wang Wei), the Bush administration nevertheless refused to call off future spy missions in the region. And though a measured executive letter of apology was issued, leading to the crew's release, the Chinese government rejected U.S. demands to return the downed spy plane. Within this politically charged milieu, the stage was set for an inevitable Chinese-U.S. foreign policy conflict.[4] Significantly, the incident marked the first foreign policy crisis in the George W. Bush presidency, portending the East Asian focus of U.S. military strategy at the turn of the twenty-first century.

Indeed, with emergent economic dominance and increased political importance, buttressed by an ever-growing industrial complex and strengthened military arsenal, China appeared to be the principal threat to U.S. national security. Concomitantly, the Hainan Island incident was geopolitically reminiscent of the Vietnam War. Located just west of the Gulf of Tonkin, Hainan Island was geographically near the site of the alleged August 2, 1964, "North Vietnamese attack" on the *U.S.S. Maddox*. The *U.S.S. Maddox* incident proved a foundational foreign policy event for the Lyndon Baines Johnson administration, which used the assault as a pretext for war. Soon after, the president issued the Gulf of Tonkin Resolution, which signaled the beginning of the eleven-year Vietnam War.

The 2001 conflict with the communist Chinese nation-state, Hainan Island's geographic proximity, and the political back-and-forth potently gestured toward cold war déjà vu, despite the fall of the Berlin Wall and the dissolution of the Soviet Union. For these reasons, if the Hainan Island incident echoes Vietnam War–era geopolitics, then the M-17 Hanoi crash unavoidably harkens back to the war's unresolved conclusion. The previous year (2000) marked the twenty-fifth anniversary of the fall of Saigon and the symbolic end of the Vietnam War. Fittingly, Vietnamese refugee-turned-U.S.-citizen Viet D. Dinh authored a March 16,

2000, *Wall Street Journal* op-ed titled "Coming to Grips with Vietnam," commemorating and contemplating the war's ongoing legacy.

The Model Minoritization of Viet Dinh

Born on February 22, 1968, in Saigon, Viet Dinh was intimately familiar with the U.S. cold war effort. His father, Phong Dinh, was a South Vietnamese Air Force pilot. Following the fall of Saigon in 1975, Dinh's father was imprisoned in a reeducation camp until his 1978 escape. That year, Dinh, his mother, and six older siblings, along with eighty-five other refugees, left Vietnam. As revealed in a May 10, 2001, *Orange Country Register* article, the Dinh family braved "storms, hunger, and gunfire in the South China Sea," and endured twelve days without food or water until they reached the Malaysian shore. Even then, the Dinh family faced more hardship. "Met by gunfire and cast back into the South China Sea," Dinh and his siblings swam to shore, "sure their boat could not withstand another sea voyage."[5] Their mother Nguyen stayed aboard, destroying the boat with an axe so that the family could remain in a Malaysian refugee camp.

The Dinh family (minus their father and a sister) eventually made their way to Portland, Oregon, where they subsisted as migrant farmers who worked the region's strawberry fields. The Mount St. Helens eruption in 1980 profoundly impacted the Pacific Northwestern agricultural industry, forcing yet another Dinh family relocation to Fullerton, California. To make ends meet, Viet Dinh worked in fast food restaurants, and taught himself English by reading *The Hardy Boys* and *Nancy Drew*. A teenaged transnational actor, Dinh sent a portion of his service industry earnings to his sister and father in Vietnam. Dinh's father finally came to the United States in 1983. With an extra household wage earner, Dinh quit his after-school jobs and focused on his studies. He attended Harvard College and furthered his postgraduate study at Harvard Law School. In 1992, while a law school student, Dinh successfully negotiated his sister's relocation from a Hong Kong refugee camp.[6]

Taken together, Dinh's familial story—and his meteoric rise from Vietnamese refugee to Harvard Law School graduate—coincides with the late twentieth-century master narrative of other Asian/Asian American "model minorities" who either came to the United States as refugees or whose parents were first-generation immigrants. Concurrently, this model minority master narrative intersects with an analogous reading of Jewish American identity. These immigrants were to varying degrees the focus of an August 31, 1987, *Time* magazine headline, "Those Asian-American Whiz Kids." The cover story, "Education: The New Whiz Kids," examined the phenomenon of Asian American academic achievement, which "appear[ed] to be another success story for the American dream, an example of the continuing immigrant urge to succeed and of the nation's ability to thrive on the dynamism of its new citizens."[7] Acknowledging the resurgence of anti-Asian "yellow peril" resentment and the homogenizing nature of the model minority stereotype, *Time* reporter Brand nevertheless reasoned, "even with these problems, many Asian-American students are making the U.S. education system work better for them than it has for any other immigrant group since the arrival of East European Jews began in the 1880s."[8]

Presupposing the assimilation of East European Jews and the correlative systemic manipulation of education by Asian/Asian American students, Brand implies that Asian Americans, like their model minority Jewish predecessors, are naturalized subjects ("new" U.S. citizens) engaged in the pursuit and fulfillment of the American dream. Though not featured in the *Time* magazine story, Dinh's story certainly adhered to its basic narrative of Asian American perseverance, hard work, and success. After law school, Dinh worked as a law clerk to Judge Laurence H. Silberman on the U.S. Court of Appeals and Supreme Court Justice Sandra Day O'Connor. He joined the academic ranks in 1996, where he became the first and only Vietnamese American law professor at Georgetown University Law Center.[9] While at Georgetown, Dinh was the codirector of the Asian Law and Policy Studies program. His legal expertise and personal story made him a seemingly perfect candidate to write "Coming to Grips with Vietnam."

Given the venue, Dinh's "Coming to Grips with Vietnam" was concentrated on the region's economic landscape. The essay nonetheless begins with Secretary of Defense William Cohen's trip to Vietnam, the first such visit by a defense secretary since the war's end. The former refugee Dinh maintains that Cohen's trip "raises delicate issues for America, for Vietnam and for the millions of people affected by the conflict. . . . For America, this year marks a quarter century since our defeat. Despite all the talk of healing, of mistakes, even of apologies, Vietnam remains deeply ingrained in the American psyche as a gentle reminder of our fallibility."[10] Stating that 2000 "marks a quarter century since *our* defeat" (emphasis added), Viet Dinh reminds readers that the war was forged through an alliance between the United States and the Republic of Vietnam (South Vietnam). The war's enduring psychological legacy is made apparent in Dinh's assertion that despite all the talk of healing, of mistakes, even of apologies, Vietnam remains deeply ingrained in the American psyche.

Conversely, the American War in Vietnam continues to haunt Dinh's former country of origin. This bilateral reading is made visible in Dinh's more extensive claim that the

> U.S. was not alone in its defeat. Our ally, the Republic of Vietnam, and more broadly the people of Vietnam, also lost. The end of the war marked the beginning of a new life for hundreds of thousands of boat people—my family among them—who risked their lives to find freedom elsewhere. Those who remained saw the continuation of war via border conflicts with China and the invasion of Cambodia, severe shortages wrought by economic mismanagement, and the loss of basic freedom and dignity. . . . Fortuitous public compassion made me a U.S. citizen, a rider on the wave of prosperity. But the people of Vietnam remain the most impoverished in the world.[11]

Alluding to "hundreds of thousands of boat people" and with the related admission that his family was among them, Dinh implicitly articulates his transnational location vis-à-vis the Vietnam War. A boat person who "risked his life to find freedom elsewhere," Dinh necessarily crossed nation-state borders en route to "freedom" and "prosperity." Representative of a post-Vietnam War flow of bodies, Dinh is a transnational subject formed from the multivalent U.S./Republic of Vietnam defeat. Simultaneously, Dinh's vocalization of U.S. selfhood is contrasted with the Vietnamese who remained. The victims of communist foreign policy and mismanagement, those who remained suffered "the loss of basic freedom and dignity."

The use of "our defeat" and "our fallibility" hints at another transnational dimension to the war's impact. Such currents of psychic trauma operate in tandem with the flow of refugees into the United States as a result of "our defeat." The persistence of "failure" in spite of talk of healing, of mistakes, even of apologies bespeaks a conservative cold war logic wherein success is mapped according to democratic triumph. Additionally, the mention of economic mismanagement is fixed to an equally conservative reading of communism through failed fiscal policy.

Still, this is not to suggest a total reading of failure vis-à-vis Vietnam. As Dinh reveals, this collective articulation—which bonds an extant nation-state to a now nonexistent one—is joined to his own experience as a boat person or Vietnamese refugee. On the one hand, a forced transnational subject at age ten, Dinh as stateless noncitizen embodies the failure of the South Vietnamese cause. On the other hand, Dinh's successful conversion to American selfhood (as refugee-turned-citizen) exemplifies a "winning" combination of affect and capitalist faith. The marriage of emotion to American citizenship is made clear in Dinh's contention that "fortuitous public compassion made me a U.S. citizen, a rider on the wave of prosperity." Granted access to economic prosperity through naturalization, Dinh is the emblematic communist Vietnamese refugee rehabilitated through flows—or "waves"—of democratic virtue and economic prosperity.

Dinh's deliberate use of "public compassion" parallels Republican presidential frontrunner George W. Bush's political platform of "compassionate conservatism," which fixed "liberal" concerns about human rights and welfare to corporate models of efficiency.[12] In addition, the connection between Dinh and the president certainly did not end at the level of semantics. Politically, the two shared an undeniable belief in and commitment to neoconservative principles. Neoconservative thought depends on the domestic reduction of government programs and the foreign policy use of military/economic power in the global spread of "democracy" and "free markets," and Dinh's article makes plain those tenets. A confirmed "patriot" willing to eschew a home in communist Vietnam for capitalistic prosperity in the United States, firmly committed to the U.S. imperial project abroad, the thirty-four-year-old Dinh becomes a model representative of turn-of-the-twenty-first-century neoconservative Republicanism.

Furthermore, as a veteran neoconservative legal practitioner, Dinh worked closely with Senator Alfonse M. D'Amato (R-NY) during the Senate investigation of President Bill Clinton's "Whitewater" hearings (1994–1995) and was a constant presence in Clinton's impeachment trial (1998). Most remarkable, regardless of the fact that naturalized citizens cannot ascend to the presidency, Dinh managed to have a hand in deciding the executive victor, having written a "friend-of-the-court" Supreme Court brief on behalf of pro-Bush Florida voters in *Bush v. Gore* (2000).[13] Consequently, Viet D. Dinh's nomination for assistant attorney general in the Office of Policy Development came as no surprise to long-time Bush supporters and neoconservative Republicans, who openly speculated that the Vietnamese American candidate could someday be the first Asian American justice in the nation's highest court.[14]

Confirming Whiteness: Viet Dinh and Michael Chertoff

On May 10, 2001, Republican senator Peter Domenici (New Mexico) enthusiastically introduced the judicial nominee Viet Dinh, who "wiped tears from his eyes as [the New Mexico senator] chronicled his remarkable journey from a 10-year-old fleeing Vietnam in a boat to a law professor facing a congressional panel."[15] During the closing arguments of Dinh's confirmation hearing, Domenici told President Pro Tempore Strom Thurmond and members of the Judiciary Committee that before them was "a Vietnamese scholar who just twenty-three years ago was a young man out on a boat at sea who could just as well have drowned, and we never would have heard from him. But because of a loving family around him, they eventually ended up American citizens." The cause and effect relationship Domenici establishes—wherein a "loving family" is a necessary ingredient for "American citizenship"—joins affective relationships of love to state-authorized U.S. selfhood. At the same time, Domenici's use of "Vietnamese scholar" instead of the more accurate label "Vietnamese American scholar" destabilizes (through non-inclusion) the New Mexico senator's subsequent assertion of U.S. citizenship. Regardless, Domenici's characterization of Dinh's voyage from refugee to U.S. citizen as "a spectacular American story" makes possible a reading of the Dinh family narrative through U.S. cold war politics and Kissinger-era realpolitik.

Dinh's familial story highlights the constant cold war deployment of U.S. military power in the service of spreading democracy around the globe. Individually, Viet Dinh as Americanized, naturalized subject becomes the U.S. foreign policy byproduct of "benevolent assimilation" whereby the formerly inimical is made a present-day "friend of the regime." A cold war warrior at the tender age of ten, Dinh's commitment to the U.S. nation-state must have struck a chord with the Senate's pro tempore president Thurmond, who almost twenty-five years earlier (in 1975) shouted his support for South Vietnam's Saigon regime from a bullhorn.[16] Resisting communist totalitarianism, bearing the forceful elements of the South China Sea, and waiting patiently for refugee sponsorship, Dinh's triumphant story of survival concludes with the candidate's U.S. naturalization. In his closing remarks to the committee, Domenici asserted that "despite this tumultuous beginning, Dinh persevered . . . More than that, he excelled."[17] Central to Domenici's characterization of Dinh the nominee is a model minority "rags-to-riches" Asian-focused narrative, wherein the Vietnamese refugee turned U.S.

citizen effectively perseveres in the face of overwhelming political and environmental odds.

Reacting to Domenici's recapitulation of his life story, Dinh the nominee told the committee: "That image of my mother destroying our last link to Vietnam really stands out in my mind to this day as to the courage she possesses, but also the incredible lengths which my parents, like so many other people, have gone to in order to find that promise of freedom and opportunity."[18] The maternal act that stands out in Dinh's mind hinges on the obliteration of "our last link to Vietnam." The association Dinh expresses between his mother's physical severance of ties to Vietnam and "courage" underscores the heroic dimensions of nation-state repudiation through filial acceptance. Though unintentional, Dinh's articulation of destroying links to the country of origin motions toward the very grammar of naturalization, which obliges applicants to publicly articulate voluntary repudiations of the country of origin. Dinh's naturalization performance before the Senate Judiciary Committee—embedded in the retelling of his mother's valiant act—lacks the transnational registers apparent in his *Wall Street Journal* op-ed published the previous year.

Correspondingly, Dinh's refugee status (constructed through a forced relocation) is recast vis-à-vis "voluntary" immigrant desires to "find that promise of freedom and opportunity." Omitted from Dinh's account is any discernible loyalty to the former country of origin, Vietnam. For all intents and purposes, Dinh "remakes himself" from involuntary refugee to willing American who, like "so many other people," had gone to "incredible lengths" to come to the United States in search of the American dream. In the same way, the Senate Judiciary Committee, composed solely of white lawmakers, is both witness to Dinh's judicial confirmation and a de facto audience for his naturalization. Dinh's refugee story, forged within the crucible of failed U.S. foreign policy, is all the same well-suited to a euphemistic teleology of U.S. nationhood built on tolerance, access, and promise.

And, though Senator Domenici portrayed the nominee's story as "a spectacular American story," Dinh's biographical narrative and response make apparent a *particular* American story that draws together U.S. imperial logics of benevolent assimilation, democratic notions of virtue, and neoconservative multiculturalism.[19] This particular American story conveniently engenders a naturalized model minoritization in which the formerly communist subject becomes a U.S. patriot. Dinh's love of the U.S. nation-state is publicly emphasized through his unrelenting belief in American prosperity and passionate dislike for the communist regime in his country of origin. Quoted in a September 18, 2002, article about the Vietnamese American's rise through the political and juridical ranks, Dinh's mother told a *Los Angeles Times* reporter that her son "had a hatred of the Communists because I made him understand it was the Communists who had taken his father away from the house and put him in prison."[20] Hence, Viet Dinh's commitment to the U.S. nation-state ostensibly emerges from familial loyalty that intersects with "family values," a hallmark conservative platform issue.

The "model minoritization" of Dinh's confirmation hearing, formed through the filial Asian subject turned loyal Asian American, initially stands in conspicuous contrast to the treatment of a "fellow model minority" candidate, Jewish American Michael Chertoff. Dinh's confirmation hearings coincided with Chertoff's nomination for assistant attorney general for the Criminal Division in the Department of Justice. Notwithstanding similar political sympathies, the two candidates were presented quite differently during the confirmation hearings. Whereas Dinh's Vietnamese background was central to establishing the "story of his candidacy," Chertoff's personal narrative was for the most part absent from the confirmation hearing.

Instead, central to Chertoff's nomination was a recapitulation of his vita, which included degrees from Harvard College and Harvard Law School (like fellow nominee Viet Dinh), his previous Judicial Branch appointment, and past publications about *Miranda* and civil rights.[21] Born in Elizabeth, New Jersey, the son of Rabbi Gershon Baruch Chertoff, a Talmud scholar and former leader of the city's Congregation B'nai Israel, and Livia Chertoff, a flight attendant for El Al Israel Airlines, Chertoff also took a prominent role in the Senate Whitewater investigation as special counsel. A 1990 George H. W. Bush administration U.S. attorney appointee, Chertoff, like Dinh, was an established long-time supporter of the neoconservative Republican agenda, a fact made clear in his position in the 2000 George W. Bush campaign as a primary criminal justice advisor and active fundraiser.[22] Four years after the 2001 confirmation hearings, Chertoff would be best known not for his professional accomplishments but for his failures as the secretary for homeland security, which were the subject of congressional hearings following the disastrous FEMA response to Hurricane Katrina in 2005.

Moreover, if Dinh's confirmation hearing at times resembled a naturalization ceremony, then the absence of any discussion of Chertoff's immigrant past by the Senate Judiciary Committee gestured toward an incontrovertibly "natural" citizenship status. A native-born citizen of the United States, Chertoff exemplified a long-held "American story" of the multigenerational immigrant subject. The grandson and son of two Talmud scholars invested in studying Jewish civil and religious law, Chertoff's familial past accessed a pre-1965 Hart-Cellar Act story, which by 2001 lacked the "recent-memory" power of Dinh's 1978 refugee story of escape. Alternatively, within this context whiteness functions as a hegemonic index of privilege and power. Accordingly, Chertoff's unmarked status as a Jewish American in the confirmation hearings attests to his location within an assimilated U.S. hierarchy.[23]

Yet Chertoff's citizenship status—as an American—would ironically materialize as a contested issue among ultraconservative bloggers, hate group organizations, and anti-Israel pundits despite his neoconservative credentials.[24] Following Chertoff's 2005 nomination as secretary of the Department of Homeland Security, speculation arose in far right-wing corners as to whether Bush's pick was a "true" American citizen. Citing the candidate's matrilineal background (Chertoff's mother was an Israeli national), conspiracy theorists vociferously challenged Chertoff's allegiance to the United States. Such attacks, which quickly assumed anti-Semitic tones and recapitulated racist arguments about a "Jewish global conspiracy," repeatedly mentioned the "fact"that Israeli law allowed non-native Jews citizenship status. Whereas Dinh's maternal recollection was largely accepted because it reproduced a story of repudiation of Vietnam, vital to the Chertoff controversy was Chertoff's mother, who allegedly, through reproduction, created a foreign and possibly traitorous body.[25]

This de jure citizenship, wherein the child of an Israeli national was presumably automatically granted political nation-state status, was never authenticated by mainstream presses and media outlets. In fact, the charge of dual citizenship was denied by Chertoff himself. Situated within a more expansive framework, the accusation of disloyalty via dual citizenship intersects with a century-long anti-transnational logic. On the one hand, such a reactionary line of reasoning characterized Chertoff as an Israeli citizen because of birthright (as the son of an Israeli national). On the other hand, the would-be homeland security secretary was an "American" by birthplace (in Elizabeth, New Jersey). The contestation over Chertoff's supposed dual citizenship, predicated on familial affiliation, highlights the still probationary limitations of Jewish Americanness within the dominant twenty-first-century U.S. imaginary.

Even so, Dinh and Chertoff were successfully confirmed by a 96–1 and 95–1 Senate vote, respectively (with the sole dissent coming from the newly elected Democratic senator from New York, Hillary Rodham Clinton). All in all, Dinh and Chertoff—despite discernible differences in the content of the 2001 Senate Judiciary confirmation hearings—were implicitly and explicitly read as two naturalized model minorities. For the Vietnamese American Dinh, his status as a model minority was confirmed in accordance with a pro-U.S. cold war/Vietnam War–era narrative and Horatio Alger "refugee rags to U.S. citizen riches" story. For the Jewish American Chertoff, his model minorityhood initially afforded the candidate an unquestioned American citizenship. If the political task before literary producers Abraham Cahan, Edith Maude Eaton, Mary Antin, and Israel Zangwill was to legitimize the immigrant U.S. citizen, then it would appear in the cases of Dinh and Chertoff that their twentieth-century arguments had reached fruition and resolution by 2001.

What is more, the very strategies each used to challenge assertions of inassimilability and perpetual foreignness—constructed through citizenship grammar, pledges of allegiance, and naturalization rhetoric—are apparent in the Dinh-Chertoff confirmation hearings. At stake for each candidate (admittedly at very different points) is the proof of one's loyalty to the nation-state through legible means of repudiation and negation. In Dinh's case, such refutation involved the cold war and communist Vietnam. In the Chertoff circumstance, the denial of Israeli political affiliations functioned as requirement for his continued political U.S. citizenship. Still, the questions around Chertoff's citizenship in particular make evident the bifurcated Jewish immigrant body as expressed in Eva Hoffman's *Lost in Translation* and underscore the political work left to be done at the level of identity politics. Concurrently, the cold war, post–civil rights dimensions that necessarily inflected the Dinh hearings in particular attest to the voluntary affiliations of Gish Jen's protagonist Mona and politics of containment in Chin Y. Lee's *Flower Drum Song.*

In the face of such "citizenship trials," it is therefore all the more striking that both Dinh and Chertoff would, in less than four months, be at the forefront of writing one of the most far-reaching pieces of immigration regulation into law: the 2001 USA PATRIOT Act. Despite the progressive politics that arguably made possible the confirmation of two "minority" candidates, Dinh and Chertoff would take on the more conservative anti-immigrant work of Murkherjee's heroine Jasmine, whose U.S. selfhood is predicated on and strengthened through her ability to enforce the "closed door" desires of the state. Whether such work took the form of law or the shape of a border fence, both Justice Department employees would be responsible for demarcating the U.S. nation in the opening decade of the twenty-first century.

A Question of Security: Demarcating the Nation

> *A truck and a keen sense of horse-trading had provided a good living for Herman Fine. He bought from and sold primarily to Japanese hotel-keepers and grocers. No transaction was made without considerable haggling and clever maneuvering, for the Japanese . . . were a shifty lot whose solemn promises frequently turned out to be groundwork for more extended and complex stratagems to cheat him out of his rightful profit. Herman Fine listened to the radio and cried without tears for the Japanese, who, in an instant of time that was not even a speck on the big calendar, had taken their place beside the Jew. The Jew was used to suffering. The writing for them was etched in caked and dried blood over countless generations upon generations. The Japanese did not know. . . . The Jap-Jew would look in the mirror this Sunday night and see a Jap-Jew.*
>
> —JOHN OKADA, *NO NO BOY*

At the beginning of September 2001, with a U.S. foreign policy agenda largely focused on the "China question," the Bush administration turned its domestic attention to the increasingly difficult "immigration question." As had haunted previous administrations, what to do with foreign bodies would persist as a touchstone issue for President George W. Bush, who on the campaign trail repeatedly promised immigration reform. Even after the passage of the 1986 Immigration Reform and Control Act, which granted 2.6 million undocumented immigrants amnesty, and the 1996 Immigration Law Amendments, which legislatively strengthened provisions for policing and deporting immigrants, immigration remained a "front and center" issue, directed primarily at the estimated three million undocumented workers from Mexico.[27] Amid a resurgent nativism revealed through amplified calls to build a wall between Mexico and the United States, the second president Bush attempted (at least publicly) to mediate a more "compassionate conservative" response to the immigrant issue.

On September 5, 2001, the White House prepared for its first official meeting with a foreign head of state. The summit, which came out of the American president's oft-repeated campaign assertion that "U.S. foreign policy begins at home," involved President Vicente Fox of Mexico.[28] Over an intense two-day period, which included an unprecedented joint cabinet session between Mexican and U.S. officials, Bush and Fox eventually agreed to further bilateral talks about temporary worker programs, free trade agreements, and immigration regulation. As the Bush/Fox meeting drew to a close, the White House optimistically issued a U.S./Mexico joint statement on September 6, 2001, pronouncing that:

> Both Presidents agreed that U.S.-Mexican relations have entered their most promising moment in history. Our governments are committed to seizing the opportunities before us in this new atmosphere of mutual trust. The depth, quality and candor of our dialogue is unprecedented. It reflects the democratic values we share and our commitment to move forward boldly as we deepen this authentic partnership of neighbors.[29]

Stressing promise, trust, candor, and democratic values, the Bush White House release foretold a new vista in Mexico/U.S. relations built on collective goals and mutual agreements about undocumented Mexican immigrant bodies. Addressing what many anti-immigrant advocates considered the perilous porosity of the Mexico/U.S. border, the White House statement temporarily eschewed a delineated "us versus them" understanding in favor of neighborly characterizations and mutual understandings of democratic virtue.

In spite of benevolent bilateralism on the immigration policy horizon, the September 11 attacks on the World Trade Center and Pentagon five days later unquestionably reconfigured national discussions over immigration and irrefutably changed the direction of U.S. foreign policy. Memories of the Hainan Island incident and its subsequent political machinations quickly faded from national and political memory. The story of the 9/11 hijackers—as unlawful and infiltrating immigrants—not only outlined the perimeters of the War on Terror but also delineated a connected "war on immigration." Allowed admission to the nation through "limitless" open-door visa programs, the hijackers took disastrous advantage of a purportedly too-permeable U.S. immigration policy.

Central to the War on Terror was the Bush Administration's assault on the transnational flows of bodies into the nation. Regardless of the fact that all but one of the hijackers came from Saudi Arabia, U.S. foreign policy centered its sights on other nations in the Middle East—in particular Afghanistan, Pakistan, Iraq, and Iran. Following suit, Arab and South Asian American men in the United States were targeted, fingerprinted, and tracked. As many contemporary scholars and some media outlets at the time noted, the treatment of Middle Eastern and South

Asian/American subjects echoed of the racialized management of Japanese and Japanese Americans six decades prior.

Responding to critiques of the administration's racial/religious profiling of both U.S. citizens and immigrants by alleged ethnic activists, historians, and politicians, Asian American conservative pundit and Fox News fixture Michelle Malkin authored *In Defense of Internment: The Case for Racial Profiling in World War II and the War on Terror* (2004).[30] Tired of such individuals "repeatedly play[ing] the World War II internment card after the September 11 attacks," Malkin argued that:

> The Bush Administration's critics have equated every reasonable measure to interrogate, track, detain, and deport potential terrorists with the "racist" and "unjustified" World War II internment policies of President Roosevelt. To make amends for this "shameful blot" on our history, both Japanese-American and Arab/Muslim-American activists argue against any and all uses of race, ethnicity, nationality, and religion in shaping current homeland security policies. Misguided guilt about the past continues to hamper our ability to prevent future terrorist attacks.[31]

Though Malkin's *In Defense of Internment* was panned for its historical inaccuracies and bombastic claims, her "defense" of the Bush administration's interrogation and detainment of "potential terrorists" makes plain the neoconservative War on Terror strategy.[32] Written three years after the planes crashed into the World Trade Center Towers, the Pentagon, and a Shanksville, Pennsylvania field, Malkin's contentions capture the neoconservative moment. Opportunistically drawing on the recent memory of the 9/11 attacks, neoconservative lawmakers used the threat of "imminent attack" to justify its expansion of U.S. military power. The neoconservative assault on civil rights and civil liberties in the aftermath of the attacks corresponded to a platform that called for the delimitation of the "domestic."

Spearheading initiatives that facilitated increased border patrol, interrogation, detainment, and deportation, the Department of Homeland Security brought into one bureaucratic space the multifaceted police work of the Immigration and Natuaralization Service (INS) and the Department of Justice. Whereas the Fox/Bush meeting days before September 11 motioned toward a possible opening up of borders via temporary worker programs, the post-9/11 creation of the Department of Homeland Security answered the reactionary call to rid the country of pathogenic elements and once again "shut the door." Mediating the "threat over there" alongside "threats over here," the turn-of-the-twenty-first-century focus on immigration regulation and discussions about immigrant bodies bring to light an increasingly rigid construction between the foreign-born, the native-born, and the naturalized.

Specifically, for those foreign-born and/or naturalized, the question of citizenship relied on the legibility of what constituted an "American" body. For Muslims/Muslim Americans, Middle Eastern/Middle Eastern Americans, and South Asian/South Asian Americans, the administration's intimation of an immigrant fifth column harkens back to Malkin's aforementioned justification of internment. Such characterizations also make evident a racialized terrorist script that in turn fueled attacks on mosques, personal assaults, and hate speech. For those outside of those scripts (like Dinh and Chertoff), the nonterrorist "friend of the state" was afforded unquestioned U.S. citizenship and, by extension, the hegemonic power of whiteness.[33] The classification of "Americans" versus "non-Americans" was forged via fears over "legality" and "security." The judicial treatment of both legal and undocumented immigrants as lawless, heretofore uncontrolled threats to U.S. nationhood and national security expose a War on Terror imaginary marked by the inflexible redrawing of boundaries, the increased policing of national spaces, and the heightened concern to standardize movement across borders.

Unmaking Americans: The USA PATRIOT Act and Immigration Policy

The push to stem post-1965 waves of immigration makes available a crucial context in which to contemplate Viet Dinh's political position in the Bush administration's War on Terror. Cynically renamed "Viet Spin" by critics because of the assistant attorney general's penchant for political maneuvering, Dinh found renewed relevance within a multivalent matrix of "us versus them" allegations, anti-immigrant sentiment, and anti-Arab and anti-South Asian anxiety.[34] As a refugee made good, Dinh's nonwhite racial identity and non-U.S. birthright offered conservatives an immigrant story that carried the potential to deflect assertions of nativism, counter allegations of racism, and support claims of U.S. exceptionalism and "progress."

In addition, Dinh's commitment to idealized democracy and hawkish U.S. foreign policy was in sync with prevailing neoconservative platforms. Specifically, Dinh's racial diversity, refugee past, and affective patriotism fit a conservative cooptation of multiculturalism focused on identity difference and ideological sameness. As many have noted, the George W. Bush cabinet was among the more racially (though not ideologically) diverse cabinets ever assembled. Nevertheless, Condoleeza Rice, Alberto Gonzales, and others were very much committed conservatives. Similar to Dinh with regard to his strategic deployment of the Vietnam War, Rice had on at least one occasion (in a *60 Minutes* interview), likened the civil rights movement to the U.S. position in the War on Terror.[35]

As a 2002 *Los Angeles Times* article titled "At Home in War on Terror" makes clear, Dinh had become a powerful member of the Bush administration "brain trust" after 9/11. Stressing that he "did not sign up for war," Dinh nonetheless maintained that after September 11 "it's a profound honor really to serve your country in a time of crisis. I can't imagine a better place for me to be right now."[36] Dinh's vocalization of "patriotic honor" calls to mind his earlier performance during the Senate Judiciary Committee hearings and officious function at the Ellis Island naturalization ceremony. Further, the assistant attorney general's pronouncement of national service speaks directly to a post-September 11 sense of public duty in the face of terrorism. Most significant, this same articulation evokes naturalization via the citizenship oath's requirement of loyalty and service.

As a model minority, a model citizen, and a naturalized subject, Dinh publicly voices a willingness to "serve and protect" the U.S. nation. Such declarations are reminiscent of the naturalization oath, which requires successful applicants to make the following promise:

> I will support and defend the Constitution and laws of the United States of America against all enemies, foreign and domestic; that I will bear true faith and allegiance to the same; that I will bear arms on behalf of the United States when required by the law; that I will perform noncombatant service in the armed forces of the United States when required by the law; that I will perform work of national importance under civilian direction when required by the law; and that I take this obligation freely without any mental reservation or purpose of evasion; so help me God.[37]

Accordingly, Dinh's declaration of service echoes to varying degrees required U.S. selfhood. Though Dinh would not militarily "bear arms on behalf of the United States," the assistant attorney general "performed work of national importance under civilian direction." And, Dinh's performance of noncombatant service in the armed forces would take the form of regulating bodies deemed "enemy combatants" in the administration's War on Terror.

Explicitly, Dinh's "work of national importance" took form in the 2001 Uniting and Strengthening America by Providing Appropriate Tools Required to Intercept and Obstruct Terrorism Act (the aforementioned USA PATRIOT Act). Co-authored with fellow judicial nominee Michael Chertoff, the USA PATRIOT Act was passed six weeks after the 9/11. Spanning 342 pages, hastily written, and quickly approved in the spirit of "homeland security," the Dinh-Chertoff legislative act dramatically reshaped U.S. domestic and foreign policy to fit contemporaneous neoconservative politics. Ironically, the legislative purview of the act makes problematical the issue of "defending the Constitution," for it distinctively limited constitutional protections for citizens and noncitizens alike.

Committed to the Bush principle that "U.S. foreign policy begins at home," the Dinh-Chertoff PATRIOT Act legislatively revised the lines between immigration law and U.S. initiatives abroad. Expanding the reach of governmental power vis-à-vis U.S. citizens, the PATRIOT Act made possible the extensive policing of multiple bodies and groups through rubrics of war and terrorism. Within this politicized backdrop, Dinh's self-characterization as a subject willing to serve his country (implicitly along with Chertoff) is principally built on the creation and wholesale support of mechanisms intended to limit civil liberties, heighten immigration regulation, and punish through denaturalization (apparent in deportations of those deemed dangerous to the nation-state). Thus, Dinh (and to a lesser extent Chertoff) "remade" himself again, transforming from cold war warrior to frontline soldier in the post-September 11 War on Terror.

Crucial to the PATRIOT Act was the question of state-legitimized selfhood, inclusive of affiliations to and rights afforded by a political nation-state.[38] At the same time, the regulation of foreign bodies made possible through the act forces a legislative reading through immigrant frames. The key surveillance provisions of the PATRIOT Act—which codified the means through which terrorists could be apprehended domestically as well as abroad—necessarily engaged immigration and immigrant rights. As Nancy Chang, senior litigation attorney at the Center for Constitutional Rights, argues:

> The executive branch's ability to conduct surveillance and gather

> intelligence, places an array of new tools at the disposal of the prosecution, including new crimes, enhanced penalties, and longer statutes of limitations, and grants the Immigration and Naturalization Service (INS) the authority to detain immigrants suspected of terrorism for lengthy, and in some cases indefinite, periods of time. And at the same time that the Act inflates the power of the executive [branch], it insulates the exercise of these powers from meaningful judicial and Congressional oversight.[39]

The new home order created by the PATRIOT Act eliminated constitutional protections for immigrants (especially with regard to due process) and enabled the INS to detain noncitizen suspects for seven days before bringing criminal charges. The act made legislatively feasible the detention of immigrants without scrutiny. Analogous to the treatment of enemy combatants in Guantanamo Bay, those domestically detained could be held without charge and without access to a court of law for a period of up to six months.[40]

While the PATRIOT Act did not introduce new deportation legislation per se, it did give local, state, and federal agencies the power to ascertain immigrant threats to the nation. At the level of denaturalization logics, the Dinh-Chertoff act did strengthen—through enforcement—a specific provision in the 1996 immigration laws. This provision, whereby an immigrant (or alien) who had committed an "aggravated felony" was subject to arrest and deportation, became a functioning apparatus for retroactively ridding the nation of "undesirable bodies." The term "aggravated felony" was at best inexact, impacting a wide array of individuals. Crimes that fell into this category included bad check writing (or kite-checking), forgery, tax evasion, domestic abuse, and more severe felonies such as assault, drug-trafficking, robbery, and murder.[41]

A month after the passage of the PATRIOT Act, Michael Chertoff, the assistant attorney general in charge of the criminal division, was asked by the Senate Judiciary Committee to respond to allegations that the Bush administration was failing to "respect the checks and balances that make up our constitutional framework." Answering Senator Patrick J. Leahy (D-Vermont), Chertoff averred, "Are we being aggressive and hard-nosed? You bet we are. In the aftermath of September 11, how could we not be?"[42] At issue in the hearings was the unilateral strategy of the administration vis-à-vis the detainment and interrogation of alleged terrorist suspects without Congressional approval. Following the passage of the PATRIOT Act, the Bush administration issued a number of executive orders, including one that gave the president the right to try a suspected terrorist before a secret military tribunal that could, on two-thirds majority vote, impose the death penalty. Within a month, the Justice Department had questioned thousands of men from Middle Eastern countries and monitored conversations between lawyers and some defendants. The same week of the Senate Judiciary hearings, the Justice Department for the first time disclosed the names of ninety-three individuals in custody under federal criminal charges, but Chertoff's superior—Attorney General John Ashcroft—refused to release the names of another 548 people arrested on charges of violating immigration regulations.

Analogous though not identical to the legislative treatment of World War II internees, the combination of surveillance and implied loyalty oaths in the USA PATRIOT Act parallels the multilateral efforts facilitated by President Franklin Delano Roosevelt's Executive Order 9066, which facilitated the mass detainment of Japanese/Japanese Americans. The subsequent recruitment of Japanese/Japanese American men through the 1943 War Relocation Authority leave clearance program further parallels the "patriotic" dimensions of the Dinh-Chertoff act. On January 29, 1943, the War Relocation Authority sent out a press release detailing an application process for exiting the camps. Those interested in leaving were required to register and fill out an application. Among other questions on the 1943 Leave Clearance Application, the following two questions proved most significant for men of Japanese descent: "Are you willing to serve in the armed forces of the United States on combat duty wherever ordered?" and "Will you swear unqualified allegiance to the United States of America and faithfully defend the United States from any or all attack by foreign or domestic forces, and forswear any form of allegiance or obedience to the Japanese emperor, to any other foreign government, power, or organization?"[43] Both questions grammatically reflect the naturalization oath.

In particular, the willingness to "serve" is central to the first question, which directly interrogates the desire of the applicant to militarily defend the U.S. nation-state. The second question is in actuality three separate inquiries that use, as a primary subject, the practice of U.S. citizenship. At issue initially is the problem of allegiance vis-à-vis the Japanese/Japanese American applicant. The issue of allegiance is reconfirmed and revised to ascertain affective willingness to "faithfully defend the United States," which evidently references the first question about military service. The requirement to "forswear any form of allegiance" replicates the previous condition to "swear unqualified allegiance." Altogether, this citizenship polemic, which demands "unqualified allegiance to the United States," uses the grammatical structure of the naturalization oath by requiring applicants to declare their love of country, defend the nation, and repudiate alleged transnational connections to Japan.

Simultaneously, to answer in the positive is to engage in a naturalized rhetoric of state-authorized U.S. citizenship. Conversely, negative responses were, as the imprisonment of so-called "no no boys" reveals, judged by the state as unpatriotic and anti-American acts. As a grammatical consideration of the Leave Clearance Application makes visible, the codification of loyalty to the nation followed a logic of repudiation. The grammar of post-Pearl Harbor citizenship adhered to a linguistic relationships wherein U.S. loyalty was necessarily established in contradiction to Japanese affiliations. Repudiation—which carries connotations of denial and refusal—is relevant to the politicized rhetoric that accompanied justifications of the PATRIOT Act.

The PATRIOT Act has understandably been analyzed through anti-neoconservative critiques focused primarily on the policing of civil liberties. Yet the very tenets that undergird it—establishing loyalty through covert surveillance and the delimitation of specific free speech freedoms—harkens back to previous denaturalization efforts and foregrounds a citizenship-oriented reading. In other words, at stake in the act's prevailing narrative is the rhetorical distinction it makes between American citizens and "enemies of the state." Integral to both the Dinh-Chertoff act and U.S. naturalization policy is the state-authorized ability to determine those bodies suitable for selfhood. Within this context, the practices engendered by the PATRIOT Act and extant naturalization law implicitly echoed past restrictionist policies and nativist arguments about "real Americans" and loyal citizens, paving the way for the removal of U.S. selfhood (denaturalization). From the surveillance of foreign students to the categorization of "terrorist aliens," the act attempted to determine through politically unbridled scrutiny, containment, and detainment "immigrant enemies."

Read through the rubrics of immigration, the PATRIOT Act naturally speaks to the grammar of immigration policy and naturalization law. As a domestic and foreign enterprise forged through the transnational routes (inclusive of countries of origin, foreign policy initiatives, and imperial endeavors), twentieth-century immigration policy is constructed through largely rigid languages of regulation and containment. The regulation rhetoric that necessarily undergirds immigration policy was historically unyielding in naturalization law, which from the outset collapsed the space between geographic borders (or ethnic classifications) and racial characterizations. Initially articulated in 1790 to include "free white persons," naturalization law adhered to a binary racial logic well into the twentieth century. And, the PATRIOT Act, which similarly deploys such binaries, makes visible the demarcated dimensions of immigration law and citizenship discourse into the twenty-first century.

Resistive Acts and Progressive Conclusions

Indeed, Socioeconomic and cultural anxieties over immigrant bodies and their ability to move through borders fueled and continue to fuel immigration politics. Such politics reflect a century-long national dialectical struggle over thresholds, constitutive of open-door versus closed-door debates. Nevertheless, as evident in the work of authors included in *Modeling Citizenship*, the border was indeed challenged. In turn, these challenges—which strategically deployed the state-authorized requirements of naturalization—signal a potential resistive politics focused on viable and undeniable citizenship. Such resistive politics, which take place in the public imaginary of the published page, reveal the contradictions of U.S. nationhood and the limitations of U.S. selfhood, and foreground possibilities for change.

The political work of model minority writers through constitutional due process and citizenship is reflected in the larger arena of political protest at the turn of the twenty-first century. Of the many activists who challenged the PATRIOT Act, Japanese American Fred Korematsu makes most apparent a politics of resistance that militates against model minoritization and naturalized complicity. If Viet Dinh and Michael Chertoff represent the apex of naturalized neoconservatism and the failure of "identity politics" to push for systemic change, then Fred Korematsu's six-decade-long story of denaturalization, retroactive absolution, and political protest engenders an alternative resistance formed through the removal of citizenship.

Fred Korematsu chose not to go to a processing center for Japanese/Japanese American evacuees in accordance with Franklin D. Roosevelt's February 19, 1942, issuance of Executive Order 9066. On May 30, 1942, Korematsu was arrested and sent to Tanforan processing center. Korematsu was then transferred to the Topaz internment camp in Utah. Protesting his arrest and forced relocation, the Japanese American internee filed a lawsuit against the U.S. government, maintaining that his constitutional rights as a U.S. citizen had been violated. His conviction and internment was upheld in a lower court, where Korematsu was found guilty of violating the order and sentenced to five years probation.[44] He appealed the lower court's ruling, and in 1944 *Korematsu v. United States* was heard before the Supreme Court.

In a 6–3 decision, the Supreme Court upheld the constitutionality of Executive Order 9066, stating that Korematsu's orders for evacuation did not reflect "hostility to him or his race." The conviction stood and would remain on Korematsu's record for the next forty years. Largely forgotten until the civil rights movement, Fred Korematsu was silent about his internment experience. However, as the Japanese American redress movement gathered political steam in the late 1970s and early 1980s, attention returned to the Koreamtsu case. In 1982, a legal team headed by Dale Minami sought to overturn Korematsu's conviction, successfully doing so in 1984. The ruling reinvigorated the redress movement, and the Reagan administration issued an official U.S. government apology. In 1988, Congress passed the Civil Liberties Act, which afforded reparations for surviving internees. A decade later, in 1998, President Bill Clinton awarded Korematsu the Presidential Medal of Freedom, the highest honor given to a civilian. Recognizing Fred Korematsu's position as a civil rights activist, the president averred, "In the long history of our country's constant search for justice, some names of ordinary citizens stand for millions of souls—Plessy, Brown, Parks. To that distinguished list we add the name of Fred Korematsu."[45] Ironically, all those mentioned by the president "sought justice" precisely because they were denied the rights of U.S. citizens.

It would be easy to read Korematsu's twentieth-century struggle through the essentialized frame of identity politics. However, central to Korematsu's case—from the 1944 Supreme Court ruling to the 1998 Presidential Medal of Freedom ceremony—is the issue of denaturalization. Reclaiming his rights as a U.S. citizen in the face of internment, Korematsu challenged the racialized regulation of bodies. Despite his model minority status, the Japanese American nonetheless vocalized protest. And, though *Korematsu v. United States* was on the surface about Japanese American selfhood, it would resurface after 9/11 as a powerful reminder of overreaching government power, abuse, and state-sanctioned removals of citizenship.

Sixty years after *Korematsu v. United States,* the internment plaintiff wrote an amicus curiae brief on behalf of the defendant in *Rumsfeld v. Padilla*. In the brief, Korematsu drew on his own denaturalization experiences, stressing that allowing the Bush Administration (including Viet Dinh and Michael Chertoff) to "decide unilaterally who to detain, and for how long" would cause "our country will repeat the same mistake of the past."[46] The court, ruling in favor of the defendant, restored citizenship, confirming the right of U.S. citizens to due process and civil rights protection. Additionally, the court's ruling afforded similar rights to Guantanamo Bay detainees, who up to that point were juridically stateless.

If Fred Korematsu's Supreme Court case and civil rights activism speak to both twentieth- and twenty-first-century citizenship struggles, then Palestinian American poet, political activist, and slam artist Suheir Hammad, like the other authors included above, articulates (through writing) a similar agenda. In particular, Hammad implicitly uses the politics of denaturalization as a means to a justice-oriented end. In "First Writing Since," Hammad attempts to make verbal sense of her experiences as a noncitizen Arab American in a post-9/11 imaginary. A spoken word poem divided into seven parts, Hammad begins: "There have been no words. / I have not written one word. / no poetry in the ashes south of canal street. / no prose in the refrigerated trucks driving debris and dna."[47] Rendered silent by the 9/11 attacks and politically voiceless because of her Arab American-ness, Hammad nonetheless finds a resistive voice as the poem continues. Such expression is globally expanded to include both Americans and non-Americans impacted by the War on Terror.

Stressing that those "who will pay" will be "women, mostly colored and poor," Hammad observes:

> women will have to bury children, and support themselves through grief. "either you are with us, or with the terrorists"—meaning keep your people under control and your resistance censored. Meaning we got the loot and the nukes. / in america, it will be those amongst us who refuse blanket attacks on the shivering. those of us who work toward social justice, in support of civil liberties, in opposition to hateful foreign policies.[48]

Hammad's purposeful deployment of the Bush administration rhetoric, reminiscent of Viet Dinh's interview in the opening epigraph, is made less stable through definition. The women (who lack selfhood modifiers) are in effect stateless subjects. Drawing on the binary grammar of "either/or," implicit in "American" versus "terrorist," Hammad highlights the neoconservative imperial logics that give rise to the use of military power embodied by "the nukes" and built on the "loot" of U.S. capitalism. Hammad's articulation of "control" and "censorship" establishes the stakes for resistance, which will be based on poetic—and therefore publicly enunciated—refusal.

In this regard, the Palestinian American poet performs a statelessness (confirmed by her admission that she feels "less American" and more "New York") and revises the repuditative requirements of naturalization to fit a post-9/11 social justice order. Hence, like Korematsu, Hammad underscores the limitations of nation-state affiliation and naturalized complicity. Hammad draws on the power of refusal, vocally opposing "hateful foreign policies." Her denaturalized position further enables a non-state-authorized support of "social justice" and "civil liberties." Eschewing state-sanctioned citizenship, Suheir Hammad amends through selfhood the immigrant-focused activism of Abraham Cahan, Mary Antin, Edith Maude Eaton, and Israel Zangwill. At the same time, within a post-September 11 world of mixed feelings, the poet's initial ambivalence speaks to Gish Jen's *Mona in the Promised Land*, Chin Y. Lee's *The Flower Drum Song*, and Eva Hoffman's *Lost in Translation*. Most important, in foregrounding an alternative global citizenship, predicated on transnational civil rights, antiracist politics, and anti-imperial logics, Suheir Hammad signals a new, unbounded space for justice, modeling a progressive template for twenty-first century immigrant acts.

Epilogue: "A Sense of Loss and Anomie": Model Minorities and Twenty-First-Century Citizenship

For a while, we assumed that all Indians were geniuses. Then, in the 1980s, the doctors and engineers brought over their merchant cousins, and we were no longer so sure about the genius thing. In the 1990s, the not-so-brilliant merchants brought their even-less-bright cousins, and we started to understand why India is so damn poor . . . sometime after I left [Edison, New Jersey], the town became a maze of charmless Indian strip malls and housing developments. Whenever I go back, I feel what people in Arizona talk about: a sense of loss and anomie and disbelief that anyone can eat food that spicy.

—JOEL STEIN, "MY OWN PRIVATE INDIA"

In July 2010, *Time* magazine published an op-ed authored by Jewish American cultural critic and sometimes-comedian Joel Stein entitled "My Own Private India."[1] Focused on shifting demographics in a post-1965 Hart-Cellar Act America, "My Own Private India" commences with nominal and thematic allusions to Gus Van Sant's dystopic film *My Own Private Idaho* (1991).[2] Just as Van Sant's Shakespeare-inspired production drew its narrative power from a story of two drifters searching for refuge in an inhospitable landscape, "My Own Private India" is shaped by a profound disconnection with Edison, New Jersey, Stein's self-proclaimed hometown. Divergently, whereas *My Own Private Idaho* reveals a sense of hopelessness within a homogenous West, Stein's "My Own Private India" concentrates its less-than-idealized attention on South Asian immigrants, who are the principal source of Edison's alienhood and Stein's concomitant alienation.

Indeed, as the opening epigraph underscores and the rest of "My Own Private India" makes clear, Edison is by and large characterized as a foreign landscape, composed of charmless Indian strip malls and housing developments. The alleged foreign takeover of New Jersey's modest metropole (population 100,000) foregrounds Stein's paradoxical immigration politics, epitomized by the author's claim that he is "very much in favor of immigration everywhere in the U.S. except Edison, N.J." Without a doubt, Stein's sardonic nativism hit a relevant chord amid a backdrop of increasing population anxiety and regulation, redolent in restrictive anti-immigration acts such as Arizona's infamous SB 1070.[3] Notwithstanding the article's political timeliness, "My Own Private India" was also incontrovertibly controversial.

Specifically critiqued for its cavalier use of racial slurs, casual references to racial violence, and relatively facile arguments about contemporary "immigrant questions," Stein's op-ed drew ire from progressives, pro-immigration activists, and South Asian Americans.[4] Putting aside briefly such valid criticisms, "My Own Private India" nonetheless functions as a significant bellwether for twenty-first-century debates over sentimental selfhood, socioeconomic naturalization, and the "making of new Americans." Written from the perspective of an anti-immigration advocate, assuming the guise of white nostalgia and white alienation, and distrustful of transnational bodies and globalized frames, Stein's op-ed recuperates past nativist discourses and revises them to fit a conservative multiculturalist agenda. Equally provocative, Stein's own location as a Jewish American model minority is eschewed in favor of an unmarked white selfhood forged through the racialization of another model minority group: Asian Americans. Indeed, Stein's racialized and often racist arguments about the changing face of U.S. citizenship tactically use the affective power of immigration to structure feelings of dislocation, defamiliarization, and denaturalization.[5] In so doing, "My Own Private India" renders identifiable the contested contours of race, ethnicity, and nation in a supposedly postracial, post–Barack Obama age.

Correspondingly, central to "My Own Private India" is a dislocating sense of loss and anomie forged in the crucible of foreign-born difference. Suggestive of a "social instability resulting from a breakdown of standards and values," anomie is etymologically embedded in alienation. Moreover, drawing on Stein's use of the term, "anomie" bespeaks a societal breakdown born out of immigration.[6] Stein's Edison is thus cast as an economic, sociocultural casualty of the 1965 Immigration and Nationality Act (a.k.a. Hart-Cellar Act), which enabled the en bloc arrival of an estimated twenty million immigrants from Latin America, Central America, and the Eastern Hemisphere (Asia). Satirically rooted, conceived, and produced, "My Own Private India" is strategically forgetful of U.S. immigration history and politics. As Stein problematically recounts, "Lyndon Johnson's 1965 immigration law raised immigration caps for non-European countries. LBJ apparently had some weird relationship with Asians in which he liked both inviting them over and going over to Asia to kill them." The flippancy of Stein's historicization with regard to monumental immigration legislation and costly U.S. foreign policy eschews political complexity in favor of hipster "newspeak."

Such quick-witted yet nonetheless politicized dismissals are time and again employed in "My Own Private India," and Stein purposefully uses irony to disremember troubling aspects of past racial discrimination. In the process, the writer puts forth an incomplete, essentialized reading of Asian immigration as an undifferentiated byproduct of mid-century domestic and foreign policy. To that end, Stein reads the Hart-Cellar Act as a paradox of thresholds and limits, situated between inviting Asians over and killing them. With no historical acknowledgement and with little attention paid to the heterogeneity of Asian America, including distinct ethnicities, histories, and cultures, Stein fails to note important transnational connections between "wars in Asia" and Asian immigrants.

In contrast to Stein's superficial examination of "Lyndon Johnson's 1965 immigration law," it is important to recall how cold war imperialism and civil rights activism played key roles in the changing of racialized immigration policy. Indeed, the Hart-Cellar Act was very much a consequence of foreign policy and domestic civil rights, for it was intended to bolster assertions of U.S. democratic virtue abroad and reconcile those claims within the United States. In the face of historicity, the unavoidable transnational registers of immigration policy (revealed in politics "over there" and policies "over here") are for the most part ignored in "My Own Private India." Instead, Stein's consideration of the extant "immigration problem" evaluates modern-day globalization by way of dominant U.S. ethnoracial logics. In establishing the contemporary "foreignization" of a "typical American" city, Stein avers that Edison has become "home to one of the biggest Indian communities in the U.S." Not only is Edison a significant destination within the Indian diaspora; his modest hometown is "as familiar to people in India as how to instruct stupid Americans to reboot their Internet routers." Stein irreverently accesses an expansive (and exploitative) global service economy which from the outset pits Indians (and by proxy, Indian Americans) against "stupid Americans." However, as "My Own Private India" continues, the nativist joke is largely on Indians and Indian Americans. Such ethnoracial hostilities reconfirm and concretize Stein's homeland alienation.

As important in "My Own Private India" is the role of space in the examination of globalization and race. Accordingly, the Edisonian's disaffection from his hometown is chiefly mapped via allusions to and acts of consumption. As Stein maintains,

> My town is totally unfamiliar to me. The Pizza Hut where my busboy friends stole pies for our drunken parties is now an Indian sweets shop with a completely inappropriate roof. The A&P I shoplifted from is now an Indian grocery. The multiplex where we snuck into R-rated movies now shows only Bollywood films and serves samosas. The Italian restaurant that my friends stole cash from as waiters is now Moghul, one of the most famous Indian restaurants in the country. There is an entire generation of white children in Edison who have nowhere to learn crime.

Circumscribed by multiple levels of "unfamiliarity," Stein's examples of spatial and demographic change—evident in reconditioned restaurants, converted grocery stores, and refurbished strip malls—constitute a dislocating "domestic-turned-foreign" narrative. Similarly, recognizable (and purportedly natural) "American" locations (Pizza Hut, the A&P, the multiplex, and the Italian restaurant) are concomitantly denaturalized by Indian immigration, influence, and assimilation.

Concentrated on sites of economic exchange and consumption, Stein employs late-century readings of transnationalism predicated on the unimpeded movement of bodies, commodities, and capital across borders. Equally crucial, in stating that "an entire generation of white children . . . have nowhere to learn crime," Stein commemorates white criminality while lamenting brown capitalism. In contrast to Neil Diamond's *Jazz Singer* celebration of immigration flows characteristic of the late 1970s and early 1980s, "My Own Private India" underscores an acute nativist feeling born in the aftermath of the North American Free Trade Agreement (NAFTA), in the shadow of September 11 attacks, and at the forefront of contemporary ultraconservative Tea Party platforms. Within this reactionary economic and political milieu, the "corruption" of the U.S. marketplace—made plain in the racialized "colonization" of Edison, New Jersey, by foreign bodies, businesses, and commodities—reinforces Stein's racialized assertion that he feels "what people in Arizona talk about: a sense of loss and anomie and disbelief that anyone can eat food that spicy."

Such disbelief that anyone can eat food that spicy further casts Indians and Indian Americans in accordance to incomprehensible geopolitical, multicultural frames. On one level, Stein's feeling of normlessness highlights an "us versus them" binary and signals a more expansive white sense of anomie. On another level, Stein (like past anti-immigration advocates who imagined a monolithic white past) privileges a homogenous reading of "the way things were" through racial nostalgia. Divergently, Stein's nostalgic evocation—suggested by a "sense of loss"—undeniably relies on the erasure of Jewish American difference. This ethnic eschewal occurs, to use George Lipstiz's model, through the author's "possessive investment in whiteness."[7] Besides, Edison is not just "India" but Stein's "*own private* India," which calls to mind privatization, capitalism, and possession. This individual ownership is grammatically supported by Stein's use of first-person pronouns and possessives ("I" and "my"). In a more collective manner, Stein's whiteness is situated alongside an expressed kinship with an entire generation of white children. Such whiteness, antithetically placed against Indianness, bridges (via race and class) the gap between the "Generation X" Stein and next-generation "Millennials."

Likewise, Stein's sense of loss and anomie is fixed to a two-sided tension about Indians and Indian Americans, who are both model minorities and perpetual foreigners. Substantiating a reading of "My Own Private India" as native-born complaint and anti-immigrant lament is Stein's incorporation of a degenerative immigrant succession narrative, which operates in stark contrast to the abovementioned generational whiteness. In "My Own Private India," post-1965 model minoritized Indian subjects (e.g., doctors and engineers) are quickly replaced over the course of two decades by less idealized, "not-as-brilliant" merchants in the 1980s and their "even-less-bright cousins" in the 1990s. Articulating generational descent, inclusive of subsequent immigration and marked by lessening economic viability, Stein characterizes three waves of South Asian immigration via denaturalized bodies that are no longer model minorities. In turn, these undesirable bodies are symptomatic of a disruptively disturbing nonwhite Edison. Increasingly working class and "un-American," such merchants and cousins racially legitimate Stein's confident classed declaration about "why India is so damn poor."

Returning to Stein's recollection of the past, the article's white-focused disaffection belies a violent racial history that impacted New Jersey's South Asian/South Asian American population. Particularly problematic is the treatment of anti-Asian violence in "My Own Private Idaho," which resembles a shorthand account of individualized (and physically nonthreatening) racist acts. According to Stein, the mass influx of South Asian immigrants prompted less than tolerant reactions, and his "townsfolk started calling the new Edisonians 'dot heads.'" A fellow student, as Stein relates, "drove down an Indian-dense street yelling for its residents to 'go home to

India.' In retrospect, I question how good our schools were if 'dot heads' was the best racist insult we could come up with for a group of people whose gods have multiple arms and an elephant nose." The "Indian-denseness" of the street corroborates Stein's previous assertions that Edison has become "India," yet the initial purpose of the passage—to adequately acknowledge nativist declaration and racial slur—is for the most part lost. In the place of racialized victims, Stein privileges white perpetrators, who are verbally critiqued but not morally condemned.[8] Instead, Edison's school system is satirized through "best racist insults," which fail to take full advantage of religious difference. By conflating two Hindu gods (Ganesh and Shiva), Stein denaturalizes further his hometown's nonwhite residents via racist name-calling and theologically insensitive articulation. Thus, for white Edisonians like Stein, the en masse demographic shifts that prompted racial attacks nonetheless make "palatable" the nativist sentiment felt by "people in Arizona."

If Stein relegates racist acts to the educational site (embodied by "fellow students"), then "My Own Private India" also actively disremembers the particulars of New Jersey's racially violent past, exemplified by a series of bias crimes committed by the self-named Dotbuster gang. As the racist name suggests, the Dotbusters targeted South Asians and South Asian Americans. In 1987, the Dotbuster attacks turned deadly. Tragically, thirty-year-old bank manager Navroze Mody was fatally beaten by some members of the gang, who during the attack reportedly chanted "Hindu! Hindu!"[9] Soon after, twenty-eight-year old Kaushal Saran was also brutally attacked and ended up in a coma. Such incidents eventually led to the passage of New Jersey's landmark Bias Crimes Law in the early 1990s.[10] This history of racial violence brings to light the political limitations at work in "My Own Private India," which eschews social justice in favor of conservative mediations on "white anomie."

Accordingly, Stein's reactionary and incomplete examination of Indian migration privileges a hopeless reading of Edison as immigrant-dominated dystopia. Not only is Edison indelibly marked by Indianness. Its South Asian/South Asian American population is markedly (and exceptionally) unassimilable. Distinctively, Stein argues, "unlike previous waves of immigrants, who couldn't fly home or Skype with relatives, Edison's first Indian generation didn't quickly assimilate (and give their kids Western names)." With regard to assimilation, Edison's first Indian generation is characterized even more negatively than previous waves of immigrants because of global telecommunication technologies (such as Skype), which enable the persistence of transnational affiliations.

Notwithstanding assumed inassimilability, "My Own Private India" closes with an incongruous kinship between Italians and Indians. Noting that "current Facebook photos of students at my old high school, J. P Stevens. . . look like the Italian Guidos I grew up within the 1980s," Stein contends that such "Guindians" have "assimilate[ed] so wonderfully that if the Statue of Liberty could shed a tear, she would. Because of the amount of cologne they wear." Inconsistent with the article's previous conflations of Italianness and whiteness, Stein nevertheless relies on a racialized reading of "Italian Guidos" that assumes a denaturalized register. And, despite declarations of "wonderful assimilation," these so-called Guindians are by and large "assimilated foreigners" who prompt tears of irritation from the iconic Mother of Exiles. This disconcerting comparison between Italians and Indians bespeaks a conservative multiculturalism which superficially acknowledges difference while insisting on an essentialized sameness.

In drawing to a close, and as "My Own Private India" makes clear, notwithstanding analogous characterizations within the dominant imaginary, at stake in current immigration debates is a conservative politics of white victimhood based on an "understandable" anomie of racialized anxiety. In other words, "My Own Private India" is on the whole an expression of legible nativism against South Asians and South Asian Americans. This empathetic reading of anti-immigration sentiment is substantiated by Joel Stein's response to the flood of emails and letters that followed *Time*'s online publication of "My Own Private India." Apologetically, Stein writes:

> I truly feel stomach-sick that I hurt so many people. I was trying to explain how, as someone who believes that immigration has enriched American life and my hometown in particular, I was shocked that I could feel a tiny bit uncomfortable with my changing town when I went to visit it. If we could understand that reaction, we'd be better equipped to debate people on the other side of the immigration issue.

In the face of Stein's contrite response, what emerges is a reiteration of dominant rubrics at work in "My Own Private India." Indeed, Stein's admission of feeling "a tiny bit uncomfortable" with demographic shifts produces a call to "understand that reaction" of "people on the other side of the immigration issue." With no specific mention of race, with no acknowledgement of anti-Asian racism, and with an emphasis on individual feelings, Stein attempts to ameliorate criticism through affect.

Though "shocked" by his own reaction, Stein implicitly issues an appeal to empathize not with victims of nativist, racist policy, and violence but with perpetrators.

In contrast, Sandip Roy offers an alternative identification that makes possible a more progressive coalition politics along the lines of immigration. To be sure, the antibrown frames expressed in "My Own Private India" are not limited to New Jersey's Indian/Indian American population. As Sandip Roy rightfully contends, for Stein and "Edison's old timers,"

> brown is brown. Too many curry shacks is not that different from too many taquerias. We are all Mexicans now. When Joel Stein goes to Edison, he "feels" what people in Arizona talk about. It's not about the papers you carry inasmuch as the "I-am-not-against-immigration-just-illegal-immigration" folks would have you believe. It is about the way you look, the food you eat, the accent you have. It is about the sense that you are taking over the strip mall. And, this American anxiety about its browning will not change.[11]

Focused on the affective dimensions of the contemporary immigration debate, Roy highlights the extent to which the perceived alien body structures feelings of anxiety and unfamiliarity. If "brown is brown," then Stein's negotiation of immigration brings to light the tenets of twenty-first-century nativism, which commences with an impending socioeconomic "brown peril."

Unintentionally, Roy's response underscores a link between the turn of the twentieth century and the turn of the twenty-first century. If W.E.B. Dubois presciently and evocatively argued that while the problem of the twentieth century was one of the "color line," then the dilemma facing the twenty-first century is the crisis of the "border line." Racially determined, and simultaneously focused on distinctions of nativity, illegality, and naturalization, such "border line" polemics—apparent in initiatives like SB 1070 and articles like "My Own Private India"—make visible the volatile and still-unresolved contours of U.S. citizenship. Alternatively, as "model minorities" and "perpetual foreigners," Jewish Americans and Asian Americans destabilize the dominant discourse around immigration, which evaluates citizenship potential according to frames of exclusion and politicized integration. Such unfixed questions of selfhood underscore the conditional foundations of U.S. nationhood, which time and again returns to immigration and the issue of how "Americans" are made by way of law, politics, and cultural production.

Notes

Preface

1. See David Kehr, "Review: *The Jazz Singer*," *Chicago Reader*, December 1980, http://www.chicagoreader.com/chicago/the-jazz-singer/Film?oid=1052131. A much earlier version of this preface, titled "Fathers, Sons, and Symbolic Ethnicity: Considering Two Generations of *The Jazz Singer*," appeared in the online magazine, *Magazine Americana*, http://www.americanpopularculture.com/archive/film/neil_diamond.htm. The film was directed by Richard Fleischer and released by Paramount Pictures, it premiered on December 19, 1980.

2. Brooklyn-born Richard Fleischer (1916–2006) was known primarily for his science fiction/fantasy productions, which included *Conan the Destroyer*, *Red Sonja*, and *Soylent Green*. He won an Oscar in 1947 for *Design for Death*, a documentary feature. Screenwriter Herbert Baker (1920–1983), known for his work with *The Danny Kaye Show*, was also the chief writer for two Elvis Presley films (*King Creole* and *Loving You*). *The Jazz Singer* would be Baker's final screenwriting credit. Neil Diamond (born in 1941) grew up in Brooklyn and was the Jewish Polish/Russian American son of a dry-goods merchant. Diamond was a top-selling singer/songwriter at the time of *The Jazz Singer*'s release. Other notable cast members included Sir Laurence Olivier in the role of Cantor Rabinovitch (the father) and the seasoned performer Lucie Arnaz (the daughter of Lucille Ball and Desi Arnaz) as Molly, Diamond's Gentile love interest.

3. Sociologist and critic Yen Le Espiritu uses Diamond's "America" to frame her reading of three immigration texts: *Immigrant America: A Portrait*, by Alejandro Portes and Ruben G. Rumbaut; *Becoming a Citizen: Incorporating Immigrants and Refugees in the United States and Canada*, by Irene Bloemraad; and *Unruly Immigrants: Rights, Activism, and Transnational South Asian Politics in the United States*, by Monisha Das Gupta. See "'They're Coming to America': Immigration, Settlement, and Citizenship," *Qualitative Sociology* 32.2 (June 2009): 221–227.

4. These readings were taken from reviews written by critics Hal Erikson, Paul

Brenner, and an unidentified *TV GUIDE* reviewer. Paradoxically, the film's star (Diamond) was nominated for a Golden Globe and a RAZZIE, which recognizes the worst performances in the entertainment industry.

5. See Paul Brenner, "The Jazz Singer," *All Movie Guide*, http://www.allmovie.com. Two other remakes of *The Jazz Singer* included a 1953 Danny Thomas version and a 1959 made-for-television remake starring Jerry Lewis. This humdrum reading was echoed by *New York Times* film commentator Janet Maslin, who maintained that Diamond's "transition from the Lower East Side bathrobes to Hollywood's V-necked sweaters with nothing underneath is made all too smoothly. . . . [It would] be no less preposterous if he started in Hollywood and wound up on the Lower East Side than it is right now. And that way, at least it would be *new*" (emphasis added). See Janet Maslin, "Movie Review: *The Jazz Singer*," *New York Times*, December 19, 1980.

6. As Chris Vials astutely notes, the miniseries signaled a seminal moment in American consciousness of the Judeocide.

7. Maslin, "Movie Review: *The Jazz Singer*."

8. Mass media magnate Henry Luce, publisher of *Time* and *Life*, referred to the twentieth century as the "American century."

9. Lauren Berlant, "Citizenship," in *Keywords for American Cultural Studies*, Bruce Brugett and Glen Hendler, eds. (New York: New York University Press, 2008), 37–38.

10. See the INS (Immigration and Naturalization Service) home page, December 15, 2001, http://www.ins.usdoj.gove/text.aboutins/statistics/LegisHist/553.htm.

11. Jerry Phillips's work on Herman Melville's phenomenological engagement with risk is especially illuminating, for he examines the interplay between capitalistic enterprise and adventure narratives.

12. Interestingly, Neil Diamond's allusion to the flag and the Statue of Liberty is reminiscent of Emma Lazarus's well-known, oft-quoted poem that is engraved in the statue's pedestal foundation, "The New Colossus." The poem, in its entirety, reads: "Not like the brazen giant of Greek fame, / With conquering limbs astride from land to land; / Here at our sea-washed, sunset gates shall stand / A mighty woman with a torch, whose flame / Is the imprisoned lightening, and her name / Mother of Exiles. / From her beacon-hand / Glows world-wide welcome; her mild eyes command / The air-bridged harbor that twin cities frame. / 'Keep ancient lands, your storied pomp!' cries she / With silent lips. 'Give me your tired, your poor, / Your huddled masses yearning to breathe free, / The wretched refuse of your teeming shore. / Send these, the homeless, tempest-tost to me, / I lift my lamp beside the golden door!'" http://www.libertystatepark.com/emma.html.

13. Michael Rogin, *Blackface, White Noise* (Berkeley: California University Press, 1996), 168. Additionally, *The Jazz Singer*'s final scene (along with its plot) is reminiscent of Israel Zangwill's 1908 play, *The Melting-Pot*, which is discussed in chapter 2.

14. In *Klezmer America* (2008), Jonathan Freedman furthers this reading of Diamond's now iconic immigrant composition vis-à-vis pro-immigration rallies in 2006.

15. "My Country, 'tis of Thee" at times functioned as the national anthem until the official adoption of Francis Scott Key's "The Star Spangled Banner" by Congress in 1931.

16. The Hasidic movement began in Eastern Europe (Poland and Ukraine), which incidentally reflects Diamond's own ethnic background.

17. Straus Square (formerly Rutgers Square) was an important site for turn-of-the-twentieth-century Jewish immigrants, who gathered for political meetings and rallies. The closing scene in the opening montage—a close-up of a street sign marking "Eldridge Street," continues the film's homage to Jewish American history, in that the street is home to the Eldridge Street Synagogue, the first such building of worship in the United States and New York. Constructed by Eastern European Jews in 1887, the building foreshadows the human story that follows, which charts the rise of the Eastern European Jewish American protagonist Jess Robin.

18. Inderpal Grewal and Caren Kaplan, "Postcolonial Studies and Transnational Feminist Practices," *Jouvert: A Journal of Postcolonial Studies* 5.1 (Autumn 2000). http://www.english.chass.ncsu.edu.

19. The original *Jazz Singer* was based on Samson Raphaelson's short story, "Day of Atonement," which appeared in *Everybody's Magazine* in 1922. In the original film and story, the traditional father dies of heartbreak caused by his son's desire to pursue a life on the stage. In the 1980 version, the father lives, allowing father and son to reconcile.

20. See "Becoming a Citizen," August 12, 2010. http://www.unitedstatesimmigration.info/becoming_a_citizen.html.

Introduction

Nicholas Lehmann, "Jews in Second Place: When Asian-Americans Become the 'New Jews,' What Happens to the Jews?" *Slate*, June 25, 1996, http://www.slate.com/id/2378. Eric Liu, *The Accidental Asian: Notes of a Native Speaker* (New York: Random House, 1998), 145.

1. I want to thank Min Hyoung Song for initially bringing this text to my attention.

2. George Packer, "From the Mekong to the Bayous" (review), *New York Times*, June 7, 1992, http://www.nytimes.com/1992/06/07/books/from-the-mekong-to-the-bayous.html.

3. At the 2009 Modern Language Association conference in Philadelphia, Susan Edmonds astutely noted parallel "civil war" structures in Lan Cao's *Monkey Bridge* (1997).

4. Robert Olen Butler, *A Good Scent from a Strange Mountain* (New York: Penguin, 1992), 126.

5. United States Congress, "An Act to Establish a Uniform Rule of Naturalization" (March 26, 1790), 1 Stat. 103–104. Edited version: Linda Grant De Pauw, et al., eds., *Documentary History of the First Federal Congress of the United States of America, March 4, 1789—March 3, 1791*. 14 vols. to date. Baltimore: Johns Hopkins University Press, 1972–1995. 6: 1516–1522.

6. As will be discussed later, African Americans were granted the right to naturalize in 1870. The Indian Citizenship Act of 1924 enabled an en masse naturalization of Native Americans.

7. Gary Okihiro, *Common Ground: Reimagining American History* (Princeton: Princeton University Press, 2001), xiii.

8. There is much debate over whether or not the resettlement of Jews in England occurred during Oliver Cromwell's reign as Lord Protector in England. According to a December 9, 2005, *Guardian* article by Elaine Glaser, no official policy had been

established for the resettlement of this population. Further, the story of Cromwell's role in lifting such a ban largely occurs during the latter part of the nineteenth century, with the mass emigration of European Jews from the continent as a consequence of pogroms and increasingly violent anti-Semitic sentiment. See "Oliver Cromwell and the Jews: A Correction," http://www.guardian.co.uk/world/2005/dec/09/religion.uk.

9. Leon Hühner, "Naturalization of Jews in New York under the Act of 1740," reprinted from the *Publications of the American Jewish Society* 13 (1905). The lack of consistency in colonial naturalization policy is apparent in the case of two Rhode Island Jewish merchants—Aaron Lopez and Isaac Elizer—who attempted to gain citizenship in 1762. Although naturalized citizenship was granted to previous Jewish subjects, the applications of Lopez and Elizer were denied by the Superior Court of Rhode Island, eventually prompting both applicants to go to other colonies (Massachusetts and New York, respectively) to successfully naturalize. Both applicants initially appealed the ruling at the level of the colonial legislature, which returned jurisdiction to the colonial court. Revealingly, as a justification for the ruling, the legislature maintained in the case of Lopez that "Inasmuch as the said Aaron Lopez hath declared himself by religion a Jew, this Assembly doth not admit himself nor any other of that religion to the full freedom of this Colony. So that the said Aaron Lopez nor any other of said religion is not liable to be chosen into any office in this colony nor allowed to give vote as a free man in choosing others." The declaration of Lopez's religious affiliation as a Jew therefore served as the primary impediment to naturalization in Rhode Island, which further prohibited the applicant's participation in "any office in this colony" and effectively disallowed a participatory role in the franchise. The connection between naturalized subject and voting citizen would reemerge in an 1854 California case, *People v. Hall*, which is discussed in chapter 1.

10. A. H. Carpenter, "Naturalization in England and the American Colonies," *American Historical Review* 9.2 (January 1904): 293.

11. The significance of this relatively new transit to citizenship was not lost on Jewish subjects living in the United States at the time of the 1790 law. For instance, Portuguese immigrant and Jewish leader Moises Seixas directly confronted the benefit of such religious omission in his letter to George Washington on August 17, composed roughly five months after the passage of the 1790 naturalization law. Speaking on behalf of the Newport, Rhode Island, Jewish community, Seixas's letter to the president alluded to the past colonial-era denial of Aaron Lopez and Isaac Elizer, two Jewish applicants for naturalized citizenship. Seixas professed: "Deprived as we heretofore have been of the invaluable rights of free Citizens, we now with a deep sense of gratitude to the Almighty disposer of all events behold a Government, erected by the Majesty of the People—a Government, which to bigotry gives no sanction, to persecution no assistance—but generously affording to all Liberty of conscience, and immunities of Citizenship: deeming every one, of whatever Nation, tongue, or language equal parts of the great governmental Machine"; Moises Seixas, "Letter to George Washington," August 17, 1790, Manuscript Division, Library of Congress, http://www.loc.gov/exhibits/treasures/trm006.html.

12. In the case *In re Ah Yup* (1878), the Court ruled that Chinese applicants were "aliens ineligible for citizenship" because they were neither a "free white person" nor someone of "African descent." This case is examined in chapter 1.

13. Takao Ozawa, "Naturalization of a Japanese Subject" (undated brief, University

of California, Los Angeles Japanese American Research Project Collection, Japanese Foreign Ministry Documents, reel 39). Though Takao Ozawa had originally filed for naturalized citizenship in 1914, it was not until 1922 that his case was heard before the Supreme Court.

14. Ian Haney Lopez examines the codification of whiteness via legal cases involving naturalization applicants; *White by Law: The Legal Construction of Race* [1996] (New York: New York University Press, 2006). This issue of legal whiteness also functions as an entrée into Matthew Frye Jacobson's work on "probationary white subjects" during the first massive wave of immigration (1880—1924) and in the twentieth century.

15. Franklin Odo, "Supreme Court: *Takao Ozawa v. United* States, November 13, 1922." *The Columbia Documentary History of the Asian American Experience* (New York: Columbia University Press, 2002), 181.

16. "Americanizing Immigrant Jews," *New York Times*, January 5, 1922, 88. Charles S. Bernheimer was perhaps best known for his study *Russian Jew in the United States: Studies of Social Conditions in New York, Philadelphia and Chicago* (1905).

17. Michael C. LeMay and Robert Elliott Barkan, *US Immigration and Naturalization Laws and Issues: A Documentary History* (Westport, Conn.: Greenwood, 1999), 133.

18. Okihiro, *Common Ground*, xiv.

19. Liu, *The Accidental Asian*, 75.

20. Lopez, *White by Law*, 64–65.

21. As Asha Nadkarni notes in "World Menace: National Reproduction and Public Health in Katherine Mayo's *Mother India*," *American Quarterly* 60.3 (September 2008): 805–827, the religious category of "Hindu" was synonymous with South Asian racial identity.

22. Lopez, *White by Law*, 64–65.

23. In *United States v. Wong Kim Ark* (1898), the Supreme Court ruled that those born in the United States—regardless of their would-be eligibility for naturalized citizenship—maintained a *jus solis* citizenship states.

24. Min Hyoung Song, "The Children of 1965: Allegory, Postmodernism, and Jhumpa Lahiri's *The Namesake*," *Twentieth-Century Literature* 53.3 (Fall 2007): 353. Song uses Lee Edelman's notion of the "Child" to discuss the symbolic function of children in conceptions of futurity.

25. In *Karma of Brown Folk* (Minneapolis: University of Minnesota Press, 2001), Vijay Prashad uses W.E.B. Dubois's famous "problematic" argument in *Souls of Black Folk*. In particular, Dubois is asked how "it feels to be a problem." Prashad revises this to fit a model minority frame, noting that Asian Americans must consider "what it means to be a solution."

26. Song, "The Children of 1965," 353.

27. "Success Story of One Minority Group in the U.S." Originally published December 26, 1966, in *U.S. News and World Report*; included in *Asian American Studies: A Reader*, Jean Yu-Wen Wu and Min Song, eds. (New Brunswick: Rutgers University Press, 2000), 158.

28. William Petersen, "Success Story, Japanese-American Style," *New York Times Magazine*, January 9, 1966, 32.

29. It is interesting to note Petersen's dismissal of student activism and protest; a conservative, he stresses that few Japanese Americans were involved.

30. Petersen, "Success Story, Japanese-American Style," 42.

31. Neela Banerjee, "In Jews, Indian-Americans See Role Model in Activism," *New York Times* October 2, 2007, http://www.nytimes.com/2007/10/02/us/02hindu.html.

32. Jonathan Freedman, "Transgressions of a Model Minority." *Shofar* 23.4 (Summer 2005): 72.

33. Yen Le Espiritu, "Homes, Borders, and Possibilities," in *Asian American Studies Now: A Critical Reader,* Jean Yu-Wen Shen Wu and Thomas C. Chen, eds. (New Brunswick: Rutgers University Press, 2010), 604–605. Originally published in *Home Bound: Filipino American Lives across Cultures, Communities, and Countries* (Berkeley: University of California Press, 2003).

34. Priscilla Wald, "Naturalization," in *Keywords for American Cultural Studies,* Bruce Burgett and Glenn Hendler, eds. (New York: New York University Press, 2007), 174.

35. Ibid., 170–171.

1 / "Who May Be Citizens of the United States"

1. "News of the Week," *German Reformed Messenger (1851–1867),* December 6, 1854, http://chroniclingamerica.loc.gov/lccn/sn87090458/. The first epigraph above is from *People v. Hall* 4 Cal. 399 (California Supreme Court 1854), http://www.uchastings.edu/racism-race/people-hall.html. The second epigraph is from an editorial in *Harper's Weekly,* May 15, 1858, "Who May Be Citizens of the United States," 306, http://immigrants.harpweek.com.

2. See *People v. Hall.*

3. U. S. Grant and A. Rawlins, *Official Records of the War of the Rebellion: Official Records of the Union and Confederate Armies.* Series I, vol. 17, part 2, Government Printing Office, 1880: 424. Grant issued the order in response to an emergent black market trade involving cotton production in the Confederacy. The practice was widespread, yet Jewish Americans did not constitute the majority of illegal traders. The act drew immediate fire from Jewish Americans, who rightfully viewed it as an anti-Semitic declaration of disloyalty. It was never put into practice; Jewish leaders organized protests across the Union, and Grant revoked the order on January 6, 1863.

4. In *Whiteness of a Different Color: European Immigrants and the Alchemy of Race* (Cambridge: Harvard University Press, 1998), Matthew Frye Jacobson examines the social construction of whiteness vis-à-vis immigration policy. Focused on what he terms "probationary" groups, Jacobson maps how particular groups were afforded whiteness via law and culture at distinct moments in American history.

5. Known before and after the Civil War as a staunch civil rights advocate, Sumner is best remembered for his antebellum role in a North/South conflict. Specifically, Sumner had (true to form) delivered a fiery abolitionist speech on May 22, 1856, provoking South Carolinian congressman Preston Brooks to deliver a caning to the Massachusetts Republican the same day. In the postbellum period, Sumner continued to advocate for "no discrimination on account of color."

6. See Charles Sumner, *The Works of Charles Sumner,* vol. 13 (Boston: Lee and Shepard, 1880). In remarks delivered to the Senate on July 2 and July 4, 1870, Sumner mentions a bill intended "to amend the Naturalization Laws and to punish crimes

against the same" (474). Central to the legislative proposition was the seemingly unstoppable nature of New York's Tammany Hall. Under the tutelage of Democrat William "Boss" Tweed, the political machine was notorious for its strategic use of immigrants, whom it deployed en masse at the polls. Correspondingly, the would-be amendment was intended on one level to prevent "election frauds perpetrated through the instrumentality of unnaturalized or illegally naturalized aliens" (474). 7. See ibid., 481.

8. The issue of Chinese citizenship contrasted with African American selfhood would reemerge in *Plessy v. Ferguson*, the now infamous case that established the constitutionality of Jim Crow "separate but equal" law. Justice John Marshall Harlan issued the dissenting opinion in the case, and noted that the Chinese were afforded a citizenship unavailable to African Americans.

9. Briefly, the Thirteenth Amendment abolished slavery; the Fourteenth Amendment confirmed constitutional rights, equal protection, and due process for all citizens; and, the Fifteenth Amendment provided suffrage for African American men.

10. See Thomas Jefferson, "Declaration of Independence," http://www.loc.gov/exhibits/jefferson/jeffdec.html.

11. See Sumner, *Works*, 13: 482.

12. Ibid.

13. Women were at last given the right to vote on August 18, 1920, with the ratification of the Nineteenth Amendment.

14. See Sumner, *Works*, 13: 482–483. As historian Moon-Ho Jung argues, the 1870 naturalization law authorized whiteness for working-class European immigrants while denying—precisely through noninclusion—access for Chinese immigrants. In *Coolies and Cane: Race, Labor, and Sugar in the Age of Emancipation* (Baltimore: Johns Hopkins University Press, 2006), Jung examines the making of race through class struggle and formation during the era of Reconstruction.

15. Ibid.

16. This is not to suggest that African Americans had full access to equal protection and due process. As would become clear, the rise of Jim Crow law along with the dissolution of Reconstruction would perpetuate asymmetrical power relationships and inequities for the next century. Symbolically, such inequities would be legally dismantled with the 1954 ruling in *Brown v. Board of Education*.

17. Lopez, *White by Law*.

18. See http://www.wvu.edu/~lawfac/jscully/Race/documents.

19. Significantly, the 1875 Page Act was the first restrictive immigration law enacted. It was not geared specifically to Chinese women; instead, undesirables included contract labor from China, Japan, or Korea; alleged prostitutes; and convicts. The passage of such a law reflected a shift in immigration jurisdiction. In 1875, the U.S. Supreme Court ruled the primacy of the federal government in the making of immigration policy, a verdict that necessarily foregrounds the congressional passage of the Page Act.

20. Sucheng Chan, *Asian Americans: An Interpretative History* (Ann Arbor: Twayne, 1991).

21. Susan Koshy, *Sexual Naturalization: Asian Americans and Miscegenation* (Stanford: Stanford University Press, 2004), 8.

22. Asian exclusion was not limited to the Chinese. For example, the 1907

Gentleman's Agreement concerned Japanese immigrants; it was an agreement orchestrated between the Japanese and U.S. governments by which the Japanese would not issue visas or passports to Japanese laborers intent on emigrating to the United States. Korean emigrants, considered Japanese subjects after 1905, were also excluded from immigration access to the United States.

23. *The Independent* was first published in 1848. "In the Land of the Free" was originally published in *Independent* 67 (September 2, 1909): 504–508. Interestingly, *The Independent* also published work by well-known Sinophobic writer Jack London.

24. Edith Maude Eaton, *Mrs. Spring Fragrance and Other Writings*, ed. Amy Ling and Annette White-Parks (Urbana: University of Illinois Press, 1995). *Mrs. Spring Fragrance* was originally published in 1912.

25. Amy Ling, "Edith Maude Eaton (Sui Sin Far) 1865–1914," in *The Heath Anthology of American Literature: Late Nineteenth Century: 1865–1910*, ed. Paul Lauter. 5th ed. Boston: Houghton Mifflin Harcourt, 2004: 494.

26. I want to thank Jerry Phillips and Mary Gallucci for their reading of race and gender in the chapter. The frame of householding used in the chapter emerges from a discussion about nineteenth-century empire and domesticity.

27. See *The Independent* 68 (March 10, 1910): 518–523.

28. Koshy, *Sexual Naturalization*.

29. In turn, it is through a domestic plot that Eaton naturalizes "the Chinese husband." Liu Kanghi's naturalization through romantic frames is matched by a geographic naturalization of Chinatown as familiar space. Indeed, Chinatown remains unnamed in "The Story of One White Woman Who Married a Chinese," and the only geographic clue is found in a letter sent by her first husband to her new home on "204 Buchanan Street" (74).

30. Mark Twain, *Roughing It*, vol. 1 (New York: Harper and Brothers, 1871), 105. Mark Twain is, of course, the pen name for Samuel Langhorne Clemens.

31. Mark Twain, "Concerning the Jews," *Harper's Monthly Magazine* (September 1899), http://www.harpers.org/archive/1899/09/0026214.

32. The federal immigration reform of 1907 reflected, in its expansion of exclusion, increasing anxiety over multiple types of immigrant bodies, taxing individual immigrants $5 per head and denying entry to "imbeciles, feeble-minded persons, unaccompanied children under 17 years of age, and persons who are found to be and are certified by the examination surgeon as being mentally or physically defective, such mental and physical defect being of a nature which may affect the ability of such aliens to earn a living." See William Dillingham, *Abstracts of Reports of the Immigration Commission: With Conclusions and Recommendations and Views of the Minority* (Washington, D.C.: Government Printing Office, 1911), 9.

33. Donald Weber, *Haunted in the New World: Jewish American Culture from Cahan to The Goldbergs* (Bloomington: Indiana University Press, 2005).

34. Robert M. Dowling, *Slumming in New York: From the Waterfront to Mythic Harlem* (Urbana-Champaign: University of Illinois Press, 2007), 131. Dowling refers to *Yekl* as a novelistic treatment. However, given its relatively short length (89 pages), I place it within the genre of the novella.

35. Henry James, *The American Scene* (New York, Harper and Brothers, 1907).

36. The chapters in *Yekl* are as follows: "Jake and Yekl" (Chapter 1); "The New York Ghetto" (Chapter 2); "In the Grip of His Past" (Chapter 3); "The Meeting" (Chapter 4);

"A Paterfamilias" (Chapter 5); "Circumstances Alter Cases" (Chapter 6); "Mrs. Kavarsky's Coup d'Etat" (Chapter 7); "A Housteop Idyl" (Chapter 8); "The Parting" (Chapter 9); "A Defeated Victor" (Chapter 10).

37. Abraham Cahan, *Yekl and the Imported Bridegroom and Other Stories of the New York Ghetto* (Mineola, N.Y.: Dover, 1970), 9.

38. Robert G. Lee, *Orientals: Asian Americans in Popular Culture* (Philadelphia: Temple University Press, 1999)

39. Karen Renner's work on nineteenth-century antebellum novels provocatively engages caveat emptor frames in the making of U.S. citizenship.

40. Cahan, *Yekl and the Imported Bridegroom*, 372.

2 / Interrupted Allegiances

The first epigraph is from an anonymous review entitled "New Zangwill Play Cheap and Tawdry." Joe Kraus uses the same review in "How *The Melting Pot* Stirred America: The Reception of Zangwill's Play and Theater's Role in the American Assimilation Experience," *MELUS*, 24:3 (Fall 1999) 3–19, though he focuses his analytical attention on assimilation and not state-authorized naturalization. The second quotation is from a *New York Times* review by Idwal Jones, "Chinatown Patriarch," May 19, 1957, BR17.

1. William McKinley, "December 21, 1898 Address," *The Statutes at Large of the United States of American from 1897 and March 1899*... vol. 30 (Washington, D.C.: U.S. Government Printing Office, 1899). 1396.

2. See Amy Kaplan's *The Anarchy of Empire* (Cambridge: Harvard University Press, 2005), Allan Isaac's *American Tropics* (Minneapolis: University of Minnesota Press, 2006), and Victor Bascara's *Model-Minority Imperialism* (Minneapolis: University of Minnesota Press, 2006).

3. Priscilla Wald, "Naturalization," in *Keywords for American Cultural Studies*, Bruce Brugett and Glen Hendler, eds (New York: New York University Press, 2008), 174.

4. Jules Chamtezky, "Beyond Melting Pots, Cultural Pluralism, Ethnicity: Or Déjà Vu All over Again." *MELUS* 16.4 (Winter 1989–90): 3–17.

5. Elaine Kim, *Asian American Literature: An Introduction to the Writings and Their Social Context* (Philadelphia: Temple University Press, 1982), 106.

6. There is very little critical writing about the novel. Elaine Kim, Christina Klein, and Robert G. Lee briefly mention it, and Kim's treatment is by far the most extensive. Two recently published literary encyclopedias—*Dictionary of Literary Biography: Asian American Writers* (Farmington Hills, Mich.: Thomas Gale, 2005) and *The Greenwood Encyclopedia of Multiethnic American Literature* (Westport, Conn.: Greenwood, 2005)—make no mention of C. Y. Lee. Most attention has been paid to the stage adaptation of the novel.

7. See *Official Catalogue and Guide Book to the Pan-American Exposition* (Buffalo, N.Y.: Charles Ahrhart, 1901).

8. Theodore Roosevelt, "Proclamation 465—Announcing the Death of William McKinley, *September 14, 1901*." John T. Woolley and Gerhard Peters, *The American Presidency Project* (Santa Barbara), http://www.presidency.ucsb.edu/ws/?pid=69370.

9. Joseph Buklin Bishop, *Theodore Roosevelt and His Time Shown in His Own*

Letters [1920] (Whitefish, Mont.: Kessinger Publishing, 2008), 473–474. Roosevelt wrote this letter days before his death on January 6, 1919.

10. See Gary Gerstle's *American Crucible: Race and Nation in the Twentieth Century* (Princeton: Princeton University Press, 2002) and Mai Ngai's *Impossible Subjects: Illegal Aliens and the Making of Modern America* (Princeton: Princeton University Press, 2004). Both Gerstle and Ngai compellingly link nationalistic and imperialistic discourses over the course of the twentieth century.

11. Hermann Hagedorn, ed., *The Theodore Roosevelt Treasury: A Self-Portrait from His Writings* (New York: Putnam, 1957), 325.

12. See Maurice Wohlgelenter, *Israel Zangwill: A Study* (New York: Columbia University Press, 1964). Neil Larry Shumksy, in "Zangwill's *The Melting Pot*: Ethnic Tension on Stage," *American Quarterly* 27.1 (March 1975), 29–41, and Joe Kraus, in "How *The Melting Pot* Stirred America," also explore Roosevelt's enthusiastic response vis-à-vis contemporary domestic ethno-racial politics.

13. Israel Zangwill, *The Melting-Pot* (New York: Macmillan, 1909).

14. "New Zangwill Play Cheap and Tawdry."

15. J. Hector St. John Crevecoeur, "Letter III," in *Letters from an American Farmer*, reprinted from the original ed., with a prefatory note by W. P. Trent and an introduction by Ludwig Lewisohn (New York: Fox, Duffield, 1904), 54–55.

16. Wohlgelenter, *Israel Zangwill*, 176.

17. Zangwill, *The Melting-Pot*, 151.

18. See INS home page, December 15, 2001, http://www.ins.usdoj.gove/text.aboutins/statistics/LegisHist/553.htm.

19. See M. M. Bakhtin, *The Dialogic Imagination: Four Essays* (Austin: University of Texas Press, 1982).

20. Wohlgelenter, *Israel Zangwill*, ix.

21. As is evident in correspondence between Mary Antin and Israel Zangwill, the two authors shared a trans-Atlantic connection. Indeed, Zangwill would provide editorial advice to Antin and wrote an early review of her work. See Evelyn Salz, ed., *Selected Letters of Mary Antin* (Syracuse: Syracuse University Press, 2000).

22. Kraus, "How *The Melting Pot* Stirred America."

23. Benedict Anderson, *Imagined Communities: Reflections on the Origin and Spread of Nationalism*, rev. and extended ed. (London: Verso, 1993), 81.

24. Kraus, "How *The Melting Pot* Stirred America," 3–4.

25. Mai Nagai, "From Colonial Subject to Undesirable Alien: Filipino Migration, Exclusion, and Repatriation, 1920–1940," in *Re/collecting Early Asian America*, Josephine Lee and Matsukawa Lim, eds. (Philadelphia: Temple University Press, 2002), 112–113.

26. Dean Acheson, "Speech on the Far East," January 12, 1950, http://teachingamericanhistory.org/library/index.asp?document=1612.

27. Pat McCarran, *Congressional Record*, March 2, 1953, 1518.

28. Chin Y. Lee, *The Flower Drum Song* [1957] (New York: Penguin Books, 2002), 3.

29. In the novel version, "Mei-Li" is spelled "May Li." For the consistency, I have elected to use the former spelling.

30. In a 2004 interview with Andrew Shin, Chin Y. Lee (1917—) reflected on his most famous literary production. Lee, a first-generation Chinese American who emigrated from China during the 1940s to attend university, revealed his intent with regard to *The*

Flower Drum Song. He maintained, "You know, this is an immigrant country. People are here from all over the world. I think Americans are naturally very curious about foreign culture. But you have to present foreign culture in many ways. Academically, which means that when students attend university, they should be reading books about foreign culture. But you have to present it another way, in a very interesting way, on the stage, in novels, in movies. So if you have an interesting story and you write a stage play or novel, or produce a film, you almost open a window for Americans to peek in and you get their interest and they will enjoy it. This is how you present foreign culture—not in an academic way, but in an entertaining way"; Andrew Shin, "Forty Percent Is Luck: An Interview with C. Y. Lee," *MELUS* 29 (Summer 2004): 95.

31. Master Wang has "two servants and a cook whom he had brought from Hunan Province" and "the only 'impure' elements in his household [according to the omniscient narrator] were his two sons, Wang Ta and Wang San, especially the latter, who had in four years learned to act like a cowboy and talk like the characters in a Spillane movie. At thirteen he had practically forgotten his Chinese" (*Flower Drum Song*, 4).

32. Robert G. Lee, *Orientals* (Philadelphia: Temple University Press, 1997), 175.

33. Frank Chin, Jeffery Paul Chan, Lawson Fusao Inada, and Shawn Wong, eds., *Aiiieeeee!: An Anthology of Asian American Writers* [1974] (Washington, D.C.: Howard University Press, 1983), x.

34. Robert G. Lee in *Orientals* takes this notion of menace further with regard to the Rodgers and Hammerstein version of *The Flower Drum Song*, maintaining that the musical's heteronormative focus on family and the ability of Asian immigrants and Asian Americans to assimilate into the larger U.S. body politic as model minorities assuaged anxieties about the aforementioned "red menace," the "yellow menace" (Asian immigrants), and the "white menace" (homosexuality).

3 / Utopian and Dystopian Citizenships

The epigraphs are from Mary Antin, *They Who Knock at Our Gates* (Boston: Houghton Mifflin, 1914), 27, and David Hollinger, *Postethnic America: Beyond Multiculturalism* [1995] (New York: Basic Books, 2000), 118–119.

1. On October 14, 1912, at a campaign stop in Milwaukee, Roosevelt was shot by saloon owner John Schrank.

2. See http://www.pbs.org/newshour/bb/politics/july-dec09/immigration_08-28.html.

3. Daniel J. Tichenor, *Dividing Lines: The Politics of Immigration Control in America* (Princeton: Princeton University Press, 2002), 136–137.

4. Woodrow Wilson, *A History of the American People* (New York: Harper and Brothers, 1902).

5. Quoted in http://www.wilsoncenter.org/events/docs/immigration-essay-intro.pdf. From "Wilson Says Big Problems Face America: Governor Gives Address at Dinner of Friendly Sons of S. Patrick," a news report of an after-dinner address in Elizabeth, New Jersey, March 18, 1912, in *The Papers of Woodrow Wilson*, Arthur S. Link, ed. (Princeton: Princeton University Press, 1977), 24: 252.

6. Robert Constantine Jr., ed., *Gentle Rebel: Letters of Eugene V. Debs* (Urbana: University of Illinois Press, 1995), xxxi.

7. Matthew Frye Jacobson, *Barbarian Virtues: The United States Encounters Foreign Peoples at Home and Abroad (1876–1917)* (New York: Hill and Wang, 2000), 86.

8. Mary Antin, *From Plotzk to Boston* (Boston: W. B. Clarke, 1899), 8.

9. Gish Jen is the pseudonym for Lillian G. Jen. In this chapter, I will be referring to Jen by her last name and by her pseudonym.

10. The move toward eugenics during the Progressive Era is clearly and compelling articulated in Asha Nadkarni's "Eugenic Feminism: Asian Reproduction in the U.S. National Imaginary," *Novel* 39.2 (Spring 2006): 221–244.

11. The Dillingham Commission consisted of the chair, Senator William P. Dillingham (Vermont), Senator Henry Cabot Lodge (Massachusetts), Senator Asbury Latimer (South Carolina, replaced in 1910 by Senator LeRoy Percy of Mississippi), and U.S. representatives Benjamin Howell, William S. Bennet, and John L. Burnett. Secretary of Labor Charles P. Neill, Jeremiah Jenks (professor, Cornell University), and William R. Wheeler of the California Commission of Immigration were also a part of this body. In 1912, Jenks left Cornell and was professor of economics at New York University.

12. Jeremiah W. Jenks and W. Jett Lauck, *The Immigation Problem: A Study of American Immigration Conditions and Needs* (New York: Funk and Wagnalls, 1922).

13. Madison Grant, *The Passing of the Great Race: or, the Racial Basis of European History* (New York: C. Scribner, 1916).

14. "Does the Pot Melt It? Can the Immigration into This Country Be Assimilated?—It Could Be Once, but Can It Now?" *New York Times*, February 11, 1912, BR61.

15. Such conditions coincide with analogous "literacy test" calls by the Immigration Restriction League.

16. "Does the Pot Melt It?"

17. Asha Nadkarni, "'World-Menace': National Reproduction and Public Health in Katherine Mayo's *Mother India*," *American Quarterly* 60.3 (September 2008): 805–827.

18. Mary Antin, *The Promised Land* (Boston: Houghton Mifflin, 1912).

19. Randolph Bourne, "Trans-National America," *Atlantic Monthly* 118 (July 1916): 93.

20. Ibid. Responding to anti-German (and by extension anti-immigration) sentiment concomitant with the emergence of World War I on the global stage, Randolph Bourne published "Trans-National America" (1916). Bourne argued that the United States had yet to achieve its promise, immigrants were integral to achieving that promise, and pushed for a reading of U.S. citizenship through cosmopolitanism (creating citizens of the world) and dual citizenship.

21. Antin's pro-immigrant activist moves within the literary imaginary of *The Promised Land* are circumscribed by genre. In other words, despite her metonymic role as a representative subject (that is, a singular immigrant who stands in for millions of immigrants), Antin must nonetheless restrict her narrative to individual experiences and recollections that in turn speak to her evolution from immigrant to American. Nevertheless, *The Promised Land* addresses the malleability of the immigrant subject through the bildungsroman, which in the memoir echoes the performative and affective dimensions of naturalization. The literary and thematic foci on citizenship are continued in Antin's more overtly political *They Who Knock at Our Gates,* published in 1914. The pro-immigrant, pro-assimilationist stance apparent in a series of essays in *They Who Knock at Our Gates* can be read as a textual supplement to lectures she

gave at the turn of the century. According to Werner Sollors (in the 1997 Penguin edition of *The Promised Land*), the topics of these lectures included "The Responsibility of American Citizenship," "The Civic Education of the Immigrant," "The Public School as a Test of American Faith," "Jewish Life in the Pale: A Lesson for Americans," and "The Zionist Movement" (xxxv). Antin, *Promised Land*, 358.

22. Evelyn Salz, ed., *Selected Letters of Mary Antin* (Syracuse: Syracuse University Press, 2000), xvi.

23. Quoted in Thomas Cieslik, David Felsen, and Akis Kalaitzidis, eds., *Immigration: A Documentary and Reference Guide* (Westport, Conn.: Greenwood, 2009), 77.

24. It is important to note that the 1921 Immigration Act, an emergency provision passed by Congress, established a quota system by which annual immigration from any country could not exceed 3 percent of the number of persons of that nationality who had been in the United States in 1910, and the law cut immigration from 800,000 to 300,000 in a single year. Passed three years later, the Johnson-Reed Immigration Act (or the National Origins Act), banned immigration from East Asia entirely and reduced the quota for Europeans from 3 to 2 percent. Because the quota system was based on the census of 1890, when there were far fewer southern and eastern Europeans in the United State, immigration flow was cut almost in half, to 164,000 a year.

25. Quoted in "Three Decades of Mass Immigration: The Legacy of the 1965 Immigration Act," September 1995, http:www.cis.org/articles/1995/back395.html.

26. From Lyndon B. Johnson, *Public Papers of the Presidents of the United States* (Washington, D.C.: U.S. Government Printing Office, 1966), 1037–1040, quoted in "Three Decades of Mass Immigration."

27. "Three Decades of Mass Immigration."

28. Ibid.

29. Ibid.

30. Gwendolyn Mink, *Whose Welfare?* (Ithaca: Cornell University Press, 1999), 109.

31. Quoted in Roger Daniels, *Coming to America: A History of Immigration and Ethnicity in American Life*, 2nd edition (New York: Harper Perennial, 2002), 340.

32. Ibid.

33. Pyong Gap Min, ed., "Asian Immigration: History and Contemporary Trends," in *Asian Americans: Contemporary Trends and Issues*, 2nd edition. (Thousand Oaks, Cal.: Pine Forge Press, 2006), 26.

34. C. N. Le, "The 1965 Immigration Act." In *Asian-Nation: The Landscape of Asian America*, May 21, 2009, http://www.asian-nation.org/1965-immigration-act.shtml.

35. "Three Decades of Mass Immigration."

36. The story that serves as the basis for the novel *Mona in the Promised Land* is entitled "What Means Switch?", which appeared in the May 1990 issue of *Atlantic Monthly*, 76–80.

37. Gish Jen, *Typical American* (New York: Plume, 1992), 3.

38. Rachel Lee, "Gish Jen and the Gendered Codes of Americanness." *The Americas of Asian American Literature: Gendered Fictions of Nation and Transnation* (Princeton: Princeton University Press, 1999).

39. Gish Jen, *Mona in the Promised Land* (New York: Vintage, 1997), 3.

40. In Jen's first novel, *Typical American*, the reader is given the background for

both Ralph and Helen's names; more specifically, Ralph, who immigrates to the United States to pursue a graduate degree in engineering, is told by the administrative assistant in the department office that he needs "an English name." Though he arrives as Yifeng Chang, he is renamed "Ralph" by the administrative assistant. In the case of Helen, her name is chosen by Ralph's older sister Theresa, because it both resembles her Chinese name Hailan, and is reminiscent of Helen of Troy.

41. The contestation over civil rights and representation was further apparent at the 1968 Summer Olympics in Mexico City. American track and field athletes Tommie Smith and John Carlos had attempted to organize black athletes around a civil rights–oriented boycott against the United States. Failing to do so, the two athletes competed and won the gold and bronze medals in the 200 meters track and field event. As the U.S. national anthem played, Smith and Carlos accepted their medals in bare feet, wore beads, and held black-gloved firsts in the air to bring attention to poverty in African American communities, honor victims of slavery and racism, and perform the Black Power salute, respectively. Their actions were met with intense outrage, and the International Olympic Committee (IOC) forced the U.S. Olympic Committee to withdraw the two athletes from other events. Additionally, Smith and Carlos were expelled from the Olympic team and the summer games.

42. The use of the term "symbolic ethnicity" within this frame diverges from Herbert Gans's application. Gans attributes such moments to third- and fourth-generation immigrant subjectivities, and I am using the term in relation to a first-generation characterization.

43. Anita Mannur, *Culinary Fictions: Food in South Asian Diasporic Culture* (Philadephila: Temple University Press, 2009).

44. Begona Simal Gonzalez, "The (Re)Birth of Mona Changowitz: Rituals and Ceremonies of Cultural Conversion and Self-Making in *Mona in the Promised Land*," *MELUS* 26.2 (Summer 2001): 225.

45. Jen's use of Jewish and Chinese identities in *Mona in the Promised Land* manifests in character histories and settings, which places the Chinese American Chang family in a predominantly Jewish American neighborhood; this sets the stage for Mona's voluntary ethno-religious shift. Andrew Furman observes, "Mona could have chosen a number of minority cultures through which to forge her own unique American identity. The pervasiveness of Jewish culture in Scarshill and its attractiveness to her convince Mona to appropriate Judaism." Mona views Jewish identity as one that is both readily accessible and, at the same time, emblematic of an immigrant American identity. Throughout the course of the novel, Mona constantly discusses the ways in which "Jewish is American," and "American is Jewish." The connection Mona makes between Jewish and American identities is ironic, however, given previously mentioned discourses about the Jewish subject as inassimilable and un-American. See Andrew Furman, "Immigrant Dreams and Civic Promises: (Con-)Testing Identity in Early Jewish American Literature and Gish Jen's *Mona in the Promised Land*," *MELUS* 25 (Spring 2000): 212.

46. James Yin and Shin Young, *The Rape of Nanking* (Chicago: Innovative Publishing Group, 1996).

47. See Michael Omi and Howard Winant, *Racial Formation in the United States: From the 1960s to the 1980s* (New York: Routledge, 1986).

48. Similarly, Fernando—a Latino cook who works in the Chang restaurant—is

also prohibited from full access to the nation. Alfred is accused of stealing a silver flask from the Gugelstein home. In fact, as Jonathan Freedman notes, Fernando actually steals the flask. According to Freedman, "Fernando's crime clears Alfred, but it's not necessarily clear that the racial problematics are resolved in a more enlightened way as a result" (*Klezmer America*, 299).

4 / Reading and Writing America

1. Envisioned in 1876 by French abolitionist, writer, and politician Édouard René de Laboulaye as an enduring symbol of French/U.S. revolutionary kinship, the Statue of Liberty honors one hundred years of U.S. nationhood (emblematized by the Declaration of Independence). After a decade of planning, site visits, and labor negotiations, French sculptor Frédéric Auguste Bartholdi's statue eventually found her way to Liberty Island (formerly Bedloe's Island) in New York Harbor. Officially "Liberty Enlightening the World," the soon-to-be immigrant icon arrived in 217 crates in 350 pieces. Over a span of four months, the 151-foot "mother of exiles" was reassembled atop an American-built star-shaped pedestal. See "The Statue of Liberty: A New York Attraction," http://www.newyorkjourney.com/statue_of_liberty.htm.

During the first year of Reagan's administration, the French-American Committee for the Restoration of the Statue of Liberty was established in conjunction with the National Parks Service. By 1984, the restoration began in earnest, following an $86 million fundraising effort. For the next two years, the statue was shrouded in scaffolding as American and French crews rushed to replace 1,350 iron spikes, refurbish the torch, and strip seven layers of paint in time for the centennial anniversary.

A four-day event, "Liberty Weekend" began on July 3 with Reagan's address and concluded on July 6 with an all-out music review (complete with 200 Elvis Presley impersonators) in New Jersey's Giants Stadium. The Fourth of July would feature Independence Day firework splendor, though July 5 took a more somber and contemplative tone, reflected in the planned scholarly summit on the meaning of liberty and the Central Park performance by the New York Philharmonic. See Richard Stengel, "The Party of the Century." *Time*, July 7, 1986, http://www.time.com/time/magazine/article/0,9171,961667,00.html.

2. Stengel, "The Party of the Century."

3. See U.S. Census Bureau, "New York City," http://quickfacts.census.gov/qfd/states/36/3651000.html.

4. Sam Roberts, "New York City Census Profile Shows Stark Changes in Decade," *New York Times*, June 22, 1993, http://www.nytimes.com/1993/06/22/nyregion/new-york-city-census-profile-shows-stark-changes-in-decade.html?pagewanted=1.

5. See Census Bureau, "New York City." Also see Fernanda Santos, "Mayor Orders New York to Expand Language Help," *New York Times*, July 23, 2008, http://www.nytimes.com/2008/07/23/nyregion/23translate.html.

6. Quoted in Lavina Dhingra Shankar and Rajini Srikanth, eds., *A Part, Yet Apart: South Asians in Asian America* (Philadelphia: Temple University Press, 1998), 59.

7. Alan E. Eliason, "One Illegal Alien Every 35 Seconds," *New York Times* (Letters), April 29, 1986, A26.

8. Robert Lindsey, "As Flow of Illegal Aliens Grows, Complaints Mount in the West," *New York Times*, April 21, 1986, 24.

9. Ibid.

10. Ibid.

11. Robert Pear, "President Signs Landmark Bill on Immigration: Law Offers Legal Status to Many Illegal Aliens," *New York Times*, November 7, 1986. A12.

12. Despite its successful passage, the 1986 Simpson-Mazzoli Act would, in retrospect, be deemed a failure largely because it did little to stem the flow of undocumented bodies into the United States. Critiqued in particular for its amnesty provisions, the IRCA faced a lack of funding at the level of enforcement and administration. More significant, though a legislative "consensus" had been reached, members of Congress maintained in hindsight that "the fundamental problem is that the nation has reached no consensus on immigration." In a revealing 1994 statement, IRCA architect Alan Simpson avowed, "Every time one of us starts talking about more effective immigration controls, somebody else throws up the Statue of Liberty, how we're a nation of immigrants and all of that. . . . The debate takes on tinges of racism, emotion." See Joel Brinkley, "Two in Congress Who Fought to Improve Immigration Policy," *New York Times*, September 15, 1993, http://www.nytimes.com/1994/09/15/us/two-in-congress-who-fought-to-improve-immigration-policy.html.

13. Bharati Mukherjee, *Jasmine* (New York: Ballantine, 1989), 124.

14. Eva Hoffman, *Lost in Translation* (New York: Penguin, 1989), 89 and 198.

15. Pear, "President Signs Landmark Bill on Immigration."

16. Michael Gorra, "Call it Exile, Call it Immigration," review, *New York Times*, September 10, 1989, http://www.nytimes.com/1989/09/10/books/call-it-exile-call-it-immigration.html.. *Jasmine* is an expanded novelistic treatment of the title short story character in the author's previous collection, *The Middleman and Other Stories*

17. See front matter for *Jasmine*.

18. Ibid.

19. Gayatri Chakravorty Spivak, "Three Women's Texts and a Critique of Imperialism," in *Critical Inquiry*, Special Issue: "Race," Writing, and Difference, ed. Henry Louis Gates, Jr., 12.1 (Autumn 1985): 243–261. The focus of Spivak's original criticism is on Mukherjee's pre-*Jasmine* work. Also, see Ajiz Ahmad, *In Theory: Classes, Nations, Literatures* (London: Verso, 1994).

20. The opening epigraph reads: "The new geometry mirrors a universe that is rough, not rounded, scabrous, not smooth. It is a geometry of the pitted, pocked, and broken up, the twisted, tangled, and intertwined."

21. Patricia Chu, *Assimilating Aliens: Gendered Strategies of Authorship in Asian America* (Durham: Duke University Press, 2000).

22. Koshy, *Sexual Naturalization*, 25.

23. Ibid., 135.

23. Ibid., 136.

24. The move toward an official U.S. language began even before the birth of the nation. In 1757, Benjamin Franklin, responding to the number of German-speaking Pennsylvanians in his colony, proposed one of the first English-only initiatives at the level of the colonial legislature.

25. James Crawford, "What's Behind Official English?" in *Language Loyalties: A Sourcebook on the Official English Controversy* (Chicago: University of Chicago Press, 1992), 172. Also see "U.S. English" at http://us-english.org.

26. Quoted in Crawford, "What's Behind Official English?" 172. Also see Southern

Poverty Law Center, "Memo to WITAN IV Attendees from John Tanton," http://www.splcenter.org/intel/intelreport/article.jsp?sid=125. The referendum did pass, despite the controversy, though the Arizona State Supreme Court declared the law unconstitutional in 1998. Several states have passed "official English" or "English only" initiatives, though this has yet to be done at the federal level.

27. Juan Batista Alberdi, *Obras Completas* (Buenos Aires: La Tribuna Nacional Bolivar 38, 1887), 197.

28. Eric Schmitt, "English-Only Bill Ignites Debate and Fear on Long Island," *New York Times*, February 14, 1989. http://www.nytimes/com/1989/02/14/nyregion/.

29. Hoffman, *Lost in Translation*, 79.

30. Hoffman notes that until 1957, there was a "ban on emigration, under which most of the Polish population lives," which was then "lifted for Jews. Anyone who is Jewish can now automatically get permission to leave for Israel—and everyone who is Jewish is confronted with this decision" (ibid., 83).

31. See "Display Ad 297," *New York Times*, October 1, 1989, BR10.

32. Giving out the Medal of Liberty awards was naturalized citizen and ABC News correspondent Ted Koppel. Gray was the first female president of the University of Chicago.

33. Kissinger was awarded the Nobel Peace Prize in 1973 along with North Vietnamese politician Le Duc Tho. Tho returned the prize to the Nobel Committee. He maintained that a lasting peace had not been negotiated in the region, which rendered the recognition meaningless.

34. Ronald Reagan, "Remarks at the Opening Ceremonies of the Statue of Liberty Centennial Celebration in New York, New York," 3 July 1986, http://www.reagan.utexas.edu/archives/speeches/1986/70386d.htm.

35. Irving Berlin's compositions served as the basis for the Broadway musical *This Is the Army*, which was adapted to film in 1938 and featured the actor Ronald Reagan. Following the Medal of Liberty presentation were performances by Neil Diamond and Frank Sinatra, who, respectively, sang "America" and "The House I Live In."

36. Stengel, "The Party of the Century."

37. Ronald Reagan, "Remarks at a Meeting with Asian and Pacific-American Leaders," February 23, 1984, http://www.reagan.utexas.edu/archives/speeches/1984/22384a.htm.

38. Quoted in Godfrey Mwakikagile, *Black Conservatives in the United States* (Pretoria: New Africa Press, 2006), 66. The original source for the Reagan quote emerges from MSNBC commentator Joe Davidson's June 7, 2004 op-ed entitled, "Reagan: A Contrary View," http://www.msnbc.msn.com/id/5158315/.

39. I want to acknowledge Chris Vials, who informally made this observation about a revised narrative vis-à-vis cold war politics.

40. David S. Wyman's *The Abandonment of the Jews: America and the Holocaust, 1941–1945* (New York: New Press, 1998) makes clear the extent to which U.S. immigration policy effectively barred Jewish refugees from entering the United States. Additionally and alternatively, the first day's concluding event—a televised naturalization ceremony held at Ellis Island—saliently speaks to a disconnect between the imagined and real vis-à-vis present-day immigration policy and debate.

41. The first day of Liberty Weekend concluded with televised naturalization ceremony held at Ellis Island involving 12,000 first-generation immigrants. These

would-be citizens, with Supreme Court Chief Justice Warren Berger presiding, uttered the oath that would "remake them" into Americans. The following day, the Statue of Liberty celebration took a more traditional Independence Day format, complete with fireworks, a parade of U.S. Navy ships, and a performance by the John Williams-led Boston Pops.

5 / Demarcating the Nation

The first epigraph is from "America's New War: Dinh Discusses Ashcroft's Policies; McBride, Murphy Debate Their Constitutionality; Rangel Grassley Discuss Economic Stimulus." Kate Snow (host); Viet Dinh (guest), http://www.transcripts.cnn.com/TRANSCRIPTS/0112/08/se.03.html. The second epigraph is from "Remarks by Homeland Security Secretary Michael Chertoff to the Heyman Fellows at Yale University on 'Confronting the Threats to Our Homeland,'" April 7, 2008, http://www.dhs.gov/xnews/speeches/sp_1208280290851.shtm.

1. George W. Bush, "Statement on the Helicopter Crash in Vietnam," *Public Papers of the Presidents of the United States: 2001*. Book 1. April 7, 2001, 379.

2. In 1985, during the Reagan administration, relations between Vietnam and the United States improved, enabling such recovery missions. Thomas Hawley focuses his attention on the movement, the politics, and the psychological dimensions of such recovery missions in *The Remains of War: Bodies, Politics, and the Search for American Soldiers Unaccounted for in Southeast Asia* (Durham: Duke University Press, 2005).

3. The U.S. plane, an EP-3E Aries II spy aircraft, was flying over international airspace when it collided with a Chinese F-8 fighter. Another Chinese fighter was deployed to intercept the U.S. aircraft. Though the Chinese government demanded an immediate public apology, Vice President Dick Cheney and Secretary of State Colin Powell initially rebuffed such calls. The final U.S. apology, though accepted by the Chinese government, was viewed by some as a conciliatory move and by others as a partial apology for the collision but not for the spy mission. See Brian Knowlton, "An American Apology over Downed Fighter Is Rejected by Cheney: Powell Sees Damage to U.S.-China Relations." *New York Times*, April 9, 2001.

4. Dena Bunis and Anh Do, "Ex-refugee Is Nominated for Justice Post: A Fullerton High Grad Gets Praise at His Senate Confirmation Hearing," *Orange County Register*, May 10, 2001.

5. Ibid.

6. See "Viet D. Dinh," *American Bar Association*, May 2003, http://www.abanet.org/publiced/rbvd.html.

7. David Brand, "Education: The New Whiz Kids," *Time*, August 31, 1987, http://www.time.com/time/magazine/article/0,9171,965326,00.html.

8. The connection between Asian American students and Jewish American experiences is made clear in a quote from NYU math professor Sylvain Cappell, who claimed that both groups "feel an obligation to excel intellectually." See ibid.

9. See "Viet D. Dinh."

10. Viet Dinh, "Coming to Grips with Vietnam," *Wall Street Journal*, March 16, 2000.

11. Ibid.

12. Myron Magnet, "What Is Compassionate Conservatism?" *Wall Street Journal*, February 5, 1999.

13. On December 10, 2000, the Supreme Court ruled in a 5–4 decision in favor of George W. Bush.

14. See "At Home on the War on Terror: Viet Dinh Has Gone from Academe to a Key behind the Scenes Role," *Los Angeles Times*, September 18, 2002.

15. See "Ex-refugee Is Nominated." Other members of the Senate Judiciary Committee included Republican senators Charles E. Grassley (Iowa), Arlen Specter (Pennsylvania), Jon Kyle (Arizona), Mike DeWine (Ohio), Jeff Sessions (Alabama), Sam Brownback (Kansas), Mitch McConnell (Kentucky), and the chair, Orrin Hatch (Utah). Democratic senators on the committee included Patrick Leahy (Vermont), Edward Kennedy (Massachusetts), Joseph Biden (Delaware), Herbert Kohl (Wisconsin), Dianne Feinstein (California), Russell Feingold (Wisconsin), Charles Schumer (New York), Richard Durbin (Illinois), and Maria Cantwell (Washington).

16. See "Scenes from the Late 60s," *Time*, February 10, 1975. http://www.time.com/time/magazine/article/0,9171,912797,00.html.

17. See U.S. Congressional Record, "Confirmation Hearing on the Nominations of Michael Chertoff and Viet D. Dinh to be Assistant Attorneys General," May 24, 2001.

18. Ibid.

19. See "Ex-Refugee Is Nominated."

20. See "At Home on the War on Terror."

21. See U.S. Congressional Record, "Confirmation Hearing on the Nominations of Michael Chertoff and Viet D. Dinh."

22. See Angie C. Marek, "A New Sherrif in Town," *U.S. News & World Report*, July 10, 2005.

23. Though seemingly coincidental, the confirmation of both Viet Dinh and Michael Chertoff would in hindsight prove significant at the year's close, when U.S. foreign policy and immigration law would be emerge as two significant fronts in the Bush administration's War on Terror.

24. Conservative reactionary blogs, such as Rense.com, Paleoconservativeprimer.com, and Americanfreepress.net, all reported on the alleged "dual citizenship problem." The Americanfreepress.net is listed by the Southern Poverty Law Center as a domestic hate group. Many other hate group sites claimed that Chertoff was part of a global Zionist movement.

25. According to Israeli law, children of Israeli citizens are eligible for Israeli citizenship. However, those desiring Israeli citizenship must apply for such a status. The discourse around Chertoff's citizenship is reminiscent of the more recent anti-Barack Obama, ultraconservative, "birther" movement. Those in the movement claim that the Obama presidency is invalid because the president is a naturalized and not natural-born citizen of the United States. Integral to the movement is the question of Obama's birth certificate. Though the Obama campaign released an electronic version of the certificate, those against the president claim that this is a fabrication.

26. John Okada, "Preface," *No No Boy* [1957] (Seattle: University of Washington Press, 1979), viii.

27. "Business, Labor Calling for Legalizing Undocumented Workers." September 7, 2001, http://www.cnn.com.

28. "Person of the Week: Vicente Fox." September 7, 2001, http://www.time.com/time/nation/article/0,8599,174018,00.html.

29. "Joint Statement between the United States of America and the United Mexican States," September 6, 2001. White House press release, http://www.whitehouse.gov/the-press-office/declaration-government-united-states-america-and-government-united-mexican-states-c.

30. Michelle Malkin, a Filipino American, is a prominent Fox News commentator. For information about Malkin and *In Defense of Internment,* see http://web.archive.org/web/20060206033611/http://michellemalkin.com/aboutidoi.htm.

31. Ibid.

32. The executive director of the Japanese American Citizens League, John Tateishi, released a statement on August 24, 2004, stating, "Michelle Malkin's book *In Defense of Internment: The Case for Racial Profiling in World War II and the War on Terror* is a desperate attempt to impugn the loyalty of Japanese Americans during World War II to justify harsher governmental policies today in the treatment of Arab and Muslim Americans." Japanese/American and Japanese/Canadian historian Greg Robinson, in a September 6, 2004, online op-ed that appeared in *History News Network* (hosted by George Mason University) similarly critiqued the book's less-than-accurate claims. See http://hnn.us/articles/7092.html.

33. Interestingly, in 1943, Chinese, Filipino, and South Asian immigrants were granted access to U.S. naturalized citizenship at the same time that Japanese/Japanese Americans were interned, illustrating their probationary whiteness in the face of crisis. This "opening up" of naturalization coincided with the 1943 Leave Clearance application, which is discussed in the epilogue.

34. Most recently, at the 2010 Conservative Political Action Conference (CPAC), Viet Dinh publicly stated his concern that the Barack Obama administration was "killing too many terrorists." At a CPAC national security panel, Dinh stressed the need to have an "effective detention policy . . . if we don't detain them, we don't know what they know and what they are up to." See Sam Stein, "Bush Official Criticizes Obama for Killing Too Many Terrorists," *Huffington Post,* February 19, 2010, http://www.huffingtonpost.com.

35. "Interview with Condoleeza Rice," *60 Minutes* (interviewed by Katie Couric), aired September 24, 2006, http://www.cbsnews.com/video/watch/?id=4478296n.

36. "At Home on the War on Terror."

37. "Oath of Allegiance for Naturalized Citizens," http://www.uscis.gov.

38. Meant "to deter and punish terrorist acts in the United States and around the world, to enhance law enforcement tools, and . . . other purposes," the PATRIOT Act redefined—and rigorously demarcated—what was considered "terrorist activity" to include any act "dangerous to human life" which "appears . . . to intimidate or coerce a civilian population" or "influence the policy of a government by intimidation or coercion." This paradoxical delineation, couched in vague language, was intentionally open-ended. Applicable to violent and peaceable protest, pertinent to controlling uncivil and civil disobedience, the PATRIOT Act engendered the increased use of wire taps, the seizure of library records, secret searches, and wide-reaching electronic communication surveillance. Additionally, Dinh and Chertoff's "patriotic act" conveniently expanded the scope of the Attorney General's office and the Department of Justice. The judicial arm of the U.S. government (integral to the act's enforcement) was given sole authority

to determine what constituted "terrorist" activity in the neoconservative service of national, "homeland" security. Though many of the act's original provisions were set to expire in December 2005, a consideration of some of its more salient points makes visible linkages between U.S. foreign policy abroad and denaturalized logics.

39. Nancy Chang, Center for Constitutional Rights, http://www.ccr-ny.org.

40. USA PATRIOT Act, http://epic.org/privacy/terrorism/hr3162.html.

41. The punishment of deportation was also expressed in the 1988 immigration laws, which also carried the provision about "aggravated felonies." Nonetheless, the 1988 laws limited the definition of "aggravated felonies" to serious crimes (murder, grand larceny, drug trafficking, and assault with intent).

42. Neil A. Lewis, "A Nation Challenged: The Hearings; Justice Dept. and the Senate Clash over Bush Actions," *New York Times*, November 29, 2001, http://www.nytimes.com/2001/11/29/us/.

43. See *The Asian American Encyclopedia*, volume 5, edited by Franklin Ng (Tarrytown, N.Y.: Marshall Cavendish, 1995). Asked of first-generation Japanese and second-generation Japanese Americans, the two questions force the naturalization of the former and the renaturalization of the latter (despite having U.S. citizenship). Those who answered "no" to both questions were deemed traitors to the U.S. nation-state and imprisoned.

44. See Mark Agrast, "Remembering Fred Korematsu (1919–2005)." Center for American Progress, April 1, 2005, http://www.americanprogress.org/issues/2005/05/b489061.html.

45. Ibid.

46. Ibid.

47. Suheir Hammad, "First Writing Since," *Progressive South Asian Exchange Net*, September 2001, http://www.proxsa.org/resources/9-11/Hammad-0109xx-FirstWritingSince.htm.

48. Ibid.

Epilogue

1. Joel Stein, "My Own Private India," *Time*, July 5, 2010, http://www.time.com/time/printout/0,9916,1999416,00.html.

2. Loosely based on *Henry IV* (Part I and II) and *Henry V*, Gus Van Sant's *My Own Private Idaho* features performances by River Phoenix and Keanu Reeves, who play Mike and Scott, respectively. Within an imaginary of abandonment and sexual commodification, the film follows Mike's search for his mother.

3. The exact language for SB 1070 commences as follows: "Be it enacted by the legislature of the state of Arizona: The legislature finds that there is a compelling interest in the cooperative enforcement of federal immigration laws throughout all of Arizona. The legislature declares that the intent of this act is to make attrition throughout enforcement the public policy of all state and local government agencies in Arizona. The provisions of this act are intended to work together to discourage and deter the unlawful entry and presence of aliens and economic activity by persons unlawfully present in the United States." See "SB 1070," http://www.azleg.gov/legtext/49leg/2r/bills/sb1070s/pdf. As a contemporaneous *New York Times* article summarized, SB 1070—also known as the "Support Our Law Enforcement and Safe Neighborhoods Act"—would, by means of required documentation, "identify, prosecute, and deport

illegal immigrants." See Randal C. Archibald, "Arizona Enacts Stringent Law on Immigration," *New York Times*, April 23, 2010, http://www.nytimes.com/2010/04/24/us/politics/24immig.html?_r=1.

4. Multiple South Asian American academics, activists, actors, and bloggers criticized "My Own Private India" for its racist position and inaccurate demographic claims. For example, the blog "Bangla Nation" noted that the 2000 U.S. Census reported 59.5 percent of Edison's population claimed to be "white," while only 29.1 percent claimed to be Asian. See http://bangla-nation.blogspot.com/2010/06/open-letter-to-joel-stein.html. Critical reactions to Stein's piece were not limited to the South Asian American community. Responses appeared in the *Wall Street Journal*, the *Huffington Post*, *Slate*, CNN, PBS, and *Vanity Fair*. News of Stein's article was also reported in South Asian papers and global media outlets.

5. According to Raymond Williams, "structures of feeling" refer to "meanings and values as they are actively lived and felt" and represent "characteristic elements of impulse, restraint, and tone; specifically affective elements of consciousness and relationships." Such "structures" are composed of "specific internal relations, at once interlocking and in tension." See Raymond Williams, *Marxism and Literature* (London: Oxford University Press, 1978), 132.

6. See "anomie," *Oxford English Dictionary*, http://www.oed.com.

7. George Lipsitz, *The Possessive Investment in Whiteness: How White People Profit from Identity Politics* (Philadelphia: Temple University Press, 1999).

8. The assumption of white personhood is constructed through Stein's own collective characterization of himself and his friends. Further, notwithstanding Stein's exaggerated claim of a substantial South Asian/South Asian American presence, the 2000 U.S. census still places whites in the majority.

9. Deborah Misir, "The Murder of Navroze Mody: Race, Violence, and the Search for Order," *Contemporary Asian America: A Multidisciplinary Reader*, ed. Min Zhou and James V. Gatewood, 501–517 (New York: New York University Press, 2000).

10. Fellow New Jerseyan Kal Penn (an Indian American actor) responded directly to Stein's "My Own Private India," writing about his own experiences "growing up a few miles from Edison, N.J." Revising Stein's tone to pointed effect, Penn writes, "I always thought it was hilarious when I'd get the crap kicked out of me by kids like Stein who would yell, 'go back to India, dothead!' I was always ROTFLAMAO when people would assume I wasn't American." See Kal Penn, "The 'Hilarious' Xenophobia of Time's Joel Stein," *Huffington Post*, July 2, 2010, http://www.huffingtonpost.com/kal-penn/the-hilarious-xenophobia_b_634264.html.

11. Sandip Roy, "Joel Stein and the Curry Problem," *Huffington Post*, July 1, 2010, http://www.huffingtonpost.com/sandip-roy/joel-stein-and-the-curry.

Bibliography

Acheson, Dean. "Speech on the Far East." January 12, 1950. http://teachingamericanhistory.org/library/index.asp?document=1612.

Agrast, Mark. *Center for American Progress*. April 1, 2005. http://www.americanprogress.org/issues/2005/05/b489061.htm.>

Ahmad, Ajiz. *In Theory: Classes, Nations, Literatures*. London: Verso, 1994.

Alberdi, Juan Batista. *Obras Completas*. Buenos Aires: La Tribuna Nacional Bolivar 38, 1887.

"America's New War: Dinh Discusses Ashcroft's Policies; McBride, Murphy Debate Their Constitutionality; Rangel Grassley Discuss Economic Stimulus." Kate Snow (host); Viet Dinh (guest). www.transcripts.cnn.com/TRANSCRIPTS/0112/08/se.03.html.

Anderson, Benedict. *Imagined Communities: Reflections on the Origin and Spread of Nationalism*, Rev. and extended ed. London: Verso, 1993.

Antin, Mary. *From Plotzk to Boston*. Boston: W. B. Clarke, 1899.

———. *The Promised Land*. Boston: Houghton Mifflin, 1912.

———. *They Who Knock at Our Gates*. Boston: Houghton Mifflin, 1914.

Archibald, Randal C. "Arizona Enacts Stringent Law on Immigration." *New York Times*, April 23, 2010. http://www.nytimes.com/2010/04/24/us/politics/24immig.html?_r=1.

Bakhtin, M. M. *The Dialogic Imagination: Four Essays*. Austin: University of Texas Press, 1982.

Bascara, Victor. *Model Minority Imperialism*. Minneapolis: University of Minnesota Press, 2006.

"Becoming a Citizen." August 12, 2010. http://www.unitedstatesimmigration.info/becoming_a_citizen.html.

Berlant, Lauren. "Citizenship." In *Keywords for American Cultural Studies*, Bruce Brugett and Glen Hendler, eds., 37–38. New York: New York University Press, 2008.

Bishop, Joseph Buklin. *Theodore Roosevelt and His Time Shown in His Own Letters*. [1920] Whitefish, Mont.: Kessinger, 2008.

Bourne, Randolph. "Trans-National America." *Atlantic Monthly* 118 (July 1916): 86–97.

Brand, David. "Education: The New Whiz Kids." *Time*, August 31, 1987. http://www.time.com/time/magazine/article/0,9171,965326,00.html

Brenner, Paul. "The Jazz Singer." *All Movie Guide*. http://www.allmovie.com/.

Brinkley, Joel. "Two in Congress Who Fought to Improve Immigration Policy." *New York Times*. September 15, 1993.

Bunis, Dena and Anh Do. "Ex-refugee Is Nominated for Justice Post: A Fullerton High Grad Gets Praise at His Senate Confirmation Hearing." *Orange County Register*, May 10, 2001.

Bush, George W. "Statement on the Helicopter Crash in Vietnam." *Public Papers of the Presidents of the United States: 2001*. Book 1. April 7, 2001: 379.

"Business, Labor Calling for Legalizing Undocumented Workers." September 7, 2001. www.cnn.com.

Cahan, Abraham. *Yekl and the Imported Bridegroom and Other Stories of the New York Ghetto*. Mineola, N.Y.: Dover, 1970.

———. *The Rise of David Levinsky*. [1917] New York, N.Y.: Penguin Classics, 1993.

Chametzky, Jules. "Beyond Melting Pots, Cultural Pluralism, Ethnicity: Or Déjà vu All Over Again." *MELUS* [*Multi-Ethnic Literature of the United States*] 16.4 (Winter 1989–90): 3–17.

Chan, Sucheng. *Asian Americans: An Interpretative History*. Ann Arbor: Twayne, 1991.

Chang, Nancy. "The USA PATRIOT Act: What's So Patriotic about Trampling on the Bill of Rights?" Center for Constitutional Rights. *www.ccr-ny.org*.

Chertoff, Michael. "Remarks by Homeland Security Secretary Michael Chertoff to the Heyman Fellows at Yale University on "Confronting the Threats to Our Homeland." April 7, 2008. http://www.dhs.gov/xnews/speeches/sp_1208280290851.shtm.

Chin, Frank, Jeffery Paul Chan, Lawson Fusao Inada, and Shawn Wong, eds. *Aiiieeeee!: An Anthology of Asian American Writers*. [1974] Washington, D.C.: Howard University Press, 1983.

Chu, Patricia. *Assimilating Aliens: Gendered Strategies of Authorship in Asian America*. Durham: Duke University Press, 2000.

Cieslik, Thomas, David Felsen, and Akis Kalaitzidis, eds. *Immigration: A Documentary and Reference Guide*. Westport, Conn: Greenwood, 2009.

Constantine, Robert Jr., ed. *Gentle Rebel: Letters of Eugene V. Debs*. Urbana: Illinois University Press, 1995.

Crawford, James. "What's behind Official English?" In *Language Loyalties: A Sourcebook on the Official English Controversy*. Chicago: University of Chicago Press, 1992: 171–186.

Daniels, Roger. *Coming to America: A History of Immigration and Ethnicity in American Life*. 2nd edition. New York: Harper Perennial, 2002.

Dillingham, William. *Abstracts of Reports of the Immigration Commission: With Conclusions and Recommendations and Views of the Minority*. Washington, D.C.: Government Printing Office, 1911.

Dinh, Viet. "Coming to Grips with Vietnam." *Wall Street Journal*. March 16, 2000.

Dowling, Robert M. *Slumming in New York: From the Waterfront to Mythic Harlem*. Urbana-Champaign: Illinois University Press, 2007.

Eaton, Edith Maude. *Mrs. Spring Fragrance and Other Writings*. Amy Ling and Annette White-Parks, eds. Urbana: University of Illinois Press, 1995.

Editorial, "Who May Be Citizens of the United States." *Harper's Weekly*, May 15, 1858, 306. http://immigrants.harpweek.com.

Eliason, Alan E. "One Illegal Alien Every 35 Seconds." *New York Times* (Letters), April 29, 1986, A26.

Espiritu, Yen Le. "'They're Coming to America': Immigration, Settlement, and Citizenship (Review). *Qualitative Sociology* (Netherlands) 32.2 (June 2009), 221–227.

Fleischer, Richard, dir. *The Jazz Singer*. Paramount Pictures, 1980.

Freedman, Jonathan. *Klezmer America: Jewishness, Ethnicity, Modernity*. New York: Columbia University Press, 2008.

Furman, Andrew. "Immigrant Dreams and Civic Promises: (Con-)Testing Identity in Early Jewish American Literature and Gish Jen's *Mona in the Promised Land*." *MELUS* 25 (Spring 2000): 209–226.

"German Reformed Messenger." http://chroniclingamerica.loc.gov/lccn/sn87090458/.

Gerstle, Gary. *American Crucible: Race and Nation in the Twentieth Century*. Princeton: Princeton University Press, 2002.

González, Begona Simal. "The (Re)Birth of Mona Changowitz: Rituals and Ceremonies of Cultural Conversion and Self-Making in *Mona in the Promised Land*." *MELUS* 26.2 (Summer 2001): 225–242.

Gorra, Michael. "Call It Exile, Call It Immigration." Review. September 10, 1989. *New York Times*. http://www.nytimes.com/1989/09/10/books/call-it-exile-call-it-immigration.html.

Grant, U. S. and A. Rawlins. *Official Records of the War of the Rebellion: Official Records of the Union and Confederate Armies*. Series I, vol. 17, part 2, Government Printing Office, 1880.

Grewal, Inderpal, and Caren Kaplan. "Postcolonial Studies and Transnational Feminist Practices." *Jouvert: A Journal of Postcolonial Studies* 5.1 (Autumn 2000). www.english.chass.ncsu.edu.

Hagedorn, Hermann, ed. *The Theodore Roosevelt Treasury: A Self-Portrait from His Writings*. New York: Putnam, 1957.

Hammad, Suheir. "First Writing Since." *Progressive South Asian Exchange Net*. September 2001. http://www.proxsa.org/resources/9–11/Hammad-0109xx-FirstWritingSince.htm

Hawley, Thomas. *The Remains of War: Bodies, Politics, and the Search for American Soldiers Unaccounted for in Southeast Asia*. Durham: Duke University Press, 2005.

Hoffman, Eva. *Lost in Translation*. New York: Penguin, 1989.

Hollinger, David. *Postethnic America: Beyond Multiculturalism*. [1995] New York: Basic Books, 2000.

INS home page, December 15, 2001. www.ins.usdoj.gove/text.aboutins/statistics/LegisHist/553.htm.

Isaac, Allan. *American Tropics*. Minneapolis: Minnesota University Press, 2006.

"Interview with Condoleeza Rice." *60 Minutes*. Interviewed by Katie Couric. Aired September 24, 2006.

Jacobson, Matthew Frye. *Barbarian Virtues: The United States Encounters Foreign Peoples at Home and Abroad (1876–1917)*. New York: Hill and Wang, 2000.

———. *Whiteness of a Different Color: European Immigrants and the Alchemy of Race*. Cambridge: Harvard University Press, 1998.

James, Henry. *The American Scene*. New York: Harper and Brothers, 1907.

Jefferson, Thomas. "Declaration of Independence." www.loc.gov/exhibits/jefferson/jeffdec.html

Jen, Gish. *Typical American*. New York: Plume, 1992.

———. *Mona in the Promised Land*. New York: Vintage, 1997.

Jenks, Jeremiah W., and Jett W. Lauck. *The Immigration Problem: A Study of American Immigration Conditions and Needs*. New York: Funk and Wagnalls, 1922.

"Joint Statement between the United States of American and the United Mexican States." September 6, 2001. White House press release. http://www.whitehouse.gov/the-press-office/declaration-government-united-states-america-and-government-united-mexican-states-c.

Johnson, Lyndon B. *Public Papers of the Presidents of the United States*. Washington, D.C.: U.S. Government Printing Office, 1966.

Jones, Idwal. "Chinatown Patriarch." *New York Times*, May 19, 1957.

Kaplan, Amy. *The Anarchy of Empire*. Cambridge: Harvard University Press, 2005.

Kehr, David. "Review: *The Jazz Singer*." *Chicago Reader*. December 1980.
http://www.chicagoreader.com/chicago/the-jazz-singer/Film?oid=1052131.

Kim, Elaine. *Asian American Literature: An Introduction to the Writings and Their Social Context* Philadelphia: Temple University Press, 1982.

Knowlton, Brian. "An American Apology over Downed Fighter Is Rejected by

Cheney: Powell Sees Damage to U.S.-China Relations." *New York Times*, April 9, 2001.

Koshy, Susan. *Sexual Naturalization: Asian Americans and Miscegenation.* Stanford: Stanford University Press, 2004.

Kraus, Joseph. "How *The Melting Pot* Stirred America: The Reception of Zangwill's Play and Theater's Role in the American Assimilation Experience." *MELUS* 24.3 (Fall 1999): 3–19.

Lee, Chin Y. *The Flower Drum Song.* [1957] New York: Penguin, 2002.

Lee, Rachel. "Gish Jen and the Gendered Codes of Americanness." *The Americas of Asian American Literature: Gendered Fictions of Nation and Transnation.* Princeton: Princeton University Press, 1999.

Lee, Robert G. *Orientals.* Philadelphia: Temple University Press, 1997.

Lewis, Neil A. "A Nation Challenged: The Hearings; Justice Dept. and the Senate Clash over Bush Actions." November 29, 2001. www.nytimes.com/2001/11/29/us/.

Ling, Amy. "Edith Maud Eaton (Sui Sin Far) 1865–1914." In *The Heath Anthology of American Literature: Late Nineteenth Century: 1865–1910*, ed. Paul Lauter. 5th ed. Boston: Houghton Mifflin Harcourt, 2004: 949.

Link, Arthur S., ed. *The Papers of Woodrow Wilson.* Princeton: Princeton University Press, 1977.

Lipsitz, George. *The Possessive Investment in Whiteness: How White People Profit from Identity Politics.* Philadelphia: Temple University Press, 1999.

Magnet, Myron. "What Is Compassionate Conservatism?" *Wall Street Journal*, February 5, 1999.

Mannur, Anita. *Culinary Fictions: Food in South Asian Diasporic Culture.* Philadelphia: Temple University Press, 2009.

Marek, Angie C. "A New Sherrif in Town." *U.S. News & World Report*, July 10, 2005.

Maslin, Janet. "Movie Review: *The Jazz Singer.*" *New York Times*, December 19, 1980.

McCarran, Pat. *Congressional Record*, March 2, 1953, 1518.

McKinley, William. "December 21, 1898 Address." In *The Statutes at Large of the United States of America from 1897 and March 1899 and Recent Treaties, Conventions, Executive Proclamations, and the Concurrent Resolutions of Two Houses of Congress.* Vol. 30. Washington, D.C.: U.S. Government Printing Office, 1899. Copy courtesy of the U.S. Library of Congress, Asian Division.

Min, Pyong Gap, ed. "Asian Immigration: History and Contemporary Trends." In *Asian Americans: Contemporary Trends and Issues.* 2nd ed. Thousand Oaks, Cal.: Pine Forge Press, 2006.

Mink, Gwendolyn. *Whose Welfare?* Ithaca: Cornell University Press, 1999.

Misir, Deborah. "The Murder of Navroze Mody: Race, Violence, and the Search for Order." In *Contemporary Asian America: A Multidisciplinary Reader*, ed.

Min Zhou and James V. Gatewood. New York: New York University Press, 2000: 501–517.

Mukherjee, Bharati. *Jasmine*. New York: Ballantine, 1989.

Mwakikagile, Godfrey. *Black Conservatives in the United States*. Pretoria: New Africa Press, 2006.

Nadkarni, Asha. "Eugenic Feminism: Asian Reproduction in the U.S. National Imaginary." *Novel* (Spring 2006): 221–244.

———. "'World-Menace': National Reproduction and Public Health in Katherine Mayo's *Mother India*." *American Quarterly* 60.3 (September 2008): 805–827.

"New Zangwill Play Cheap and Tawdry." *New York Times*, September 7, 1909.

"News of the Week." *German Reformed Messenger (1851–1867)* December 6, 1854. http://chroniclingamerica.loc.gov/lccn/sn87090458/

Ng, Franklin, ed.*The Asian American Encyclopedia*. Vol. 5. Tarrytown, N.Y.: Marshall Cavendish, 1995.

Ngai, Mae. "From Colonial Subject to Undesirable Alien: Filipino Migration, Exclusion, and Repatriation, 1920–1940." In *Re/collecting Early Asian America*, ed. Josephine Lee, and Matsukawa Lim. Philadelphia: Temple University Press, 2002.

———. *Impossible Subjects: Illegal Aliens and the Making of Modern America*. Princeton: Princeton University Press, 2004.

"Oath of Allegiance for Naturalized Citizens." http://www.uscis.gov.

Official Catalogue and Guide Book to the Pan-American Exposition. Buffalo: Charles Ahrhart, 1901.

Okada, John. "Preface." *No No Boy*. [1957] Seattle: University of Washington Press, 1979.

Pear, Robert. "President Signs Landmark Bill on Immigration: Law Offers Legal Status to Many Illegal Aliens." *New York Times*. November 7, 1986. A12.

Penn, Kal. "The 'Hilarious' Xenophobia of Time's Joel Stein." *Huffington Post*. July 2, 2010. http://www.huffingtonpost.com/kal-penn/the-hilarious-xenophobia_b_634264.html.

People v. Hall. California Supreme Court, 1854). 4 Cal. 399. http://www.uchastings.edu/racism-race/people-hall.html.

"Person of the Week: Vicente Fox." September 7, 2001. http://www.time.com/time/nation/article/0,8599,174018,00.html.

Reagan, Ronald. "Remarks at the Opening Ceremonies of the Statue of Liberty Centennial Celebration in New York, New York." July 3, 1986. http://www.reagan.utexas.edu/archives/speeches/1986/70386d.htm.

Roberts, Sam. "New York City Census Profile Shows Stark Changes in Decade." *New York Times*, June 22, 1993. http://www.nytimes.com/1993/06/22/nyregion/new-york-city-census-profile-shows-stark-changes-in-decade.html?pagewanted=1.

Rogin, Michael. *Blackface, White Noise*. Berkeley: California University Press, 1996.

Roosevelt, Theodore. "Proclamation 465—Announcing the Death of William McKinley. *September 14, 1901*." In John T. Woolley and Gerhard Peters, eds., *The American Presidency I Project*, Santa Barbara, Cal. www.presidency.ucsb.edu/ws/?pid=69370.

Roy, Sandip. "Joel Stein and the Curry Problem." *Huffington Post*. July 1, 2010, http://www.huffingtonpost.com/sandip-roy/joel-stein-and-the-curry.

Salz, Evelyn, ed. *Selected Letters of Mary Antin*. Syracuse: Syracuse University Press, 2000.

Santos, Fernanda. "Mayor Orders New York to Expand Language Help." *New York Times*, July 23, 2008. http://www.nytimes.com/2008/07/23/nyregion/23translate.html.

"Scenes from the Late 60s." *Time*, February 10, 1975. http://www.time.com/time/magazine/article/0,9171,912797,00.html.

Schmitt, Eric. "English-Only Bill Ignites Debate and Fear on Long Island." *New York Times*, February 14, 1989. http://www.nytimes/com/1989/02/14/nyregion/.

Spivak, Gayatri Chakravorty. "Three Women's Texts and a Critique of Imperialism." *Critical Inquiry*. Special Issue: "Race," Writing, and Difference, ed. Henry Louis Gates, Jr., Vol 12:1 (Autumn 1985). Chicago: University of Chicago Press, 1986: 243–261

"The Statue of Liberty: A New York Attraction." http://www.newyorkjourney.com/statue_of_liberty.html.

Stein, Joel. "My Own Private India," *Time*, July 5, 2010. http://www.time.com/time/printout/0,9916,1999416,00.html.

Stein, Sam. "Bush Official Criticizes Obama for Killing Too Many Terrorists," *Huffington Post*, February 19, 2010. www.huffingtonpost.com.

Stengel, Richard. "The Party of the Century." *Time*, July 7, 1986. http://www.time.com/time/magazine/article/0,9171,961667,00.html.

Sumner, Charles. *The Works of Charles Sumner*. Vol. 13. Boston: Lee and Shepard, 1880.

"Three Decades of Mass Immigration: The Legacy of the 1965 Immigration Act." September 1995. http:www.cis.org/articles/1995/back395.html.

Tichenor, Daniel J. *Dividing Lines: The Politics of Immigration Control in America*. Princeton: Princeton University Press, 2002.

Twain, Mark. "Concerning the Jews." *Harper's Magazine*, September 1899. http://www.harpers.org/archive/1899/09/0026214.

———. *Roughing It*. Vol. 1. New York: Harper and Brothers, 1871.

USA Patriot Act. http://epic.org/privacy/terrorism/hr3162.html.

U.S. *Congressional Record*. "Confirmation Hearing on the Nominations of Michael Chertoff and Viet D. Dinh to be Assistant Attorneys General." May 24, 2001.

"Viet D. Dinh." American Bar Association, 2003. http://www.abanet.org/publiced/rbvd.html.

Wald, Priscilla. "Naturalization." *Keywords for American Cultural Studies*, ed. Bruce Brugett and Glen Hendler. New York: New York University Press, 2008.

Weber, Donald. *Haunted in the New World: Jewish American Culture from Cahan to the Goldbergs*. Bloomington: Indiana University Press, 2005.

Williams, Raymond. *Marxism and Literature*. London: Oxford University Press, 1978.

Wilson, Woodrow. *A History of the American People*. New York: Harper and Brothers, 1902.

Wyman, David. S. *The Abandonment of the Jews: America and the Holocaust, 1941–1945*. New York: New Press, 1998.

Wohlgelenter, Maurice. *Israel Zangwill: A Study*. New York: Columbia University Press, 1964.

Yin, James, and Shin Young. *The Rape of Nanking*. Chicago: Innovative Publishing Group, 1996.

Zangwill, Israel. *The Melting-Pot*. New York: Macmillan, 1909.

INDEX

The Accidental Asian (Liu), 1, 5, 10–11, 12–13, 15–16

African Americans: citizenship and, 24, 27, 59; in *Jasmine* (Mukherjee), 127; Medal of Liberty for, 149, 151; modeling and, 149, 150, 151; in *Mona in the Promised Land* (Jen), 119–120, 121, 122; naturalization and, 24, 26, 27, 187n6; whiteness and, 121, 122, 150

Ah Yup, 23, 26–28

alienation: Asian Americans and, 177–184; in *Children of the Ghetto* (Zangwill), 68; in *The Flower Drum Song* (Lee), 55, 56, 75, 80, 81, 83; in *Jasmine* (Mukherjee), 128; Jewish Americans and, 177–184; in *Lost in Translation* (Hoffman), 128, 141, 144–145, 146; in *The Melting-Pot* (Zangwill), 60, 62–63; in *Mona in the Promised Land* (Jen), 119; in "My Own Private India" (Stein), 177–184; in *Roughing It* (Twain), 39; in "Snow" (Butler), 3, 5; in "The Story of One White Woman Who Married a Chinese" (Eaton), 36–37

allegiances: Asian Americans and, 26, 116, 117, 159, 162, 170–171; assimilation and, 57; in *The Flower Drum Song* (Lee), 75, 81; identity and, 116, 117; immigration policy and, 170–171; in *The Jazz Singer* (Fleischer), xiv, xv; Jewish Americans and, 54–55, 116, 117, 162; in *The Melting-Pot* (Zangwill), 54–55, 58, 61, 63–68; in *Mona in the Promised Land* (Jen), 116, 117; naturalization and, 4–5, 6, 7–8, 26, 63–68, 159, 167; oaths of, 4–5, 6, 26, 65, 67, 71, 78, 94–95, 96, 167–168, 170–171; in *The Promised Land* (Antin), 89, 92, 94–97, 98, 99; religion and, 116, 117; USA PATRIOT Act and, 170–171; in *Yekl: A Tale of the New York Ghetto* (Cahan), 45. *See also* patriotism

Antin, Mary: Chertoff and Dinh compared with, 162; Hammad compared with, 175; Hoffman compared with, 145; Jen compared with, 105, 106, 107, 109, 112, 115, 122; in *Lost in Translation* (Hoffman), 123, 125; *The Promised Land*, 89–90, 92–101, 102; *They Who Knock at Our Gates*, 86; Zangwill compared with, 69

anti-Semitism: in American Civil War, 22–23; Chertoff and, 161; citizenship and, 161; in "Concerning the Jews" (Twain), 40–41; in *The Immigration Problem* (Jenks and Lauck), 92; in *Lost in Translation* (Hoffman), 142; in *The Melting-Pot* (Zangwill), 61, 66, 68; in *The Promised Land* (Antin), 98, 99; in *Yekl: A Tale of the New York Ghetto* (Cahan), 44

Arab Americans, 164–165, 166, 174–175
Asian Americans: in *The Accidental Asian* (Liu), 1, 5, 10–11, 12–13, 15–16; alienation and, 177–184; allegiances and, 26, 116, 117, 159, 162, 170–171; assimilation and, 158–160, 162, 195n34; citizenship and, 23, 24–28, 114–116, 132, 133, 137–138, 157, 158–160, 170–171, 172–174; cold war and, 103; democracy and, 71; discrimination and, 14–15; economy and, 21, 26, 28, 163; education and, 108, 154–155; employment and, 36–37, 39, 154; family and, 31–33, 107, 112, 113, 118–119, 158, 159, 160, 195n34; in *The Flower Drum Song* (Lee), 55, 56, 74–75, 76–85; in *The Flower Drum Song* (Rodgers and Hammerstein), 75–76, 84; food and, 110–111; in *A Good Scent from a Strange Mountain* (Butler), 5; holidays and, 110–111, 119; identity and, 16, 32–33, 79, 107–108, 109–110, 113–122, 129–132, 138; immigration and, 74–75, 76–85, 104–105, 114–115, 124, 126, 154–155, 156–157, 158–160, 178–179; immigration policy and, 28, 29–33, 103, 104–105, 166–167, 177–179, 184; in "In the Land of the Free" (Eaton), 29–33; in *Jasmine* (Mukherjee), 129–138; in *The Jazz Singer* (Fleischer), xiii–xiv, xv–xvi; language and, 107, 154; literacy and, 119; Medal of Liberty for, 149, 151; modeling and, 10, 12–16, 31, 39, 51, 56, 74, 79, 84, 112–113, 119, 122, 135–136, 137, 138, 149, 150, 151, 154–163, 173, 177, 178, 181, 184; in *Mona in the Promised Land* (Jen), 106–122; in "My Own Private India" (Stein), 177–184; nationhood and, 184; naturalization and, 6–8, 9–13, 23, 24–28, 29, 32–33, 35–38, 55, 73, 76–85, 117–118, 130–132, 133–138, 155, 157, 158–160, 162, 205n43; as perpetual foreigners, 181, 184; personhood and, 26–27, 39, 41; as refugees, 55, 159, 162; religion and, 113–122; Second World War and, 165, 170–171, 172–174; selfhood and, 21–22, 25, 27, 28, 32, 41, 75, 173, 184; statelessness and, 74–75, 132, 133, 157; in "The Story of One White Woman Who Married a Chinese" (Eaton), 33–38; in "Success Story, Japanese-American Style" (Petersen), 14–15; in "Success Story of One Model Minority Group in the U.S.," 13–14; suffering by, 163; testimony by, 20–23; transnationalism and, 154, 156–157, 158–160; in *Typical American* (Jen), 106; violence and, 181–182; War on Terror and, 164–165, 166; whiteness and, 10–12, 20–23, 24–28, 31–32, 36–37, 113, 114, 121, 150, 159, 166–167, 178, 180–181, 181–182, 183–184; writing and, 119
assimilation: Asian Americans and, 158–160, 162, 195n34; benevolent, 52–55, 56–60, 62, 71, 73, 85, 158–160; bodies and, xviii–xix, 18–19, 25, 53, 57, 59, 62, 64, 105, 119, 126; of Chertoff, 161, 162; of Dinh, 158–160, 162; in *The Flower Drum Song* (Lee), 53–54, 56, 74, 85; in *The Flower Drum Song* (Rodgers and Hammerstein), 84; in *The Immigration Problem* (Jenks and Lauck), 90–92; in *Jasmine* (Mukherjee), 129, 130, 135, 136; Jewish Americans and, 54–55, 161, 162; language and, 141; in *Lost in Translation* (Hoffman), 141, 143, 145, 146; as melting pot, 58–60, 61, 66–67, 70, 73, 90–92; in *The Melting-Pot* (Zangwill), 53–55, 60–71; in *Mona in the Promised Land* (Jen), 105, 111, 113, 119; in "My Own Private India" (Stein), 182–183; nationhood and, 71, 90–92; in *The Promised Land* (Antin), 88–89, 92, 94, 97, 100; refugees and, 18–19

Cahan, Abraham: Antin compared with, 100; Chertoff and Dinh compared with, 162; Hammad compared with, 175; *The Rise of David Levinsky*, 50–51, 82; *Yekl: A Tale of the New York Ghetto*, 23, 38, 41–51
character, 4–5, 6, 8, 9
Chertoff, Michael, 152, 160–163, 168–172
China, 71–72, 80, 81, 152–154, 164
Chinatown, 55, 56, 74–75, 80–82, 104–105, 192n30
Chinese Exclusion Act, 23, 28, 59, 70
Chinese problem. *See* Asian problem
citizenship: African Americans and, 24, 27, 59; anti-Semitism and, 161; Asian Americans and, 23, 24–28, 114–116,

132, 133, 137–138, 157, 158–160, 170–171, 172–174; of Chertoff, 160–162; cold war and, 53; Constitution and, 24–25; Declaration of Independence and, 24–25; of Dinh, 157, 158–160; dual, 161, 196n15; family and, 18, 158, 159, 160, 161; in *The Flower Drum Song* (Lee), 55–56, 83–85; gender and, 25; identity and, 114–116, 146; in "In the Land of the Free" (Eaton), 23; in *Jasmine* (Mukherjee), 132, 133, 137–138, 147–148; in *The Jazz Singer* (Fleischer), xiii–xiv, xxvii–xviii; Jewish Americans and, 23, 42, 45, 48–51, 54–55, 114 116, 141–142, 143, 146, 160–162; language and, 141–143, 146–148; literature and, generally, 16–19; in *Lost in Translation* (Hoffman), 141–143, 146–148; love and, 158; in *The Melting-Pot* (Zangwill), 54–55, 55–56, 61; in *Mona in the Promised Land* (Jen), 89, 109–112, 114–116, 119–120, 121; Native Americans and, 59; in *The Promised Land* (Antin), 88–89, 92, 95–96, 96–97, 98–100; in *The Rise of David Levinsky* (Cahan), 51; Second World War and, 170–171, 172–174; slavery and, 59; in "The Story of One White Woman Who Married a Chinese" (Eaton), 23; Vietnam War and, 157; voting and, 87; War on Terror and, 166, 174; whiteness and, 59, 114, 159, 161; in *Yekl: A Tale of the New York Ghetto* (Cahan), 23, 42, 45, 48–51. *See also* immigration policy; naturalization

civil rights movement: Civil Liberties Act, 173; economy and, 102; immigration policy and, 12, 101–105, 179; in *Mona in the Promised Land* (Jen), 105, 108–109, 116, 120, 121, 122; Olympics and, 198n41; Reagan and, 150; War on Terror compared with, 167

cold war: Asian Americans and, 103; China and, 72; citizenship and, 53; democracy and, 158; in *The Flower Drum Song* (Lee), 55, 56, 74, 77, 81, 82, 84–85; immigration policy and, 73, 102–105, 124, 179; in *Jasmine* (Mukherjee), 133–134; Liberty Weekend and, 151; in *Mona in the Promised Land* (Jen), 108, 110–111, 117; naturalization and, 73; Vietnam War and, 153–154, 156, 158–159, 162; War on Terror replaces, 152; whiteness and, 103

Dinh, Viet D., 152, 153–163

Eaton, Edith Maude, 23, 28–38, 39, 51, 162, 175

economy: Asian Americans and, 21, 26, 28, 163; civil rights movement and, 102; Dinh and, 155–157; in *The Flower Drum Song* (Lee), 80–82; in *The Flower Drum Song* (Rodgers and Hammerstein), 76; immigration and, xvi–xvii, 123–124, 124–125; immigration policy and, 102, 127–129; in *Jasmine* (Mukherjee), 128, 130, 137; in *The Jazz Singer* (Fleischer), xvi–xvii; in *Lost in Translation* (Hoffman), 128; in *The Melting-Pot* (Zangwill), 60; in *Mona in the Promised Land* (Jen), 121, 122; in "My Own Private India" (Stein), 177–178, 178–179, 180, 181; naturalization and, 127–129; in *The Promised Land* (Antin), 94, 97–98; Statue of Liberty and, 123–124, 124–125; Vietnam War and, 155–157; in *Yekl: A Tale of the New York Ghetto* (Cahan), 47

Ellis Island, 46–48, 63, 64, 104, 201n41, 201n42

Emergency Quota Act, 9, 88, 101

Expatriation Act, 34, 38

gender: Asian problem and, 34, 37, 38; bodies and, 25; citizenship and, 25; Constitution and, 25; denaturalization and, 34; in *Jasmine* (Mukherjee), 132, 134, 138; Liberty Weekend and, 151; selfhood and, 174–175; in "The Story of One White Woman Who Married a Chinese" (Eaton), 34–35; voting and, 191n13; War on Terror and, 174–175; womanhood, 32, 34–35

A Good Scent from a Strange Mountain (Butler), 1–5, 7, 10

Hoffman, Eva: Chertoff compared with, 162; Hammad compared with, 175; *Lost in Translation*, 123, 125, 127–129, 139, 141–148

Hollinger, David, 86, 107, 109, 122

Immigration Act of 1921, 197n24
Immigration Act of 1965. *See* Immigration and Nationality Act
Immigration and Nationality Act: in *The Accidental Asian* (Liu), 12–13; enactment of, 86, 101–105; *The Jazz Singer* (Fleischer) and, xii, xiv; in *Mona in the Promised Land* (Jen), 119; in "My Own Private India" (Stein), 178–179; naturalization in, xviii; promised land and, 124
Immigration Law Amendments, 163
immigration policy: in *The Accidental Asian* (Liu), 10–11, 15–16; allegiances and, 170–171; Asian Americans and, 28, 29–33, 103, 104–105, 166–167, 177–179, 184; Asiatic Barred Zone Act, 11, 88; assimilation in, 54, 57–60; bodies and, 28, 41, 57, 73, 101, 103, 104–105, 134, 138, 163, 164–165, 166, 169, 171, 172, 173, 192n33, 200n12; borders in, 21, 28, 100–101, 125–127, 129, 139, 162–163, 164, 165–166, 171–172, 184; Bush and, 163–166, 167, 174; Chinese Exclusion Act, 23, 28, 59, 70; civil rights movement and, 12, 101–105, 179; cold war and, 73, 102–105, 124, 179; Commission on Immigration, 90; crime and, 164, 169; democracy and, 102, 104, 140–141, 164, 166–167, 179; Dinh and, 166–172; discrimination and, 101–102; Displaced Persons Act, 55; economy and, 102, 127–129; in election of 1912, 86–88, 90; Emergency Quota Act, 9, 88, 101; employment and, 103–104, 105, 127–128, 134, 136, 139; Expatriation Act, 34, 38; family and, 31–33, 103–104, 105; in *The Flower Drum Song* (Lee), 53–54, 55, 78, 84–85; in *A Good Scent from a Strange Mountain* (Butler), 5, 10; Immigration Act of 1921, 197n24; Immigration and Nationality Act, xii, xiv, xviii, 12–13, 86, 101–105, 119, 124, 178–179; Immigration Law Amendments, 163; Immigration Reform and Control Act, 127–129, 131–132, 136, 138, 139, 163; Indochinese Migration/Refugee Assistance Act, 124; in "In the Land of the Free" (Eaton), 29–33; in *Jasmine* (Mukherjee), 127–129, 131–132, 134, 135, 136, 137–138, 147–148; in *The Jazz Singer* (Fleischer), xii–xiv, xv; Jewish Americans and, 46–48, 184, 201n41; Johnson-Reed Act, 9, 59, 88, 101; language and, 128, 139–141; Latin Americans and, 104; Liberty Weekend and, 151; literacy and, 87, 90, 91, 128; literature and, generally, 16–19; in *Lost in Translation* (Hoffman), 127–129, 147–148; marriage and, 103–104; McCarran-Walter Act, 6, 55, 72–73, 77, 103, 127; in *The Melting-Pot* (Zangwill), 53–54, 65, 69–71; melting pot and, 66–67, 100–101; modeling and, 31, 184; in *Mona in the Promised Land* (Jen), 105, 109, 111, 119; in "My Own Private India" (Stein), 177–178, 178–179; names and, 132; nationhood and, 101, 172, 184; Naturalization Act of 1790, 4–7, 21–22, 59; Naturalization Act of 1870, 7, 23, 24–28, 59; *Ozawa v. United States*, 7–8, 27; Page Act, 23, 28, 32; Parliamentary Act of 1740, 6; perpetual foreigners and, 184; personhood and, 23; preferences in, 103–104; in Progressive era, 86–88, 89–92; promised land and, 105, 124; quotas in, xv, 9, 12, 15, 73, 87, 88, 90, 92, 101–102, 103, 151, 197n24; *In re Ah Yup*, 23, 26–28, 32; Refugee Act, xiv, 124; refugees and, 104; residency in, 103–104, 128; Second World War and, 9; selfhood and, 23, 28, 101, 168–169, 171, 172, 184; sexuality and, 28; taxation in, 41; transnationalism and, 171–172; undocumented migration and, 125–129, 135, 136, 137–138; *United States v. Thind*, 11–12, 27; *United States v. Wong Kim Ark*, 36; USA PATRIOT Act, 162–163, 168–172; War Brides Act, 28; War on Terror and, 164–172, 174; whiteness and, 31–32, 100–101, 103, 140–141, 166–167, 172; in *Yekl: A Tale of the New York Ghetto* (Cahan), 46–48. *See also* naturalization
The Immigration Problem (Jenks and Lauck), 90–92, 100–101
Immigration Reform and Control Act, 127–129, 131–132, 136, 138, 139, 163
India, 177–184
Indian Citizenship Act, 187n6

Indochinese Migration/Refugee Assistance Act, 124
In re Ah Yup, 23, 26–28, 32, 188n11
"In the Land of the Free" (Eaton), 23, 29–33

Jasmine (Mukherjee): analysis of, 123, 125, 127–138; Chertoff and Dinh compared with, 162; *Lost in Translation* (Hoffman) compared with, 142, 146, 147–148
The Jazz Singer (Fleischer), xi–xix, 180
The Jazz Singer (Jolson), xi
Jen, Gish, 89–90, 105–122, 162, 175
Jewish Americans: in *The Accidental Asian* (Liu), 1, 5, 10, 12–13, 14–16; alienation and, 177–184; allegiances and, 54–55, 116, 117, 162; in American Civil War, 22–23; assimilation and, 54–55, 161, 162; citizenship and, 23, 42, 45, 48–51, 54–55, 114–116, 141–142, 143, 146, 160–162; family and, 46–51, 160, 161; food and, 62–63; in *A Good Scent from a Strange Mountain* (Butler), 5; holidays and, 115–116, 119; identity and, xii, xvii, 16, 42, 45, 50, 51, 113–122, 143; immigration and, 40–51, 92, 124, 142; immigration policy and, 46–48, 184, 201n41; in *The Immigration Problem* (Jenks and Lauck), 92; in *The Jazz Singer* (Fleischer), xii–xiv, xii, xv–xvi, xvii–xviii; the Jewish problem, 40–41, 68, 69, 92; language and, 117; literacy and, 119; in *Lost in Translation* (Hoffman), 141–142, 143, 146; Medal of Liberty for, 149, 151; in *The Melting-Pot* (Zangwill), 54–55, 55–56, 60–61, 62–63, 68–69; modeling and, 9, 10, 12–13, 14–16, 39–40, 54–55, 56, 112–113, 119, 149, 151, 154–155, 160–163, 178, 184; in *Mona in the Promised Land* (Jen), 107–108, 109–110, 112–122; in "My Own Private India" (Stein), 178, 181; nationhood and, 184; naturalization and, 6–7, 8–10, 23, 27, 41–42, 42–43, 44–51, 117–118, 155; as perpetual foreigners, 184; personhood and, 14, 40, 41, 46, 51; in *The Promised Land* (Antin), 98–100; promised land and, 98–100; as refugees, 201n41; religion and, 6, 68–69, 113–122; selfhood and, 40, 41, 42, 43, 49, 146, 184; statelessness and, 6, 60, 98–99, 143; suffering of, 163; transnationalism and, 40–41, 42–44, 48, 50, 51, 54–55; whiteness and, 6, 22–23, 27, 40, 44, 92, 113, 114, 121, 161, 178, 181; in *Yekl: A Tale of the New York Ghetto* (Cahan), 41–51
Johnson, Lyndon B., 102, 103, 104, 153, 178–179
Johnson-Reed Act, 9, 59, 88, 101

language: Asian Americans and, 107, 154; assimilation and, 57, 141; citizenship and, 141–143, 146–148; democracy and, 140–141; Dinh and, 154; education and, 144–145; in *The Flower Drum Song* (Lee), 80, 81; identity and, 143–144; immigration and, 126–127, 128, 139–143; immigration policy and, 128, 139–141; in *The Immigration Problem* (Jenks and Lauck), 91; in "In the Land of the Free" (Eaton), 29–30, 31; in *Jasmine* (Mukherjee), 127, 128, 147–148; Jewish Americans and, 117; in *Lost in Translation* (Hoffman), 127, 128, 139, 141–148; in *The Melting-Pot* (Zangwill), 62, 63, 65; in *Mona in the Promised Land* (Jen), 107, 112, 117; naturalization and, 91, 139–141, 143–148; in New York City, 124; official, 139–141; in *Ozawa v. United States*, 7; patriotism and, 139–141; in *The Promised Land* (Antin), 94–96, 98; selfhood and, 142; transnationalism and, 143, 144–145; whiteness and, 140–141; in *Yekl: A Tale of the New York Ghetto* (Cahan), 43–44, 45, 48, 49, 50. *See also* literacy; names
Lee, Chin Y.: *The Flower Drum Song*, 52, 53–54, 55–56, 74–75, 76–85;
literacy: Asian Americans and, 119; immigration and, 126–127, 128; immigration policy and, 87, 90, 91, 128; in *Jasmine* (Mukherjee), 127, 128; Jewish Americans and, 119; in *Lost in Translation* (Hoffman), 127, 128, 146; in *Mona in the Promised Land* (Jen), 112, 113, 115–116, 117, 119, 122; naturalization and, 91; in *The Promised Land* (Antin), 95–96, 100; selfhood and, 146. *See also* language

Lost in Translation (Hoffman): analysis of, 123, 125, 127–129, 139, 141–148; Chertoff compared with, 162; "First Writing Since" (Hammad) compared with, 175

McCarran-Walter Act: in *The Flower Drum Song* (Lee), 77, 84; Immigration Reform and Control Act and, 127; whiteness and, 6, 55, 72–73, 103
McKinley, William, 52–53, 54, 56, 62, 71, 73
Medal of Liberty, 148–151
melting pot: in election of 1912, 87; First World War and, 93, 100–101; in *The Immigration Problem* (Jenks and Lauck), 90–92, 100–101; in *Lost in Translation* (Hoffman), 139, 148; in *The Melting-Pot* (Zangwill), 58–60, 61, 66–67, 70; in *Mona in the Promised Land* (Jen), 110–111, 111–112; naturalization and, 73; in *The Promised Land* (Antin), 94
The Melting-Pot (Zangwill): analysis of, 52, 53–56, 58, 60–71, 84; *The Jazz Singer* (Fleischer) compared with, 186n13; *The Promised Land* (Antin) compared with, 88–89, 93, 94–95, 99
Mona in the Promised Land (Jen), 89–90, 105, 106–122, 175
Mukherjee, Bharati: *Jasmine*, 123, 125, 127–138
Muslim Americans, 164–165, 166, 174–175
"My Own Private India" (Stein), 177–184

names: immigration policy and, 132; in "In the Land of the Free" (Eaton), 32–33; in *Jasmine* (Mukherjee), 130–131, 132, 136–137; in *The Jazz Singer* (Fleischer), xiv; in *Lost in Translation* (Hoffman), 144–145; in *Mona in the Promised Land* (Jen), 107, 108, 121; in "My Own Private India" (Stein), 182–183; naturalization and, 132; transnationalism and, 130–131; in *Yekl: A Tale of the New York Ghetto* (Cahan), 42–43, 48, 50. *See also* language
nationhood: Asian Americans and, 184; assimilation and, 71, 90–92; bodies and, 69; democracy and, 53, 60; in *The Flower Drum Song* (Rodgers and Hammerstein), 75–76; immigration policy and, 101, 172, 184; in *The Immigration Problem* (Jenks and Lauck), 90–92; in "In the Land of the Free" (Eaton), 33; in *Jasmine* (Mukherjee), 130; Jewish Americans and, 184; in *Mona in the Promised Land* (Jen), 107; naturalization and, xviii, 17, 18; in *The Promised Land* (Antin), 95–96; Statue of Liberty and, 125; in *Yekl: A Tale of the New York Ghetto*, 44, 48. *See also* personhood; selfhood
naturalization: in *The Accidental Asian* (Liu), 10–11, 16; African Americans and, 24, 26, 27, 187n6; allegiances and, 4–5, 6, 7–8, 26, 63–68, 159, 167; Asian Americans and, 6–8, 9–13, 23, 24–28, 29, 32–33, 35–38, 55, 73, 76–85, 117–118, 130–132, 133–138, 155, 157, 158–160, 162, 205n43; Asiatic Barred Zone Act, 11, 88; assimilation and, 53, 57–58, 59; bodies and, xix, 9, 10, 11, 53, 57, 59, 91, 96, 127, 148, 171, 172, 173, 181; character and, 4–5, 6, 8, 9; Chinese Exclusion Act, 23, 28, 59, 70; cold war and, 73; Constitution and, 77; of Dinh, 157, 158–160, 162; economy and, 127–129; education and, 144–145, 155; Emergency Quota Act, 9, 88, 101; Expatriation Act, 34, 38; family and, 158, 159, 160; in *The Flower Drum Song* (Lee), 55–56, 76–80, 84; in *The Flower Drum Song* (Rodgers and Hammerstein), 75–76; in *A Good Scent from a Strange Mountain* (Butler), 3–5, 7, 10; in Great Britain, 6; identity and, 117–118; Immigration and Nationality Act, xii, xiv, xviii, 12–13, 86, 101–105, 119, 124, 178–179; Immigration Law Amendments, 163; in *The Immigration Problem* (Jenks and Lauck), 91–92; immigration problem and, 17; Immigration Reform and Control Act, 127–129, 131–132, 139, 163; Indian Citizenship Act, 187n6; in "In the Land of the Free" (Eaton), 23, 29, 32–33; in *Jasmine* (Mukherjee), 128–129, 130–132, 133–138; in *The Jazz Singer* (Fleischer), xiv, xviii–xix; Jewish Americans and, 6–7, 8–10, 23, 27, 41–42, 42–43, 44–51, 117–118,

155; Johnson-Reed Act, 9, 59, 88, 101; language and, 91, 139–141, 143–148; Liberty Weekend and, 148–151; literacy and, 91; literature and, generally, 16–19; in *Lost in Translation* (Hoffman), 128–129, 141, 143–148; McCarran-Walter Act, 6, 55, 72–73, 77, 103, 127; in *The Melting-Pot* (Zangwill), 55–56, 58, 60, 63–71; modeling and, 18, 157, 158–160, 162; in *Mona in the Promised Land* (Jen), 89, 109–110, 115–116, 117–118; in "My Own Private India" (Stein), 178; names and, 132; nationhood and, xviii, 17, 18; Native Americans and, 187n6; Naturalization Act of 1790, 4–7, 21–22, 59; Naturalization Act of 1870, 7, 23, 24–28, 59; oaths for, 4–5, 26, 65, 67, 71, 78, 94–95, 96, 167–168, 170–171; *Ozawa v. United States*, 7–8, 27; Parliamentary Act of 1740, 6; patriotism and, 7–8, 167; personhood and, 5, 17, 26–27; in *The Promised Land* (Antin), 88–89, 92, 93–101; *In re Ah Yup*, 23, 26–28, 32; refugees and, 159, 162; religion and, 6, 117–118; residency and, 4–5, 11, 91, 128, 134–135, 139, 150; selfhood and, xviii, 17–18, 27, 28, 167–168, 171; in "The Story of One White Woman Who Married a Chinese" (Eaton), 23, 33, 35–38; transnationalism and, 144–145; in *Typical American* (Jen), 197n40; *United States v. Thind*, 11–12, 27; *United States v. Wong Kim Ark*, 36; War on Terror and, 166, 168, 169, 171–172, 175; whiteness and, 4–8, 10–12, 24–28, 59, 87, 91–92, 100–101, 159, 172; in *Yekl: A Tale of the New York Ghetto* (Cahan), 23, 41–42, 42–43, 44–51. *See also* immigration policy

Naturalization Act of 1790, 4–7, 21–22, 59

Naturalization Act of 1870, 7, 23, 24–28, 59

oaths: in *The Flower Drum Song* (Lee), 78; in *The Melting-Pot* (Zangwill), 64, 65, 67, 71; for naturalization, 4–5, 26, 65, 67, 71, 78, 94–95, 96, 167–168; in *The Promised Land* (Antin), 94–95, 96; religion and, 6; in Second World War, 170–171; in *Yekl: A Tale of the New York Ghetto* (Cahan), 45. *See also* allegiances

Ozawa v. United States, 7–8, 27

Page Act, 23, 28, 32

The Passing of the Great Race (Grant), 90, 100

PATRIOT Act, 162–163, 168–172

patriotism: Dinh and, 167; language and, 139–141; in *The Melting-Pot* (Zangwill), 64, 65, 68, 69, 70–71; naturalization and, 7–8, 167; in *The Promised Land* (Antin), 92, 94, 95–96; Statue of Liberty and, 148; in *Yekl: A Tale of the New York Ghetto* (Cahan), 45. *See also* allegiances

People v. Hall, 20–23, 25, 27, 32, 188n9

perpetual foreigners: in *The Accidental Asian* (Liu), 11; Asian Americans and, 181, 184; bodies of, 9, 12; in *The Flower Drum Song* (Lee), 79; in *A Good Scent from a Strange Mountain* (Butler), 2, 10; immigration policy and, 184; Jewish Americans and, 184; in *Mona in the Promised Land* (Jen), 110–111, 115; in "My Own Private India" (Stein), 181; in *United States v. Thind*, 12

personhood: African Americans and, 26; Asian Americans and, 26–27, 39, 41; immigration policy and, 23; in "In the Land of the Free" (Eaton), 33; Jewish Americans and, 14, 40, 41, 46, 51; marriage and, 38; in *Mona in the Promised Land* (Jen), 119–120; in "My Own Private India" (Stein), 206n8; naturalization and, 5, 17, 26–27; in *Ozawa v. United States*, 8; in *People v. Hall*, 21; in *The Promised Land* (Antin), 94; in *The Rise of David Levinsky* (Cahan), 51; in *Roughing It* (Twain), 39; selfhood and, 23; in "Snow" (Butler), 3, 5; in "The Story of One White Woman Who Married a Chinese" (Eaton), 38; in "Success Story, Japanese-American Style" (Petersen), 14; whiteness and, 23, 24, 26–27, 28, 29, 39, 206n8; in *Yekl: A Tale of the New York Ghetto* (Cahan), 46, 51. *See also* nationhood; selfhood

Philippines, 52–53, 56, 71

The Promised Land (Antin), 88–89, 89–90, 92–101, 105, 145

questions. *See* Asian problem; immigration problem; Jewish problem quotas: Dillingham Commission and, 90; in election of 1912, 87; Emergency Quota Act, 9, 88, 101; in *The Flower Drum Song* (Lee), 78; Immigration Act of 1921, 197n24; Immigration and Nationality Act and, 12, 101–102, 103; in *The Immigration Problem* (Jenks and Lauck), 92; in *The Jazz Singer* (Fleischer), xv; Johnson-Reed Act and, 101, 197n24; Liberty Weekend and, 151; McCarran-Walter Act and, 73; in "Success Story, Japanese-American Style" (Petersen), 15

race. *See* African Americans; Asian Americans; whiteness
reading. *See* literacy
Reagan, Ronald, 123–125, 127, 129, 148–151, 173
refugees: Asian Americans as, 55, 159, 162; assimilation and, 18–19; Dinh as, 159, 162, 166–167; in *The Flower Drum Song* (Lee), 53–54, 55, 56, 74–75, 77, 78–79, 80–85; immigration policy and, 104; in *Jasmine* (Mukherjee), 133; Jewish Americans as, 201n41; in *Lost in Translation* (Hoffman), 144; in *The Melting-Pot* (Zangwill), 53–54; in *Mona in the Promised Land* (Jen), 105; naturalization and, 159, 162; Refugee Act, xiv, 124
religion: allegiances and, 116, 117; Asian Americans and, 113–122; identity and, 113–122; Jewish Americans and, 6, 68–69, 113–122; in *The Melting-Pot* (Zangwill), 60, 62–63, 67, 68–69; in *Mona in the Promised Land* (Jen), 89, 107–108, 109, 113–122; naturalization and, 6, 117–118; in *The Promised Land* (Antin), 92, 94, 99; whiteness and, 114
residency: in immigration policy, 103–104, 128; in *The Immigration Problem* (Jenks and Lauck), 91; in *Jasmine* (Mukherjee), 134–135; in *The Melting-Pot* (Zangwill), 64; in "My Own Private India" (Stein), 181–182; naturalization and, 4–5, 11, 91, 128, 139, 150; in *Yekl: A Tale of the New York Ghetto* (Cahan), 45
Roosevelt, Franklin D., 165, 170, 172
Roosevelt, Theodore, 53, 56–58, 61, 71, 73, 86–87
Russia: in *The Melting-Pot* (Zangwill), 60, 61, 62, 66; in *The Promised Land* (Antin), 89, 93, 94, 96–97, 99, 100; in *Yekl: A Tale of the New York Ghetto* (Cahan), 42–48, 50

Second World War: Asian Americans and, 165, 170–171, 172–174; citizenship and, 170–171, 172–174; in *A Good Scent from a Strange Mountain* (Butler), 2, 3; immigration policy and, 9; Liberty Weekend and, 151; in *Mona in the Promised Land* (Jen), 118
selfhood: in *The Accidental Asian* (Liu), 13, 15–16; Asian Americans and, 21–22, 25, 27, 28, 32, 41, 75, 173, 184; assimilation and, 53, 57, 59; in election of 1912, 87; family and, 158; in *The Flower Drum Song* (Lee), 75, 77, 78, 79; in *The Flower Drum Song* (Rodgers and Hammerstein), 76; gender and, 174–175; in *A Good Scent from a Strange Mountain* (Butler), 3; identity and, 146; immigration policy and, 23, 28, 101, 168–169, 171, 172, 184; in *The Immigration Problem* (Jenks and Lauck), 91–92; in "In the Land of the Free" (Eaton), 32; in *Jasmine* (Mukherjee), 127, 129, 133, 138, 147–148, 162; in *The Jazz Singer* (Fleischer), xiii–xiv, xvii, xviii–xix; Jewish Americans and, 40, 41, 42, 43, 49, 146, 184; language and, 142; literacy and, 146; literature and, generally, 18–19; in *Lost in Translation* (Hoffman), 127, 142, 143, 144, 145, 146, 147–148; love and, 158; in *The Melting-Pot* (Zangwill), 63, 64, 65, 68; in *Mona in the Promised Land* (Jen), 105, 107, 119–120; in "My Own Private India" (Stein), 178; naturalization and, xviii, 17–18, 27, 28, 167–168, 171; personhood and, 23; in *The Promised Land* (Antin), 92, 93–94; in *The Rise of David Levinsky* (Cahan), 51; Vietnam War and, 156–157; War on Terror and, 168–169, 171; whiteness and, 23, 27, 28; in *Yekl: A Tale of the New York Ghetto* (Cahan), 23, 42, 43, 49, 51. *See also* nationhood; personhood

September 11, 2001, terrorist attacks, 164, 167, 169, 174
Simpson-Mazzoli Act. *See* Immigration Reform and Control Act
Spanish-American War, 52–53, 56, 71
statelessness: Asian Americans and, 74–75, 132, 133, 157; Dinh and, 157; in "First Writing Since" (Hammad), 174–175; in *The Flower Drum Song* (Lee), 74–75; in *Jasmine* (Mukherjee), 132, 133; Jewish Americans and, 6, 60, 98–99, 143; in *Lost in Translation* (Hoffman), 143; in *The Promised Land* (Antin), 98–100; in *Rumsfeld v. Padilla*, 174; War on Terror and, 172–175
Statue of Liberty: democracy and, 124; economy and, 123–124, 124–125; history of, 199n1; immigration and, 123–125, 148–151; in *The Jazz Singer* (Fleischer), xv; Johnson at, 102, 104; Liberty Weekend and, 123–125, 148, 202n42; in *The Melting-Pot* (Zangwill), 67–68, 70; in "My Own Private India" (Stein), 183
Stein, Joel, 177–184
"The Story of One White Woman Who Married a Chinese" (Eaton), 23, 33–38
"Success Story, Japanese-American Style" (Petersen), 14–15
"Success Story of One Model Minority Group in the U.S.," 13–14
Sumner, Charles, 24–26, 39
Supreme Court: *Brown v. Board of Education*, 149; *Bush v. Gore*, 157; on federal supremacy, 191n19; *Korematsu v. United States*, 172–174; *Ozawa v. United States*, 7–8, 27; *People v. Hall*, 20; *Plessy v. Ferguson*, 44, 191n8; *Rumsfeld v. Padilla*, 174; *United States v. Thind*, 11–12, 27; *United States v. Wong Kim Ark*, 36, 189n23
Sutherland, George, 11–12

terrorism, 19, 132, 138, 152, 164–172
testimony, 20–23
They Who Knock at Our Gates (Antin), 86, 196n21
Thind, 11–12
Third World Liberation Front, 108
transnationalism: Asian Americans and, 154, 156–157, 158–160; Dinh and, 154, 156–157, 158–160; in *The Flower Drum Song (Lee)*, 55–56, *79, 81–82, 83;* in *A Good Scent from a Strange Mountain (Butler), 3,* 10; identity and, 51, 79; immigration policy and, 171–172; in "In the Land of the Free" (Eaton), 32; in *Jasmine* (Mukherjee), 129–131; in *The Jazz Singer* (Fleischer), xiv, xvi–xviii; Jewish Americans and, 40–41, 42–44, 48, 50, 51, 54–55; language and, 143, 144–145; in *Lost in Translation* (Hoffman), 143, 144–145; in *The Melting-Pot* (Zangwill), 54–55, 55–56, 61, 66–67; in *Mona in the Promised Land* (Jen), 106–107, 110–112; in "My Own Private India" (Stein), 178–179, 182; names and, 130–131; naturalization and, 144–145; in *The Promised Land* (Antin), 93–94, 96–97, 98–100; in *The Rise of David Levinsky* (Cahan), 51; Vietnam War and, 156–157; War on Terror and, 171–172; in *Yekl: A Tale of the New York Ghetto* (Cahan), 42–44, 48, 50, 51
Twain, Mark, 39–42
Typical American (Jen), 105–106, 197n40

undocumented migration: Bush and, 163–164; Chavez and, 140; employment and, 127–128, 136; identity and, 138; immigration policy and, 125–129, 135, 136, 137–138; in *Jasmine* (Mukherjee), 127–128, 131–132, 133–134, 135, 136, 137–138; in *Lost in Translation* (Hoffman), 127–128
United States v. Thind, 11–12, 27
United States v. Wong Kim Ark, 36, 189n23
USA PATRIOT Act, 162–163, 168–172

Vietnam War: cold war and, 153–154, 156, 158–159, 162; "Coming to Grips with Vietnam" (Dinh), 153–154, 155–157; in *A Good Scent from a Strange Mountain* (Butler), 1–2, 3; Hainan Island incident and, 152–154; in *Jasmine* (Mukherjee), 133–134; in *Mona in the Promised Land* (Jen), 108, 117; in "My Own Private India" (Stein), 179
violence: Asian Americans and, 181–182; in *Jasmine* (Mukherjee), 134, 135–136, 142; in *Lost in Translation* (Hoffman),

142; modeling and, 15; in "My Own Private India" (Stein), 178, 181–182, 184; in Philippine-American War, 71; War on Terror and, 152
voting, 87, 103, 191n13

whiteness: African Americans and, 121, 122, 150; Asian Americans and, 10–12, 20–23, 24–28, 31–32, 36–37, 113, 114, 121, 150, 159, 166–167, 178, 180–181, 181–182, 183–184; assimilation and, 161; bodies and, 21, 23, 25, 59, 101, 103, 105, 141, 178, 180, 181; borders and, 21, 28, 184; citizenship and, 59, 114, 159, 161; cold war and, 103; Constitution and, 24–25; crime and, 180, 181–182; Declaration of Independence and, 24–25; democracy and, 140–141; denaturalization and, 25; education and, 126; family and, 31–32; in *The Flower Drum Song* (Lee), 84, 85; in *A Good Scent from a Strange Mountain* (Butler), 4; identity and, 114; immigration and, 126, 140–141; immigration policy and, 31–32, 100–101, 103, 140–141, 166–167, 172; in *The Immigration Problem* (Jenks and Lauck), 90–92; in "In the Land of the Free" (Eaton), 31–32; Jewish Americans and, 6, 22–23, 27, 40, 44, 92, 113, 114, 121, 161, 178, 181; language and, 140–141; Liberty Weekend and, 151; in *The Melting-Pot* (Zangwill), 62, 64, 65; modeling and, 113, 150, 178; in *Mona in the Promised Land* (Jen), 113, 114, 121, 122; in "My Own Private India" (Stein), 178, 180–181, 181–182, 183–184; naturalization and, 4–8, 10–12, 24–28, 59, 87, 91–92, 100–101, 159, 172; personhood and, 23, 24, 26–27, 28, 29, 39, 206n8; religion and, 114; selfhood and, 23, 27, 28; in "The Story of One White Woman Who Married a Chinese" (Eaton), 34, 36–37; testimony and, 20–23; voting and, 87; War on Terror and, 166; in *Yekl: A Tale of the New York Ghetto* (Cahan), 44

Yekl: A Tale of the New York Ghetto (Cahan), 23, 38, 41–51

Zangwill, Israel: Antin compared with, 88–89, 93, 94–95, 99; Chertoff and Dinh compared with, 162; Hammad compared with, 175; *The Jazz Singer* (Fleischer) compared with, 186n13; *The Melting-Pot*, 52, 53–56, 58, 60–71, 84

About the Author

Cathy J. Schlund-Vials is Assistant Professor of English and Asian American Studies at the University of Connecticut–Storrs.